MEAT, POULTRY & GAME

FERRANDI Paris

Project Coordinator: Audrey Janet
Chefs: Bastien Ancelet, Alexander Dreyer, and Stéphane Jakic

Flammarion

French Edition
Editorial Director: Clélia Ozier-Lafontaine,
assisted by Salomé-Marie Ramphort
Editorial Collaboration: Estérelle Payany
Design: Alice Leroy

English Edition
Editorial Director: Kate Mascaro
Editor: Helen Adedotun
Translation from the French: Ansley Evans
Copyediting: Wendy Sweetser
Typesetting: Alice Leroy
Proofreading: Nicole Foster
Indexing: Chris Bell

Production: Julie Hautecourt
Color Separation: IGS-CP, L'Isle d'Espagnac

Printed in China by Toppan Leefung

Simultaneously published in French as
Viandes: Recettes et Techniques d'une École d'Excellence
© Éditions Flammarion, S.A., Paris, 2024

English-language edition
© Éditions Flammarion, S.A., Paris, 2024

editions.flammarion.com
@flammarioninternational

24 25 26 3 2 1
ISBN: 978-2-08-045681-6
Legal Deposit: 12/2024

FERRANDI
PARIS

MEAT, POULTRY & GAME

RECIPES AND TECHNIQUES FROM
THE FERRANDI SCHOOL OF CULINARY ARTS

Photography by Rina Nurra

Flammarion

PREFACE

For over one hundred years, **FERRANDI Paris** has taught all of the culinary disciplines to students from around the world. Following the success of our six previous works published by Flammarion—a comprehensive guide to French pâtisserie, as well as volumes focused on chocolate, vegetables, fruit and nuts, charcuterie, and the French boulangerie—it is now time to explore the art of cooking with meat, which requires both inventiveness and technical skill.

France boasts a rich variety of dishes made with beef, veal, pork, lamb, poultry, and game. These time-honored recipes and techniques are part of the French culinary heritage that our teachers are committed to preserving. Moreover, the chefs at **FERRANDI Paris** are continually enriching this repertoire with regional recipes from around France (such as *baeckeoffe*, veal blanquette, and *navarin*) and the world (vitello tonnato, moussaka, lamb tagine, and more).

Both traditional skills and creative innovation lie at the heart of **FERRANDI Paris**'s teaching philosophy. We maintain a balance between the two through strong ties to the professional world, making our school the leading institution that it is today. That is why this book not only provides delicious recipes, but also demonstrates fundamental techniques and shares expert advice. Anyone who wishes to discover the inspiring world of meat cookery, whether it be at home or in a professional kitchen, will find this volume an invaluable reference.

I extend my warmest thanks to the members of **FERRANDI Paris** who have brought this book to fruition, particularly Audrey Janet, who coordinated the project, and Bastien Ancelet, Alexander Dreyer, and Stéphane Jakić, chef instructors at the school, who have generously shared their expertise and adeptly combined technical skills and creativity to demonstrate the infinite and flavorful potential of cooking with meat.

Richard Ginioux
Executive Director of **FERRANDI Paris**

CONTENTS

INTRODUCTION

A Portrait of
FERRANDI Paris

In over one hundred years of history, **FERRANDI Paris** has earned an international reputation as one of the premier culinary and hospitality schools in France. Since its inception, the school—a member of the prestigious Conférence des Grandes Écoles and hailed "the Harvard of gastronomy" by the press—has trained generations of groundbreaking chefs and entrepreneurs who have left their mark on the industry around the world. Whether at its historic campus in the Saint-Germain-des-Prés neighborhood in Paris, or at its newer campuses in Saint-Gratien, Bordeaux, Rennes, or Dijon, this institution is dedicated to world-class teaching with the aim of training future leaders in the culinary and pastry arts, hotel and restaurant management, and hospitality entrepreneurship.

Founded more than a century ago by the Paris Île-de-France Regional Chamber of Commerce and Industry, **FERRANDI Paris** is the only school in France to offer a full range of degree and certification programs in the culinary and hospitality arts, from vocational training to the master's degree level, in addition to international programs. The school takes pride in its 99 percent exam pass rate, which is the highest in France for degrees and certifications in the sector. No matter the level, a **FERRANDI Paris** education is rigorous and combines a mastery of the basics with an emphasis on innovation, management and entrepreneurial skills, and hands-on experience in a professional environment. Committed to corporate social responsibility, **FERRANDI Paris** strives to limit its production of greenhouse gases and foster social inclusion and diversity within its establishments, while also integrating sustainable and ethical practices into the school's curriculum.

Strong Ties to the Professional World

A space for discovery, inspiration, and exchange—where the culinary arts mingle with science, technology, and innovation—**FERRANDI Paris** brings together the most prestigious and pioneering names in the hospitality sector and creative culinary world. The school trains 2,200 apprentices and students each year, in addition to three hundred international students of over thirty nationalities and two thousand adults who come to the school to perfect their skills or change careers. The one hundred instructors at the school are all highly qualified: several have received prominent culinary awards and distinctions, such as the Meilleur Ouvrier de France (Best Craftsman in France) title, and all have at least ten years of work experience in the culinary field in prestigious establishments in France

Formations d'Excellence au Tourisme (CFET), a group of institutions in France offering top-quality training in tourism-related fields.

Extensive Savoir Faire

FERRANDI Paris's expertise, combining practice and close collaboration with professionals in the field, has been shared in six previous volumes devoted to French pâtisserie (which received a Gourmand World Cookbook award), chocolate, vegetables, fruits and nuts, charcuterie, and bread and *viennoiseries*, intended for both professional chefs and amateur cooks alike. In this next book in the successful series, FERRANDI Paris now brings the art of cooking with meat into the spotlight.

Beef, veal, lamb, pork, poultry, and game

Rich in symbolic meaning, meat is central to many traditional cuisines worldwide. From selecting the best cuts of beef, veal, lamb or pork, to expertly preparing them, cooking with meat demands skill and experience, but the reward is a remarkable array of textures and flavors. In this book, FERRANDI Paris professionals share techniques and recipes for showcasing all types of meat, unlocking the secrets to succulent roast chickens, tender pot-au-feu, perfectly seasoned sweetbreads, and slow-simmered tagines, to name but a few of the delicious dishes presented. You will soon hold the keys to preparing, marinating, braising, grilling, and roasting meat like a pro.

and abroad. To give students maximum opportunities and the chance to connect with other fields and the greater global community, the school has formed collaborative partnerships with several other institutions. In France, partner schools include the ESCP Europe Business School and AgroParisTech; abroad, the school collaborates with Johnson and Wales University in the United States, the ITHQ tourism and hotel management school in Canada, Hong Kong Polytechnic University, Macao University of Tourism, and Başkent University in Turkey, among others. Since theory and practice go hand in hand, and because FERRANDI Paris strives for excellence in teaching, students also have the chance to participate in a number of official events through partnerships with several chief culinary associations in France, including Maîtres Cuisiniers de France, Société des Meilleurs Ouvriers de France, Euro-Toques, and more. In addition, the school offers numerous prestigious professional competitions and prizes, giving students many opportunities to demonstrate their skills and knowledge. A dedicated ambassador of French culture, FERRANDI Paris draws students from around the world every year and is a member of the French Interministerial Tourism Council; the Collège Culinaire de France (an association dedicated to upholding culinary craftsmanship); the Strategic Committee of Atout France (the French tourism development agency); and the Conférence des

MEAT:
THE ESSENTIALS

What is meat?

The French word for meat—*viande*—comes from the Latin *vivanda* (meaning "that which is necessary for life") and initially referred to any type of solid food. The English word "meat" has undergone a similar evolution. Over time, "meat"—like *viande*—came to exclusively refer to the edible flesh of mammals and birds. The Food and Agriculture Organization of the United Nations (FAO) defines meat as "all parts of an animal that are intended for, or have been judged as safe and suitable for, human consumption" in the *Codex Alimentarius*, or "Food Code."

In France, meat is classified into the following categories:
• **White meats:** pork (excluding charcuterie), veal, and suckling lamb.
• **Red meats:** beef, mutton, and lamb.
• **Poultry:** white meat (turkey, chicken); red meat (duck, guinea fowl, quail); and rabbit.

In English-speaking countries, and according to the World Health Organization, the term "red meat" encompasses all butchered meats except poultry, and therefore includes beef, veal, pork, mutton, and lamb. In butchery, meat is typically categorized by the type of animal it comes from. This book follows the same classification system, with chapters on beef, veal, pork, lamb, poultry, and game.

Offal or variety meats

The different stages in the slaughtering process separate the carcass and muscle cuts from other components, including waste and offal, both edible and inedible. Known as the "fifth quarter," these elements represent up to 50 percent of an animal's weight. Some by-products are used by manufacturers other than those in the food industry: hides are used to make leather, cow and sheep tallow are used in candles, soaps, and cosmetics, and animal-sourced insulin to treat diabetes is derived from cow and pig pancreases.

Edible offal, or variety meat—*abats* or *produits tripiers* in French—represent up to 15 percent of an animal's weight. These include organ meats (heart, liver, kidneys); the head (tongue, brain, cheeks or jowls); the tail; and even some muscle cuts. Edible offal is often classified into two categories:
• White offal: stomach and intestines, feet, head, sweetbreads, caul fat.
• Red offal: liver, kidneys, heart, tongue, cheeks.

Official quality labels

In Europe, there are several labels that are regularly monitored by public authorities and accredited certification bodies. In France, these include Label Rouge, Agriculture Biologique (organic farming), and the EU-wide certifications Protected Geographical Indication (PGI) and Protected Designation of Origin (PDO). These labels guarantee producers have followed precise specifications and methods and, in some cases, ensure the product's origin and typicity. In the US and UK, the "organic" label is regulated and certifies that farmers have followed sustainable, ethical methods without growth hormones or antibiotics. In the US, the term "pasture-raised" is not regulated, so can be misleading. In the UK, the Red Tractor logo certifies that meat has been responsibly sourced, safely produced, and is from animals that have been well cared for. It is important to purchase meat from trusted butchers, particularly those who can source their meat from local farmers.

Prior to cooking

To ensure tender results when roasting or grilling, **salt the meat ahead of time**. Salt affects the proteins in the muscle cells, preventing them from contracting and releasing moisture during cooking. Depending on the thickness of the meat and the cooking method, the ideal salting time before cooking can vary from 6 hours (for pork or lamb chops and poultry legs) to 10 hours (for rib steaks), or even 15 hours (for roasts, legs of lamb). It is also important to **remove meat (except for ground meat) from the refrigerator well in advance**, ideally at least 2 hours before cooking, depending on the room temperature. This prevents the meat from toughening due to temperature shock. Pat the meat dry before cooking to remove any surface moisture.

After cooking

For tender, juicy meat, it is essential to **let it rest after cooking**. This allows the muscle fibers to relax, the juices to be redistributed, and the temperature to equalize throughout. The resting time should be the same as the cooking time for roasted or grilled meats (such as steaks, duck breasts, and tied roasts) or meats cooked at low temperatures. Place the meat in a warm spot to rest, such as a stovetop corner or in the oven preheated to 120°F (50°C/Gas Mark ¼ or less) and then turned off. You can also cover it with aluminum foil, making sure the foil is tented so it does not touch the meat. Take into account the weight of the cooked piece and its cooking temperature: a large piece cooked at a high temperature will retain more heat than a small piece prepared at a low temperature.

Storing meat and offal

To ensure optimal quality and safety, meat should be kept chilled at all times. Whole cuts of meat and offal can be stored for two to three days in the coldest part of the refrigerator (32°F–37.4°F/0°C–3°C). Alternatively, they can be frozen and stored at 0.4°F (-18°C). Ground meat should be consumed within 24 hours of grinding. If the meat is vacuum-packed, it can be kept in the refrigerator for up to 10 days.

Meat trimmings and bones can be used to make flavorful broths, stocks, and jus. Leftover cooked meat is also valuable and can enrich countless recipes if stored properly. Here are some of the many uses for leftover meat:
- Sandwich fillings
- Salads
- Bolognese-type sauces for pasta
- Fillings for lasagne, cannelloni, tortellini, or ravioli
- Stuffing for vegetables
- Gratins and shepherd's pie
- Meatballs
- Fillings for spring rolls
- Fillings for empanadas, samosas, turnovers

The ABCs of storage
Always defrost meat in the refrigerator, and never refreeze it once thawed.

Type of meat	In the refrigerator	In the freezer
LAMB	Raw: 3 days Cooked: 3 days	Raw, in pieces: 6–9 months Cooked: 2–3 months
CHICKEN AND OTHER POULTRY	Raw: 2 days Cooked: 3 days	Raw, in pieces: 6 months Cooked: 2–3 months
PORK	Raw: 3 days Cooked: 3 days	Raw, in pieces, or cooked: 2–3 months
BEEF	Raw: 3 days (except ground beef: 1 day maximum) Cooked: 3 days	Raw, in pieces: 6–12 months Cooked: 2–3 months
VEAL	Raw: 2 days Cooked: 3 days	Raw or cooked, in pieces: 2–3 months
MEATS IN SAUCE	3 days	3–4 months

Beef

Beef is the meat of cattle—either steers or cows—belonging to the domesticated species *Bos taurus*. In French, the same word, "*bœuf*," is used to describe both the live animal and the meat. Meat sold under this name may come from a fifteen-month-old steer (*baby bœuf*); a young bull (*taurillon*), under twenty months old; a bull between two and five years of age (*taureau*) that has previously been used for breeding; a heifer (*génisse*)—a young cow that has never had a calf; a dairy cow; or a bull or cow sent to slaughter due to old age. The appearance and taste of the meat vary according to the animal's breed, age, and diet.

Beef, dairy, and dual-purpose cattle

There are three main types of cattle breed:
• **Beef cattle** are breeds specifically raised for meat production, and their meat is of excellent quality. This category includes suckler herds, in which the calves are left to suckle from their mothers. In France, these breeds are divided into three groups: traditional breeds (Charolais, Limousine, Blonde d'Aquitaine); regional breeds (Blanc-bleu, Parthenaise); and hardy breeds (Salers, Aubrac). Well-known beef cattle from elsewhere include Aberdeen Angus and Hereford in the UK, Angus in the US, Rubia Gallega in Spain, and Chianina in Italy.
• **Dairy cattle** are bred to produce milk and calve annually. They yield meat of average quality. Examples include Holstein, Prim'Holstein, Bretonne Pie Noir, and Jersey.
• **Dual-purpose cattle** combine the qualities of the two previous types and are equally appreciated for their milk and meat. Examples include Normande, Montbéliarde, Abondance, Tarentaise, and Simmental.

Beef quality labels

In France, the following types of beef have been granted Protected Designation of Origin (PDO) status at EU level: Taureau de Camargue, Maine-Anjou, Fin Gras du Mézenc, and Bœuf de Charolles. Others bear a Protected Geographical Indication (PGI) label: Boeuf du Bourbonnais, Boeuf de Chalosse, Boeuf du Maine, Boeuf de Bazas, Génisse Fleur d'Aubrac, and Charolais de Bourgogne. In addition, sixteen types of beef in France are Label Rouge-certified, including Bœuf Blond d'Aquitaine, Bœuf Charolais du Bourbonnais, Bœuf de Chalosse, Bœuf Fermier Aubrac, and Bœuf Fermier du Maine. Worldwide, other labels certify beef quality and protect the integrity of the name. These include the "Certified Angus Beef" label in the US, the Japanese equivalent of PGI for Kobe beef, and "Irish Grass Fed Beef," which was recently granted PGI status.

Suggested cooking and internal temperatures*

*Temperatures generally recommended in France. Note that the USDA recommends a minimum internal temperature of 145°F (63°C) for beef, veal, pork, and lamb.

Slow-cooking at 176°F–212°F (80°C–100°C) after browning	Internal temperature when removed from the oven	Internal temperature after resting for 30 minutes
EXTRA RARE (*BLEU*)	113°F (45°C)	118°F (48°C)
RARE (*SAIGNANT*)	118°F (48°C)	126°F (52°C)
MEDIUM-RARE (*À POINT*)	126°F (52°C)	133°F (56°C)
MEDIUM (*DEMI-ANGLAIS*)	135°F–140°F (57°C–60°C)	140°F–145°F (60°C–63°C)
MEDIUM WELL (*CUIT*)	145°F (63°C)	150°F (66°C)
WELL DONE (*BIEN CUIT*)	155°F (68°C)	160°F (71°C)

Veal

Veal is meat produced from young cattle aged twelve months or less (eight months in France). It is typically pale pink in color and darkens as the animals begin to consume iron-containing foods like grass. The appearance and flavor can vary based on the age of the calf, how it was reared, and its diet. In France, veal is categorized into three groups:

• *Veau sous la mère:* Veal from calves raised on small family farms and exclusively fed with their mother's milk. It makes up only 10 percent of veal production in France. It is the most tender veal and has the most delicate flavor. In the US, the term "milk-fed veal" can be misleading, as the calves are not necessarily reared on their own mother's milk and may be confined to crates, which are banned in Europe, the UK, and several US states.

• *Veau de boucherie standard:* Veal from calves raised on dairy or veal farms. The calves are separated from their mothers at two weeks of age and fed reconstituted milk powder and plant-based supplements. Their meat is fattier and less tender than the former.

• *Veau broutard:* Veal from calves fed on their mother's milk and pastured until they are weaned and fattened in specialized facilities. They are older and have darker meat. In the US and UK, veal from calves raised in this manner may be referred to as rose (or rosé), grass-fed, pastured, or pasture-raised veal.

Veal quality labels

Seven types of veal have been awarded Label Rouge status in France: Bretanin, Terre Océane, Veau d'Aveyron et du Ségala, Veau du Limousin, Veau Fermier Élevé au Lait Entier, Veau sous la Mère, and Vedelou. These are generally produced from the suckler cows of breeds such as Limousin, Gasconne, or Bazadaise. Veau du Limousin and Veau d'Aveyron et du Ségala also bear PGI labels. Veal quality labels elsewhere include Vitellone Bianco dell'Appennino Centrale (IGP) in Italy, Ternera Gallega Asturiana (IGP) in Spain, and Rosée des Pyrénées Catalanes (IGP) and Vedell des Pyrénées Catalanes (IGP) in the Catalan Pyrenees, straddling France and Spain.

Suggested cooking and internal temperatures

Slow-cooking at 176°F–212°F (80°C–100°C) after browning	Internal temperature when removed from the oven	Internal temperature after resting for 30 minutes
RARE OR PINK (ROSÉ)	133°F (56°C)	136°F (58°C)
MEDIUM-RARE (À POINT)	140°F (60°C)	144°F (62°C)
MEDIUM (BIEN CUIT)	147°F (64°C)	150°F (66°C)

Beef and veal offal

Veal offal is highly prized for its delicacy, as opposed to beef offal, which has a denser texture and a stronger flavor. Edible bovine offal includes tripe, tongue, cheeks, snouts, brains, bones (used for their marrow and for making jus), gelatin-rich extremities (like the feet), and flavor-rich extremities (such as the tail). Livers, kidneys, and hearts are also appreciated, as well as sweetbreads, which are the thymus glands and found only in calves, lambs, and kids.

Brown Veal Stock
(fond brun de veau)

Makes 8 cups (2 liters)
Ingredients
½ veal foot
3½ lb. (1.5 kg) veal bones and trimmings (hind shanks, foreshanks, and lean meat scraps)
5¼ oz. (150 g) onions, chopped
5¼ oz. (150 g) carrots, chopped
1¾ oz. (50 g) celery, chopped
2 tbsp (1 oz./30 g) tomato paste
½ head garlic, unpeeled
1¾ tsp (5 g) peppercorns
2–3 whole cloves
1 sprig thyme
1 bay leaf
3 qt. (3 liters) water

Blanch the ½ veal foot. Brown the bones and trimmings in a roasting pan in the oven preheated to 410°F (210°C/Gas Mark 6). Add onions, carrots, celery, and tomato paste to the pan and sweat in the oven for several minutes, until softened. Transfer everything in the roasting pan to a large, two-handled saucepan. Deglaze the roasting pan with a little water and pour into the saucepan. Add the garlic, peppercorns, cloves, thyme, bay leaf, and water. Simmer for 3–4 hours, skimming any foam from the surface. Strain through a fine mesh sieve.

CHEFS' NOTES: To make a **thickened brown veal stock** (*fond brun de veau lié*), stir in 3 tbsp (1 oz./30 g) cornstarch mixed until smooth with 6 tbsp (90 ml) water. To make **white veal stock** (*fond blanc de veau*), follow the recipe for white poultry stock p. 19, replacing the poultry carcasses and giblets with veal bones and trimmings.

GOOD TO KNOW
Certain muscle cuts, such as veal and beef hanger and skirt steaks, are also considered offal.

Pork

Pork, from domestic pigs, is the most widely consumed meat globally. It accounts for 38 percent of meat production worldwide, despite being prohibited in several religions. Omnivorous pigs are easy to feed, and their meat can be cured for long-term storage. Every part of the pig can be used, from the fat (lard) to the hairs (bristles)—hence the French saying *"Tout est bon dans le cochon,"* meaning no part goes to waste.

Among more than 350 breeds of pig worldwide, the most common ones in France are Large White, French Landrace, Piétrain, and Duroc. Some local heritage breeds still exist in the country, including Porc Gascon, Cul Noir du Limousin, Porc Basque, Blanc de l'Ouest, Bayeux, and the Corsican Porc Nustrale. Prized native pedigree pig breeds in the UK include Tamworth, Berkshire, Gloucester Old Spot, British Saddleback, and Welsh.

Pork quality labels

In France, 4 percent of the pork produced is Label Rouge certified, encompassing sixteen appellations such as Porc Fermier d'Argoat and Porc de Normandie. Seven products have PGI status, including Porc de Franche-Comté, Porc d'Auvergne, and Porc du Sud-Ouest. Only two products are PDO-certified: Porc Basque Kintoa and Porc Noir de Bigorre—both from preserved local breeds. Other PDO-protected heritage breeds in Europe include Italy's Cinta Senese and Portugal's Porco Alentejano.

Suggested cooking and internal temperatures

For safety reasons, it is recommended to consume pork well done, not rare, although "pink" pork is becoming increasingly accepted and common in restaurants.

Slow-cooking at 176°F–212°F (80°C–100°C) after browning	Internal temperature when removed from the oven	Internal temperature after resting for 30 minutes
LOIN (*LONGE*)	154°F (68°C)	162°F (72°C)
ROAST (*RÔTI*)	162°F (72°C)	167°F (75°C)
TENDERLOIN (*FILET MIGNON*)	154°F (68°C)	160°F (71°C)

Pork offal

With a characteristically strong flavor, pork offal has waned in popularity. Yet pork liver remains a key ingredient in pâtés, terrines, and other types of French charcuterie, as does caul fat. This fine, fat-laced membrane that surrounds the viscera is ideal for holding together stuffed and ground meat preparations such as paupiettes and crépinettes. When used to enclose stuffed rabbit or lamb saddles, caul fat melts during cooking and helps to keep the meat juicy and tender.

Lamb

The term "lamb" refers to both the meat and the animal it comes from: young domestic sheep, both male and female, typically under one year of age. Meat from a sheep aged one to two years is known as yearling meat or hogget; after two years, it is classed as mutton.

Traditionally, lamb production peaked in spring, but it is now available year-round. The taste and quality of the meat depend on the breed, geographical conditions, climate, and diet.

In France, there are three categories of lamb:

• *Agneau de lait* or **agnelet**: Known as sucking lamb in English, this baby lamb is exclusively fed on ewe's milk and slaughtered between five and six weeks of age at a weight of under 22 pounds (10 kg). The meat is exceptionally pale and tender.

• *Agneau de boucherie* or **agneau blanc**: This type of lamb is fed on cow's or ewe's milk and grains, and is slaughtered between the ages of three and five months. The meat is tender and pink.

• *Agneau gris d'herbages* or **broutard**: Fed on grass and grains, these lambs are slaughtered between the ages of six and ten months. The fattier, darker meat has a more assertive taste.

Among the more than two hundred domestic sheep breeds worldwide, some have been selected for wool (like Merinos) or leather, and others for milk (such as Lacaune, Manech, and Basco-Béarnaise) or meat production, or both in the case of dual-purpose breeds. Well-known breeds such as Southdown, Suffolk, and Texel are found in many countries, including France, which has over fifty different sheep breeds.

Lamb quality labels

In France, 18.5 percent of the lamb produced bears an official quality label. Some, such as Agneau de Lait des Pyrénées, Agneau du Limousin, and Agneau de Sisteron, have both IGP and Label Rouge certifications. Salt-meadow (pré-salé) lambs from the Bay of Mont-Saint-Michel and Baie de Somme are both PDO-protected. Raised on marsh meadows along English Channel estuaries, they graze on halophilic plants with high salinity and iodine content, giving their meat a unique flavor. Salt-meadow lamb is also produced in the UK, Canada, Germany, and the Netherlands.

Suggested cooking and internal temperatures

Slow-cooking at 176°F–212°F (80°C–100°C) after browning	Internal temperature when removed from the oven	Internal temperature after resting for 30 minutes
RARE (*SAIGNANT*)	126°F (52°C)	130°F (54°C)
MEDIUM-RARE OR PINK (*ROSÉ*)	133°F (56°C)	136°F (58°C)
WELL-DONE (*BIEN CUIT*)	147°F (64°C)	150°F (66°C)

Lamb offal

Small but flavorful, lamb offal is prized by connoisseurs. Choice bits include sweetbreads, feet, caul fat, brains, livers, kidneys, hearts, tongues, and testicles.

White Poultry Stock
(*fond blanc de volaille*)

Makes 8 cups (2 liters)
Ingredients
2¼ lb. (1 kg) poultry carcasses
(including giblets and wings)
2½ qt. (2.5 liters) water
1 onion, chopped
3½ oz. (100 g) carrots, chopped
3½ oz. (100 g) celery, chopped
1 leek, white part only, chopped
1 clove garlic
1¾ tsp (5 g) peppercorns
2–3 whole cloves
1 sprig thyme
1 bay leaf
Kosher salt

Roughly chop the carcasses and place in a large two-handled saucepan. Add the water and bring to a simmer, meticulously skimming any foam from the surface. Add the remaining ingredients, season with salt, and let simmer for 1½ hours, skimming often. Strain through a conical sieve lined with muslin to ensure the stock is clear.

CHEFS' NOTES: To make **brown poultry stock** (*fond brun de volaille*), follow the recipe for brown veal stock p. 16, replacing the veal bones and trimmings with poultry bones and wings.

Poultry

In culinary terms, the word "poultry" encompasses all domesticated farmyard birds, including both gallinaceous and web-footed fowl like chickens and ducks, respectively. It also includes certain wild game species like quails and pigeons if they are born and raised in captivity. In France, domestically bred rabbits are also considered poultry.

In France, poultry is categorized into two groups based on the darkness of its meat:
- *Chair blanche* (**white-meat poultry**): chicken, capon, poularde, turkey, and rabbit.
- *Chair brune* (**dark-meat poultry**): goose, duck, pigeon, guinea fowl, and quail.

Hens are raised for their eggs, while chickens are raised for their meat. During the holiday season, capons—male chickens castrated to make them fattier—and poulardes—pullets with the ovaries removed for the same reason—are often given pride of place on festive tables due to their tender, flavorful meat.

Poultry quality labels
The taste and quality of poultry are influenced by factors such as the type of feed, the rearing method (caged in barns or free to roam outdoors), stocking density, and slaughter age. Whenever possible, purchase Label Rouge or organic poultry, which meets higher standards in terms of how the animals were fed, treated, and raised. There are over forty PGI-protected poultry in France, including Canard à Foie Gras du Sud-Ouest, Oie d'Anjou, and Volailles d'Ancenis, de Houdan, and de Janzé. Volaille de Bresse was the world's first poultry protected by an Appellation d'Origine Contrôlée (AOC) in 1957, and it became a PDO in 1996. This PDO includes capons, poulardes, chickens, and turkeys from Bresse.

Suggested cooking and internal temperatures*

Slow-cooking at 176°F–212°F (80°C–100°C) after browning	Internal temperature when removed from the oven
RARE DUCK MAGRET OR BREAST (*SAIGNANT*)	118°F– 122°F (48°C–50°C)
MEDIUM-RARE DUCK MAGRET OR BREAST (*À POINT*)	133°F–136°F (56°C–58°C)
POULTRY BREAST	145°F (63°C)
POULTRY LEG	162°F (72°C; at the joint)
ROAST TURKEY BREAST	154°F (68°C)

*Temperatures generally recommended in France. Note that the USDA recommends a minimum internal temperature of 165°F (74°C) for poultry.

Poultry offal, or giblets

Poultry livers are key ingredients in many pâtés and terrines. Foie gras—goose or duck liver obtained by fattening the birds using traditional methods—is renowned for its smooth consistency and rich flavor. Duck and chicken gizzards are appreciated by aficionados for their firm texture and distinct flavor.

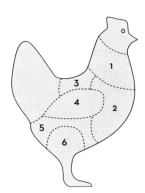

1. *Cou* / Neck
2. *Poitrine* / Breast
3. *Dos* / Back
4. *Aile* / Wing
5. *Cuisse* / Thigh
6. *Pilon* / Drumstick

Game

The term "game" refers to wild animals that can be legally hunted in their natural habitat, as well as the meat obtained from them. They are often categorized into the following groups:

• **Furred game (mammals):** hare, rabbit, wild boar, venison (deer), elk, bison.
• **Feathered game (birds):** partridge, quail, thrush, pheasant, pigeon, wild duck.

Commercial game meat may come from either wild game or farmed game (animals born and raised in captivity and then released into the wild). This is especially true for boar, pheasants, and partridges. Game meat consumption is often tied to local and family traditions, particularly during the fall and end-of-the-year holidays. These meats are popular for their distinctive and bold flavors.

Glossary of Meat Terms

BARDING: Wrapping a piece of lean meat in a thin slice of pork fatback (*barde*), tying it in place with twine. The pork fat keeps the meat moist and prevents it from drying out during cooking.

BASTING: Periodically drizzling liquid (such as pan juices, hot fat, or a sauce) over meat as it cooks, to prevent it drying out, to enhance flavor, and to encourage even cooking.

BLANCHING: Covering meats (especially offal) with cold water in a saucepan and bringing it to a boil to remove impurities. Blanching bacon removes some of the saltiness and improves the final texture.

BONING: Removing bones from meat or poultry, typically using a boning knife.

BRAISING: Slowly cooking meat in a covered pan, either in the oven or on the stove top, with sufficient liquid to ensure that the meat stays succulent. The slow cooking breaks down the collagen in the meat, making it tender and releasing its flavor.

CAUL FAT (*CRÉPINE*): A thin, neutral-tasting pork or beef membrane that looks like fine netting and is laced with fat. It is used for wrapping stuffed or ground meat preparations to hold the meat together during cooking and help keep it juicy and tender.

CHAIN: The narrow, sinewy strip of meat that runs alongside a whole beef tenderloin. It is often removed but can be trimmed and used in other recipes, including stir-fries and stews.

CHATEAUBRIAND: An exceptionally tender cut of beef from the tenderloin (fillet). Often used in English to describe the middle, prime section of the fillet. In this book, the term refers to a cut from the thick (butt) end.

CHINE BONE: A term used in butchery for an animal's backbone.

CONTISER: Seasoning poultry beneath the breast or leg skin, which encourages the flavors of the seasonings, such as fresh herbs and citrus zests, to infuse the meat.

DRESSING (POULTRY): Cleaning and trimming poultry and singing off any remaining feathers to prepare it for cooking.

FELL: The thin fascial membrane that covers animal carcasses just beneath the hide. Papery and tough, it is typically removed before cooking.

FRENCH TRIMMING (FRENCHING): Scraping meat and connective tissue off the ends of exposed bones on cuts of meat such as racks of lamb, beef, or pork. The bones are scraped clean to prevent the meat and tissue from burning during cooking and to enhance presentation.

LARDO: A classic Italian charcuterie (salumi) made by salting, seasoning, and dry-curing pork fatback. The most celebrated is *Lardo di Colonnata*.

MAGRET: Breast meat from ducks that have been fattened to produce foie gras.

MARBLING (INTRAMUSCULAR FAT): Fine streaks of fat distributed throughout muscles, between the muscle fibers. Marbling indicates that the meat will be especially tender and flavorful, as the fat melts into the meat during cooking.

ROASTING: Cooking meat using dry heat, typically in an oven. Hot air circulating around the meat browns the surface, seals in the juices, and boosts flavor.

SILVER SKIN (OR SILVERSKIN): Tough connective tissue that holds muscles together. It does not break down during cooking, so should be removed.

SPATCHCOCKING: Removing the backbone from poultry or a game bird and splaying the body flat. This encourages faster, more even cooking and crisper skin, especially if grilling or cooking on a barbecue.

TRIMMING: Removing excess fat, gristle, and sinew from a cut of meat but retaining enough of the fat to prevent the meat from drying out during cooking. This also makes it easier to carve and serve the meat.

TRUSSING: Tying poultry or a game bird with butcher's twine—with or without the use of a trussing needle—to bind the wings and legs close to the body, keeping the bird in optimal shape for cooking.

A FEW NOTES

MEAT CUTS: Some of the French cuts used in the recipes in this book do not have an exact equivalent in other countries. Suggested alternative cuts in the USA and the UK have been provided, along with the original French cut in parentheses. See also the meat cut diagrams pp. 22–23.

INSTANT-READ THERMOMETERS: Taking a meat's internal temperature is the most reliable way to determine doneness without having to cut into it and lose precious juices. For an accurate reading, insert the thermometer into the deepest part of a joint of meat or the thigh of poultry, avoiding the bone. You can also use a remote or wireless thermometer to avoid opening the oven door.

MEAT CUTS

Beef

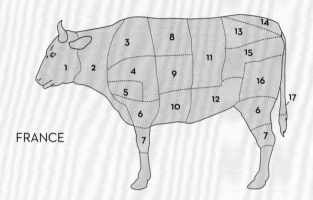

FRANCE

1. Joue 2. Collier 3. Paleron 4. Macreuse 5. Veine grasse
6. Gîte 7. Crosse 8. Côtes couvertes 9. Plat de côtes
10. Poitrine 11. Filet et aloyau 12. Flanchet 13. Culotte
14. Rumsteck 15. Tranche 16. Gîte à la noix 17. Queue de bœuf

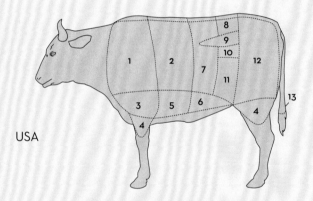

USA

1. Chuck 2. Rib 3. Brisket 4. Shank 5. Plate
6. Flank 7. Short Loin 8. Sirloin 9. Tenderloin
10. Top Sirloin 11. Bottom Sirloin 12. Round 13. Oxtail

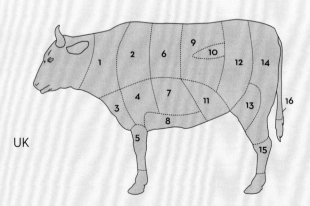

UK

1. Neck 2. Chuck and Blade 3. Clod 4. Thick Rib
5. Shin 6. Fore Rib 7. Thin Rib 8. Brisket 9. Sirloin
10. Fillet 11. Thin Flank 12. Rump 13. Thick Flank
14. Topside and Silverside 15. Leg 16. Oxtail

Veal

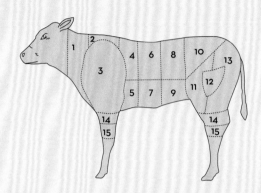

1. Collier 2. Côtes découvertes 3. Épaule
4. Côtes secondes 5. Poitrine 6. Côtes premières
7. Tendron 8. Longe 9. Flanchet 10. Quasi 11. Noix patissière
12. Noix 13. Sous-noix 14. Jarret 15. Crosse

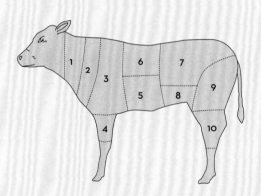

1. Neck 2. Chuck 3. Shoulder 4. Fore Shank 5. Breast
6. Ribs 7. Loin 8. Flank 9. Leg 10. Hind Shank

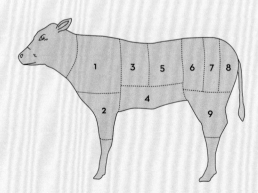

1. Shoulder 2. Fore Shank 3. Best End 4. Breast 5. Loin
6. Rump 7. Silverside 8. Topside 9. Hind Shank

Pork

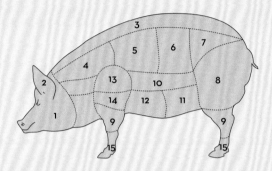

1. Tête **2.** Oreille **3.** Lard gras / gras dur / barde
4. Échine **5.** Carré **6.** Milieu de filet **7.** Pointe de filet
8. Jambon **9.** Jarret **10.** Travers **11.** Poitrine **12.** Plat de côtes
13. Palette **14.** Épaule **15.** Pieds

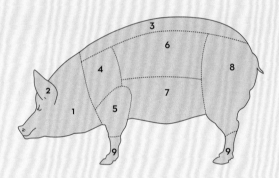

1. Head **2.** Ear **3.** Fatback **4.** Shoulder Butt
5. Picnic Shoulder **6.** Loin **7.** Spare Ribs/Belly
8. Ham **9.** Trotters

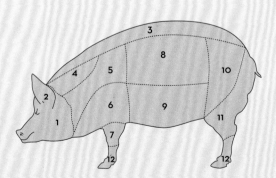

1. Head **2.** Ear **3.** Fatback **4.** Spare Rib **5.** Blade **6.** Hand
7. Hock **8.** Loin **9.** Belly **10.** Chump **11.** Leg **12.** Trotters

Lamb

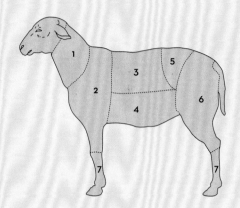

1. Collet **2.** Épaule **3.** Carré **4.** Poitrine
5. Selle **6.** Gigot **7.** Pieds

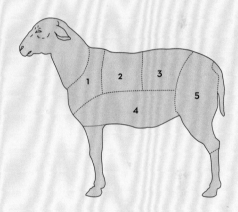

1. Shoulder **2.** Rack **3.** Loin
4. Foreshank and Breast **5.** Leg

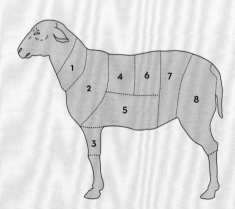

1. Scrag **2.** Shoulder **3.** Shank **4.** Best end of neck
5. Breast **6.** Loin **7.** Chump **8.** Leg

EQUIPMENT

1. Paring knife
2. Boning knife
3. Santoku knife
4. Chef's knife

5. Poultry shears
6. Carving fork
7. Honing or sharpening steel
8. Butcher's or bone saw

9. Cutting board
10. Pastry bags
11. Pastry tips
12. Butcher's twine
13. Trussing needle
14. Meat pounder or tenderizer

15. Cast-iron ridged grill pan
16. Cast-iron Dutch ovens
    of different sizes
17. Instant-read thermometer

TECHNIQUES

BEEF

Trimming Beef Tenderloin (Fillet)

Ingredients

Beef tenderloin (fillet)

Equipment

Boning knife

1 • Carefully cut along the chain (the thick strip of connective tissue running down the length of the tenderloin).

2 • Separate the chain.

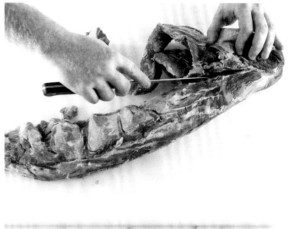

3 • Trim the sides of the tenderloin and remove the wing (the large piece of meat on the side of the butt end).

4 • Remove the chain and the chateaubriand (the long tapered section containing the butt end, center cut, and tail).

5 • Separate the chain from the chateaubriand.

6 • Holding the blade of the knife horizontal to the meat, carefully cut away just the membranes and excess fat from the chateaubriand.

Trimming Beef Tenderloin (Fillet) (continued)

7 • Turn the tenderloin over and trim off the fat on the underside.

8 • Pull the membrane away from the underside of the meat using your fingers.

9 • Holding the knife horizontal to the meat, cut away just the silver skin.

10 • The tenderloin, chain, and chateaubriand are ready to be cooked.

Preparing Côte de Boeuf (Bone-In Ribeye Steak)

Ingredients

Côte de bœuf (bone-in ribeye steak)

Equipment

Boning knife
Butcher's twine
Scissors

1 • Using the boning knife, cut into the meat around the bone, about 1½ in. (4 cm) from the end.

2 • Scrape the bone using the knife to release the meat, leaving the exposed end of the bone clean.

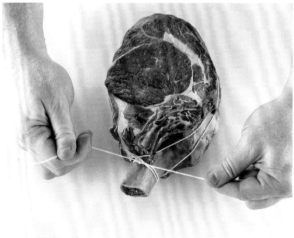

3 • Wrap a piece of twine around the bone where it joins the meat, tie a knot, then wrap the twine horizontally around the meat. Tie another knot around the exposed bone, wrap the twine around the meat again, and tie a third knot.

Preparing *Paleron* Steaks

Ingredients

Paleron (top-blade roast)

Equipment

Chef's knife

Boning knife

1 • Using the chef's knife, carefully remove the tough outer membrane.

2 • Turn the meat over to make it easier to remove the membrane.

3 • Using the boning knife, trim off the silver skin. Cut the meat into 2 equally sized pieces.

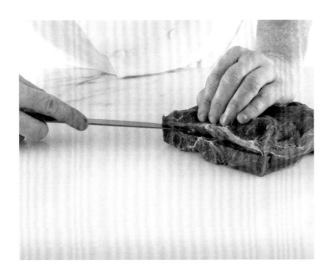

4 • Cut an incision along the silver skin running through the center of each piece of meat.

5 • Continue cutting each piece of meat in half crosswise, cutting along the silver skin.

6 • Remove the silver skin from each piece.

7 • The *palerons* are ready to be cooked.

Trimming Beef Cheeks

Ingredients
Beef cheek

Equipment
Boning knife

1 • Cut into the layer of fat covering the top of the beef cheek.

2 • Cut away the fat and silver skin all around the cheek.

3 • Remove the fat and silver skin from under the cheek as well.

4 • Release any remaining sinews.

5 • Remove these sinews completely.

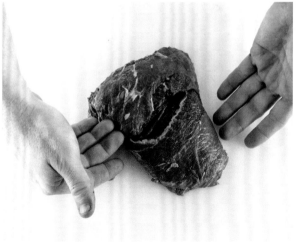

6 • The cheek is ready to be cooked.

Preparing Ground Beef Patties

Ingredients

Trimmed beef round (*rumsteck*), breast (*poitrine*),
flank (*flanchet*), or chuck (*paleron*)

Equipment

Meat grinder + grinding plate with medium-sized holes
4-in. (10-cm) hamburger rings, ¾ in. (2 cm) deep

1 • Cut the meat into approximately 1½-in. (4-cm)
pieces and pass it through the meat grinder fitted
with the grinding plate with medium-sized holes.

2 • To make each patty, fill the hamburger ring with
the ground beef, pressing it down well.

3 • Remove the ring and repeat with the remaining
ground beef.

Cutting Tournedos (Medallions)

Ingredients

Trimmed beef tenderloin (fillet)

Equipment

Chef's knife

Butcher's twine

1 • Cut the meat into 1¼-in. (3-cm) slices.

2 • Tie each slice twice all the way round with twine.

3 • The tournedos are ready to be cooked.

Tying a Boneless Beef Roast with Twine

Ingredients

Top sirloin or topside beef roast (*tende de tranche*),
or any other boneless roast

Equipment

Butcher's twine

Scissors

1 • Wrap the twine lengthwise all the way around the meat, about halfway up, gradually unwinding the twine as you go.

2 • Cross the two ends of the twine at one end of the meat.

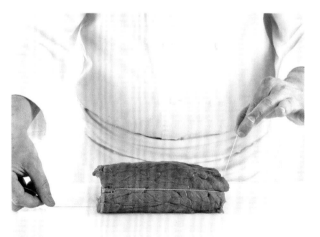

3 • Holding the short end of the twine in one hand and the long end in the other, pass the twine underneath the meat.

4 • Pull the long end of the twine up and over the meat.

5 • Tie a knot on the top.

6 • Start wrapping the long end of the twine around the meat.

7 • Continue wrapping it around the meat at regular intervals of about ¾ in. (2 cm).

Tying a Boneless Beef Roast with Twine (continued)

8 • When you get to the end, return in the opposite direction, wrapping the twine around the meat in between the intervals from the previous step.

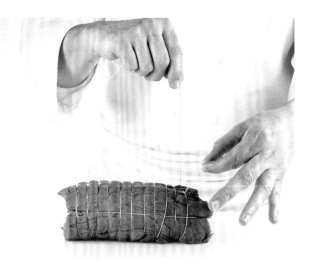

9 • Finish by making a first knot.

10 • Cut the twine.

11 • Tie a second knot and cut off the excess twine.

Cooking Beef Tongue

Ingredients

1 beef tongue

⅔ cup (150 ml) white vinegar

1 carrot, peeled

1 stalk celery

2 onions, peeled

Cloves from 1 head garlic, unpeeled

A few thyme sprigs

1 bay leaf

Salt and black peppercorns

Equipment

Chef's knife

Skimmer

Soaking time

Overnight

Cooking time

4 hours

1 • Soak the tongue overnight in a bowl of ice water in the refrigerator. The following day, cut the vegetables into ¼–½-in. (5–10-mm) pieces.

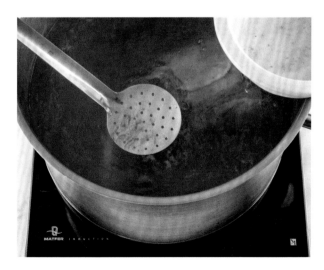

2 • Drain the tongue. Place it in a large pan of salted water and bring to a boil, regularly skimming any foam from the surface. Reduce the heat.

3 • Add the vegetables, unpeeled garlic cloves, thyme sprigs, and bay leaf. Let simmer for 4 hours, continuing to skim off any foam that rises to the surface.

Trimming Beef Tongue

Ingredients

1 cooked beef tongue (see technique p. 45)

Equipment

Boning knife

Chef's knife

1 • Trim the side of the tongue using the boning knife.

2 • Using the tip of the knife, start separating the skin from the tongue.

3 • Using the blade of the knife, cut the skin off the top of the tongue.

4 • The remaining skin will come away on its own and can be peeled off using your fingers.

5 • Using the knife, cut off the bottom part of the tongue.

6 • Cut the tongue into large pieces or chop as needed for your recipe.

VEAL

Boning a Veal Top Rump

Ingredients

Top rump of veal (*quasi*), boned

Equipment

Boning knife

1 • Using the boning knife, cut the fat off the meat.

2 • Using the tip of the knife, cut along the sinew to separate the meat.

3 • Cut off the tough, fibrous piece of meat and remove the sinew. You can use this to make a stock or jus.

4 • Cut off all the sinews and other connective tissues.

5 • Turn the meat over and repeat. Cut into the meat along the sinew.

6 • Remove the sinew.

7 • Be sure to remove all sinews and other connective tissues.

Preparing Veal Scaloppine (Escalopes)

Ingredients
Veal fillets

Equipment
Meat tenderizer
Boning knife

1 • Cut the veal fillets in half crosswise.

2 • Using a meat tenderizer, pound each piece until it is an even thickness all over.

3 • Continue pounding until each scaloppine is very thin (about ¼ in./5 mm thick).

Preparing Veal Paupiettes

Ingredients

Veal scaloppine, flattened (see technique p. 52)

Stuffing of your choice

Caul fat

Thinly sliced pork fatback (*barde de porc*)

Salt and freshly ground pepper

Equipment

Butcher's twine

Scissors

1 • Season the veal scaloppine with salt and pepper. Spoon a little stuffing into the center.

2 • Fold the bottom of each scaloppine over the stuffing, then the sides and the top.

3 • Bring the edges of each scaloppine together at the top so the stuffing is enclosed, to make a pouch.

Preparing Veal Paupiettes (continued)

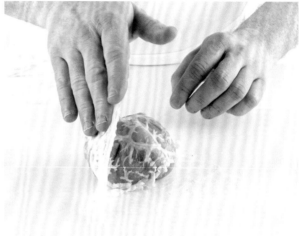

4 • Place each paupiette in the center of a piece of caul fat.

5 • Wrap the caul fat around it, folding up the bottom, then the sides, followed by the top.

6 • Wrap a strip of fatback around the sides of the paupiettes.

7 • Place 2 pieces of butcher's twine on a work surface to form an "x" shape.

8 • Add another 2 pieces of twine to form a star shape. Place a paupiette upside down in the center.

9 • Lift the opposite ends of one piece of twine over the paupiette and tie a knot. Do the same with the other 3 pieces of twine.

10 • Cut off the excess twine. Repeat with the other paupiettes. They are now ready to be cooked.

Cleaning Veal Sweetbreads

Ingredients

Veal sweetbreads

Soaking time

30 minutes–1 hour

Equipment

Chef's knife

1 • Rinse the sweetbreads in a large bowl of water, then soak them in a separate bowl filled with ice water for 30 minutes–1 hour to remove all traces of blood.

CHEFS' NOTES

To cook the sweetbreads, simply place them in a large saucepan of cold salted water, bring to a boil, and let simmer for 2 minutes. Drain the sweetbreads and plunge them into a bowl of ice water to stop the cooking.

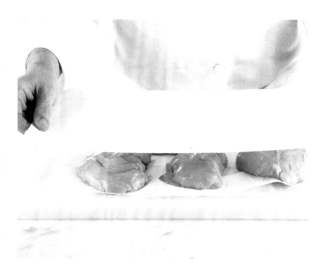

2 • Place on paper towel, cover with more paper towel, and pat dry.

3 • Using the chef's knife, gently cut along the veins and remove them.

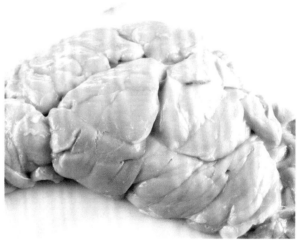

4 • Cut off the fat.

5 • Carefully remove the membrane.

Cooking Veal Tripe

Ingredients

Veal tripe

Vegetables and herbs
to make a stock (onion and
carrot, peeled and sliced
or cut into pieces; unpeeled
garlic cloves; thyme sprigs)

Salt and peppercorns

Equipment

Chef's knife

Soaking time

Overnight

Cooking time

6 hours

1 • Place the tripe in a large bowl of ice water
and soak overnight in the refrigerator.

2 • Drain the tripe and cut it into approximately
2-in. (5-cm) strips. Place the onion, carrot, garlic,
and thyme in a saucepan of water and bring
to a boil.

3 • Season with salt and peppercorns, then add
the tripe.

4 • Let simmer for about 6 hours.

Preparing Veal Kidneys

Ingredients
1 veal kidney

Equipment
Boning knife

1 • Pull away the layer of fat surrounding the kidney.

2 • Using your hands, continue to remove the fat, working your way around the kidney.

3 • Take off the membrane, too.

4 • Cut off the mass of fat using the boning knife.

5 • Cut all around the center of the kidney (renal pelvis) to remove the white parts, the fat, and the small tubes (ureters), in a single piece.

6 • Cut off as many white parts still attached to the kidney as possible.

7 • The kidney is now ready to be cooked.

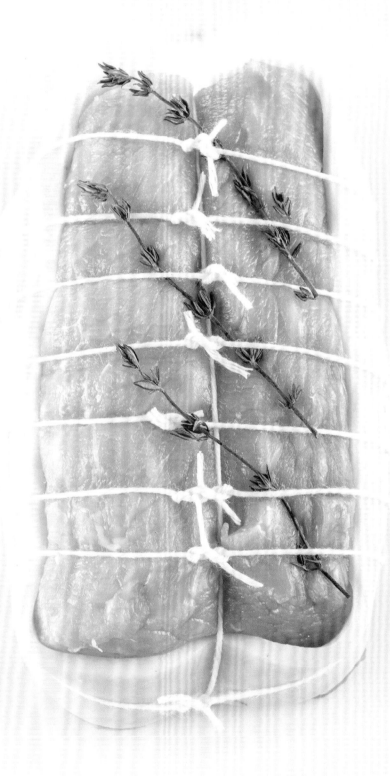

PORK

French Trimming a Rack of Pork

Ingredients

Rack of pork (*carré de porc*),
chine bone sawed through

Equipment

Chef's knife

Boning knife

1 • Using the chef's knife, cut all the way down through the rib bones.

2 • Insert the knife blade between each of the ribs on the top of the rack.

3 • Turn the rack over and do the same on the other side.

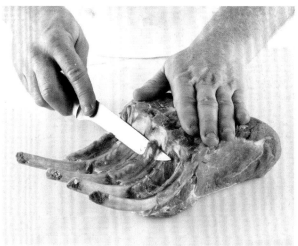

4 • Scrape each rib bone using the knife to remove all the meat.

5 • Loosen the membrane from the rib bones on the underside using the boning knife, and remove it by pulling it away.

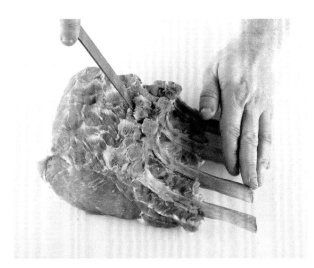

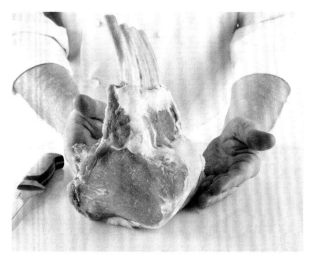

6 • Cut out any remaining pieces of backbone (chine bone).

7 • The French trimmed rack of pork is now ready to be cooked.

Cutting Pork Rib Chops

Ingredients

French trimmed rack of pork (see technique p. 64)

Equipment

Chef's knife

1 • Using a well-sharpened chef's knife, begin cutting into the meat between two ribs.

2 • Continue cutting all the way through the meat, making a clean cut without using a sawing motion. Repeat between each rib.

Tying Pork Chops with Twine

Ingredients

Pork chops (see technique p. 66)

Equipment

Butcher's twine

Scissors

1 • Wrap a piece of twine around the bone and tie the two ends together tightly in a knot.

2 • Wrap the twine all the way around the outside of the chop and tie another knot at the bone.

3 • Repeat step 2, then trim the ends of the twine, if necessary. The pork chop is ready to be cooked.

Tying a Boneless Pork Roast with Twine

Ingredients

Thinly sliced pork fatback (*barde de porc*)

Boneless pork roast (*rôti de porc*)

Equipment

Butcher's twine

Scissors

1 • Cut a wide strip from the pork fatback large enough to wrap around the roast.

2 • Pass a piece of twine underneath the meat lengthwise.

3 • Pull the twine up and over the meat, then cross it at one end.

4 • Wrap the twine around the fatback, tie a knot, and trim the ends.

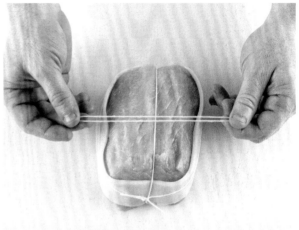

5 • Cut several pieces of twine that are more than twice as long as the roast is wide.

6 • Wrap one piece of twine around the middle of the roast crosswise and tie a knot at the top. Trim off excess twine.

7 • Continue tying pieces of twine around the meat at regular intervals as many times as necessary.

Preparing Pork Belly

Ingredients

Pork belly, bone-in (*poitrine de porc*)

Equipment

Boning knife

Chef's knife

1 • Run the blade of the boning knife beneath the bony part.

2 • Separate the meat from the bones.

3 • Remove the bony part.

4 • Using the chef's knife, cut away the leathery skin or rind.

5 • To make it easier to cut away the skin, turn the meat over once you have cut part of it away and slide the knife blade along the meat between the skin and the fat, while holding the end of the skin.

6 • Turn the meat back over and continue to cut the skin away from the fat, pulling on it as you release it.

7 • Finish cutting the skin away from the meat to remove it completely.

Preparing Pigs' Trotters

Ingredients
Pigs' trotters

Equipment
Paring knife

1 • Place a trotter upside-down and, using the knife, cut all the way down the center lengthwise.

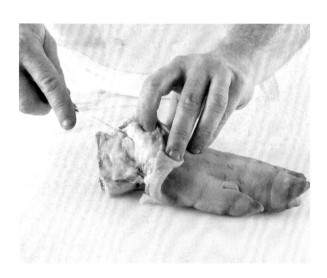

2 • Turn the trotter over and start rolling the meat away from the bone, cutting as you go.

3 • Run the knife blade along the bone to gradually separate the meat.

4 • Turn the trotter over and work your way toward the front end.

5 • Cut through the sinews and connective tissues.

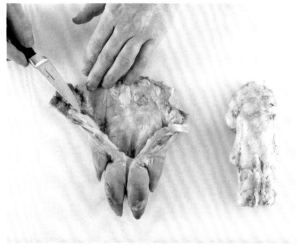

6 • Finish cutting the meat away from the bone and remove it.

7 • The trotter is now ready to be cooked.

LAMB

French Trimming a Rack of Lamb

Ingredients

Rack of lamb

Equipment

Boning knife

Chef's knife

Poultry shears

1 • Using the boning knife, remove the fell (the tough, papery membrane covering the fat).

2 • Remove the cartilage from the shoulder blade.

3 • Begin removing the thin layer of meat from the rib bones by cutting into it about halfway up.

4 • Continue by turning the rack upright and cutting through the fat and meat until you reach the rib bones.

5 • Turn the rack on one side and insert the knife between each rib.

6 • Scrape the bones with the knife until the meat comes away.

7 • Push the meat off the bones using the knife or your hand.

French Trimming a Rack of Lamb (continued)

8 • Remove the membranes inside the ribs to make the next step easier.

9 • Cut down from the top to the backbone (chine bone) to remove the large tendon so the rack will hold its shape when cooked.

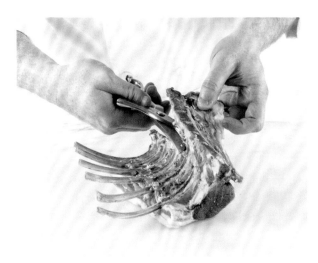

10 • Cut off the backbone using the poultry shears.

11 • Save all the trimmings to prepare a stock or meat jus.

Tying a Rack of Lamb with Twine

Ingredients

French trimmed rack of lamb (see technique p. 76)

Equipment

Butcher's twine

1 • Place the rack of lamb on a work surface with the rib bones facing upward. Pass a piece of twine underneath the meat between two ribs and tie a double knot.

2 • Do the same between each rib. The rack is now tied and ready to roast.

Cutting Lamb Chops

Ingredients

Rack of lamb, backbone (chine bone) removed

Equipment

Boning knife

Chef's knife

1 • Using the boning knife, begin cutting away the fell (the tough, papery membrane covering the fat) to remove it.

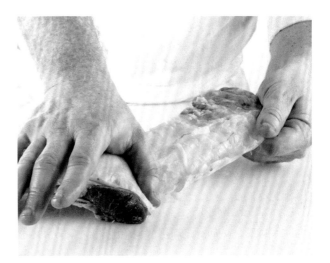

2 • Using your hands, pull the fell away from the meat to remove it completely.

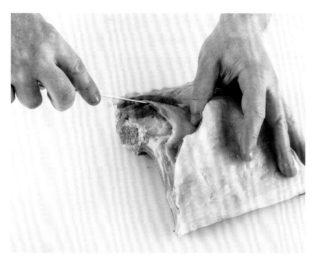

3 • Remove some of the fat and meat from the top of the ribs to reach the cartilage.

4 • Cut the cartilage off the shoulder blade.

5 • Using the chef's knife, cut between the ribs to separate the lamb chops.

6 • The lamb chops are now ready to be cooked.

Preparing a Leg of Lamb

Ingredients

Leg of lamb

Equipment

Boning knife

Butcher's saw

1 • Using the boning knife, remove the fell (the tough, papery membrane covering the fat).

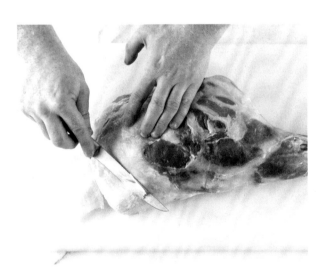

2 • Cut off part of the fat.

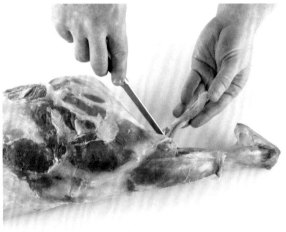

3 • Remove the tendon to make it easier to french the leg (scrape the bone clean of any meat).

4 • Make a cut in the meat around the tibia, about 3 in. (8 cm) from the end of the leg.

5 • Scrape the bone to remove the meat from it.

6 • Using the butcher's saw, cut 1¼ in. (3 cm) off the end of the leg bone.

7 • The leg of lamb is now ready to be cooked.

Preparing a Saddle of Lamb

Ingredients
Whole saddle of lamb

Equipment
Boning knife
Chef's knife

1 • Remove the kidneys from either side
of the backbone.

2 • Cut off and remove the thin outer membrane
(silver skin).

3 • Remove the fat surrounding the kidneys,
which has a strong smell.

4 • Turn the saddle over and make a cut on top down the center.

5 • Remove the fell (the tough, papery membrane covering the fat) from each side.

6 • Turn the saddle over again and remove the tenderloin (fillet) from each side. Trim the fat off the tenderloins.

7 • Cut two-thirds off the flanks (flaps).

Preparing a Saddle of Lamb (continued)

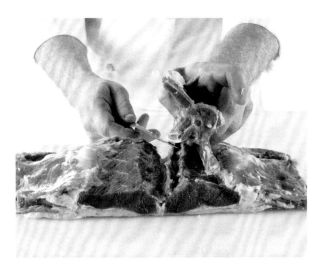

8 • Cut out the backbone (chine bone).

9 • Trim excess fat off the insides of the flanks (flaps).

Trimming Lamb Loins

Ingredients

Trimmed lamb saddle (see technique p. 84)

Equipment

Chef's knife

CHEFS' NOTES

For lamb noisettes (medallions),
cut the trimmed loins crosswise
into 1¼-in. (3-cm) slices.

1 • Cut the saddle in half between the loins.

2 • Cut the flank (flap) off each loin.

3 • Turn the flank over and score a crosshatch pattern
in the fat using the tip of the chef's knife.

Boning a Lamb Shoulder

Ingredients

Lamb shoulder

Equipment

Boning knife

1 • Using the boning knife, remove the fell (the tough, papery membrane covering the fat).

2 • Cut into the meat at the shoulder blade. Separate the meat to expose the bone.

3 • Run the knife under the shoulder blade to cut it free.

4 • Cut into the meat at the humerus bone. Separate the meat to expose the bone.

5 • Pull on the bone using your hands, as this is the easiest way to remove it.

6 • Make a cut down the center of the lower part to remove the ulna bone. Separate the meat to expose the bone.

7 • Scrape the knife along the bone to cut it free. The shoulder is boned and ready to be cooked.

Tying a Boned Lamb Shoulder with Twine

Ingredients

Boneless lamb shoulder (see technique p. 88)

Equipment

Boning knife

Butcher's twine

1 • Trim the fat off the sides of the lamb shoulder.

2 • Bring the edges toward the center and turn the shoulder over so the seam faces down.

3 • Measure a piece of twine long enough to wrap the rolled shoulder lengthwise. Pass one end of it under the meat.

4 • Tie a knot and run the twine along the sides to the other end.

5 • Tie a knot and cut the twine.

6 • Pass a piece of twine crosswise under the roast in the center and tie a knot on top. Continue tying pieces of twine around the meat at regular intervals, in the same way, as many times as necessary.

7 • The shoulder is now tied and ready to be cooked.

4 • Place the bird breast side down and cut off the head. Using the tip of a knife, cut through the skin from the neck to the shoulder blades.

5 • Cut off the neck at the top of the spine using the poultry shears.

6 • Cut out the oil (or preen) gland just above the pope's (parson's) nose at the tail end, where the spine finishes.

7 • Gently pull back the skin at the top of the bird to expose the flesh and make it easier to access the wishbone.

↪

Dressing Poultry (continued)

8 • Remove the wishbone using your thumb.

9 • Cut off the wings at the joint.

10 • Soak the feet in boiling water for 10 seconds, then rub off the dry outer layer using the dish towel.

11 • The bird is now dressed.

Gutting Poultry

Ingredients

Dressed chicken or other fowl (see technique p. 94)

Equipment

Boning knife

Tablespoon

1 • Loosen the neck skin and fold it back slightly. Insert your finger into the bird and slide it along the breastbone.

2 • To open the cavity, cut through the skin above the cloaca (the vent at the tail end of the bird).

3 • Enlarge the opening using your fingers.

Gutting Poultry <small>(continued)</small>

4 • Pull out the lungs and fat.

5 • Continue pulling to remove the remaining innards.

6 • Using the tablespoon, ensure you have removed everything.

7 • The bird is now ready to be trussed and cooked.

Flavoring or Stuffing Poultry between the Skin and the Flesh (*Contiser*)

Ingredients

Dressed and gutted chicken or other fowl
(see techniques pp. 94 and 97)

Preserved lemon slices

Thyme or rosemary sprigs

1 • Lift the neck skin up and fold it back slightly.

2 • Insert your finger between the skin and the flesh.

Flavoring or Stuffing Poultry between the Skin and the Flesh (*Contiser*) (continued)

3 • Move your fingers forward carefully to loosen the skin from the flesh without tearing it.

4 • Push several preserved lemon slices under the skin, placing them evenly.

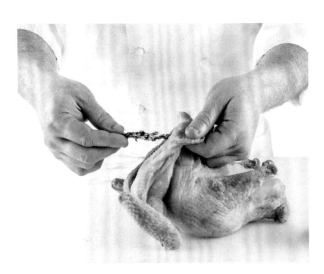

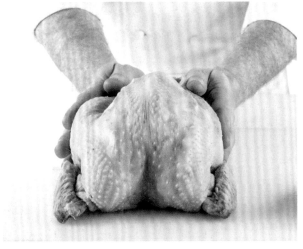

5 • Add some thyme or rosemary sprigs.

6 • Pull the skin forward over the lemon slices and thyme sprigs, tucking it under the bird and ensuring the skin is taut. The bird is now ready to be trussed and cooked.

Trussing Poultry (Slitting Technique)

Ingredients

Dressed and gutted chicken or other fowl
(see techniques pp. 94 and 97)

Equipment

Boning knife

Butcher's twine

Scissors

1 • Cut away the oil (or preen) gland just above the pope's (parson's) nose at the tail end, where the spine finishes, if necessary.

2 • Pull out the excess skin on the rump overhanging the cavity and carefully cut two small slits on either side, just large enough to fit the leg bones through to hold them in place.

3 • Tuck each leg bone into a slit, making sure the skin does not tear. Tuck the excess skin inside the cavity.

Trussing Poultry (Slitting Technique) <small>(continued)</small>

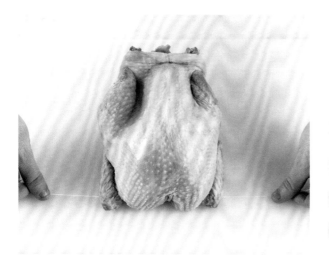

4 • Pass a piece of twine underneath the bird at the neck end.

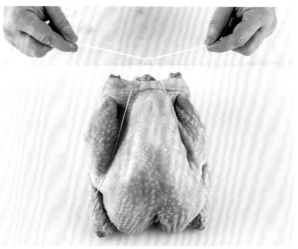

5 • Bring the twine up on each side over the wings and the breast, toward the rump, and tie in a single knot.

6 • Wrap the ends of the twine around the legs to pull them together and close the cavity. Tie a double knot and cut off the excess twine.

7 • The bird is now trussed and ready to be cooked.

Trussing Poultry (with a Needle)

Ingredients

Dressed and gutted chicken or other fowl
(see techniques pp. 94 and 97)

Equipment

Trussing needle

Butcher's twine

Scissors

1 • Thread the needle with twine. Pull the loose flap
of skin over the bird's neck cavity and tuck it under
the body. Pass the needle through the skin on top
of the right wing and the neck skin.

2 • Pass the needle through the top part of the breast,
just below the neck cavity, and the left wing,
mirroring the other side.

3 • Turn the bird over and pass the needle through
the middle of the thigh, then through the lower
part of the underside.

↳

Trussing Poultry (with a Needle) _(continued)

4 • Continue until the needle comes out through the other leg in the middle of the thigh.

5 • Remove the twine from the needle and hold both ends of it.

6 • Tie the ends in a knot.

7 • Thread the needle with another piece of twine and pass it through one side of the body underneath the thigh.

8 • Continue until the needle comes out the other side.

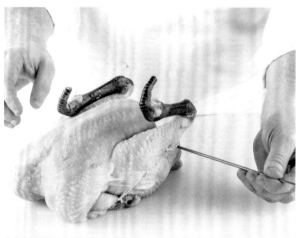

9 • Make sure it comes out in the same place under the leg.

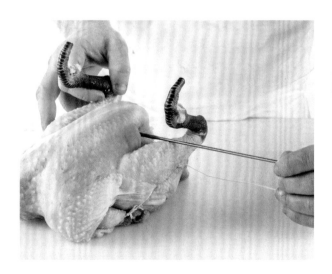

10 • Pass the needle back through the bird close to the pope's (parson's) nose above the previous exit point and the leg, all the way through to the other side.

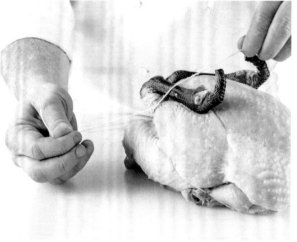

11 • Fold the feet up over the bird's back. Remove the needle, hold the twine at both ends and tie a double knot to finish.

Trussing Poultry (without a Needle)

Ingredients

Dressed and gutted chicken or other fowl
(see techniques pp. 94 and 97)

Equipment

Butcher's twine

Scissors

1 • Cut a piece of twine that is four times as long as the bird.

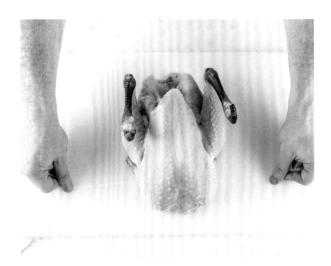

2 • Pass the twine under the bird midway between the neck and the legs.

3 • Bring the two ends of the twine up, pass them between the breast and thighs, and tie a knot.

4 • Pass the twine under and round the legs, and back up again.

5 • Tie a knot.

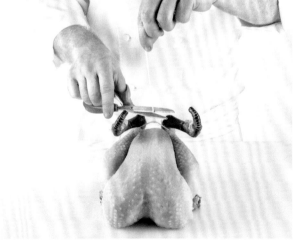

6 • Cut off the excess twine. The bird is now trussed and ready to be cooked.

Cutting Poultry in Four

Ingredients

Dressed and gutted chicken or other fowl
(see techniques pp. 94 and 97)

Equipment

Poultry shears

Boning knife

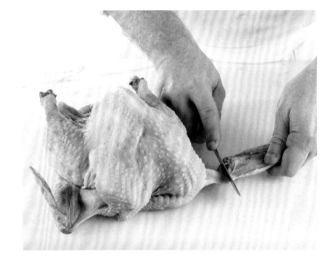

1 • Cut off the tips of the wings (save them for stock).

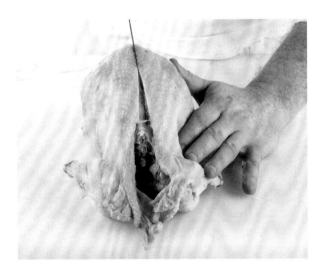

2 • Turn the bird over and cut through the skin down the length of the backbone.

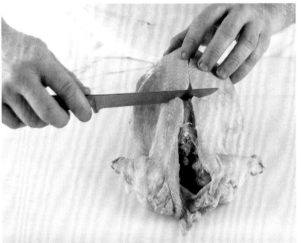

3 • Make a perpendicular cut across the bird about halfway up the spine.

4 • Cut the skin at knee level on one leg and push the thigh through the hole. Cut the skin at the groin level. Repeat for the other leg.

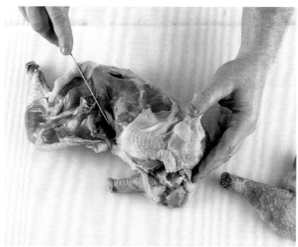

5 • Cut off each leg.

6 • Using the poultry shears, cut along the backbone to the neck, then repeat on the other side of the backbone, leaving the rib cage and two breast halves on the carcass.

7 • Turn the bird over and make a cut down the center, along the breast bone.

Cutting Poultry in Four (continued)

8 • Cut off the breast fillets with the tops of the wing bones attached.

9 • Remove the veins.

10 • Trim the fillets to remove excess fat.

Cutting Poultry in Eight

Ingredients

Dressed and gutted chicken or other fowl
(see techniques pp. 94 and 97)

Equipment

Poultry shears
Boning knife

1 • Cut the bird into 4 pieces (see technique p. 108). Cut the breast fillets in two leaving the tops of the wing bones attached.

2 • Using the boning knife, cut each thigh along the bone to separate the meat from the bone.

Cutting Poultry in Eight (continued)

3 • Remove the thigh bones by snapping the joints attaching them to the drumstick bones.

4 • Cut the boned thighs off the drumsticks.

5 • Tuck the loose skin under the thighs to give them an attractive shape.

Spatchcocking Poultry

Ingredients

Dressed and gutted chicken or other fowl
(see techniques pp. 94 and 97)

Equipment

Poultry shears

Chef's knife

Boning knife

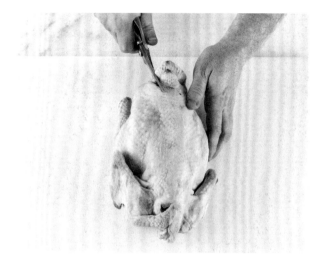

1 • Using the poultry shears, cut along one side of the backbone.

2 • Cut along the other side of the backbone.

Spatchcocking Poultry (continued)

3 • Cut out the backbone using the shears.

4 • Using the chef's knife, split open the bird at the top and bottom, so it can be opened out flat on the countertop.

5 • Using the boning knife, carefully remove the gall bladder without piercing it.

6 • Cut out all the internal organs.

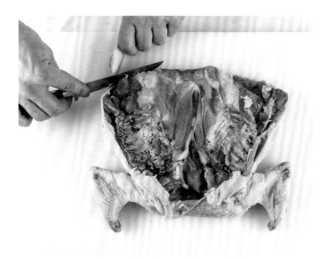

7 • Cut off the fatty parts.

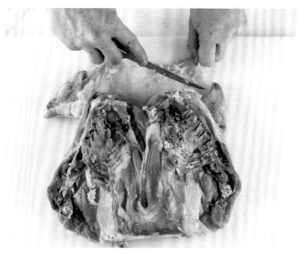

8 • Trim off excess skin.

9 • The bird is now spatchcocked and ready
to be cooked.

Boning Poultry Legs

Ingredients

Leg of a chicken or other fowl

Equipment

Boning knife

1 • Using the knife, cut along both sides of the thigh bone to release it.

2 • Do the same with the drumstick bone.

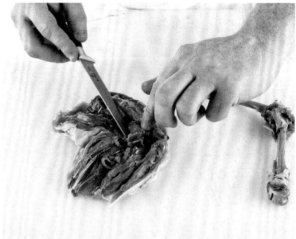

3 • Remove the bones.

4 • Redistribute the meat to fill the spaces where the bones were and to ensure the leg is of an even thickness.

5 • Close the thigh by tucking the edges of the skin underneath.

Preparing a Poultry *Jambonette*

Ingredients

Leg of a chicken or other fowl

Equipment

Butcher's saw

Boning knife

1 • Cut off the end of the leg bone using the butcher's saw.

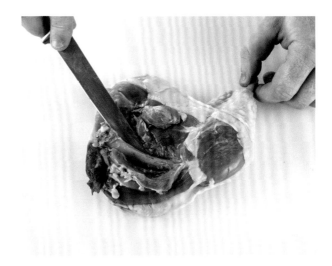

2 • Turn the leg over. Using the knife, cut along both sides of the thigh bone to release it.

3 • Remove the bone without damaging the meat, leaving the drumstick bone in place.

4 • Fold the loose skin over the top of the thigh to enclose the meat and make a neat shape.

5 • Make a cut in the skin ¾ in. (2 cm) from the top edge of the thigh. Push the drumstick bone through the hole to ensure the *jambonette* stays closed during cooking.

Boning and Stuffing a Quail

Ingredients

Quail
Stuffing of your choice

Equipment

Paring knife
Poultry shears
Trussing needle
Butcher's twine
Disposable pastry bag
Scissors

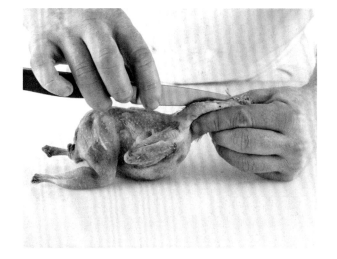

1 • Place the quail breast side down and cut off the head. Using the tip of the paring knife, cut through the skin from the neck to between the shoulder blades.

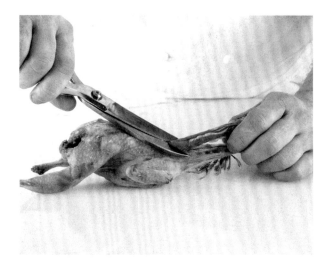

2 • Using the poultry shears, cut out the neck at the top of the spine.

3 • Cut off the wings at the joint.

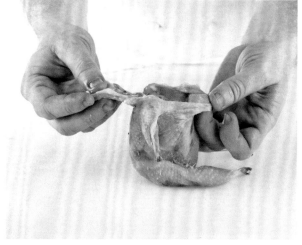

4 • Gently pull back the skin at the neck cavity to expose the meat.

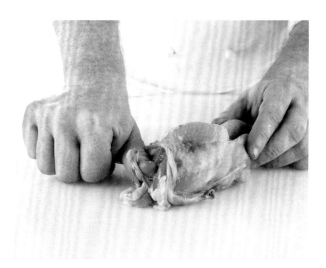

5 • Using the knife, cut along the wishbone to release it. Remove it using your fingers.

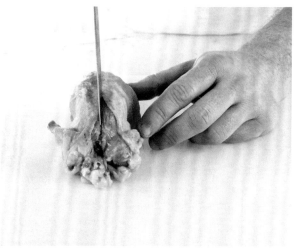

6 • Make a cut all the way down the center of the bird along the breast bone.

↪

Boning and Stuffing a Quail (continued)

7 • Cut into the skin under the wings.

8 • Using the paring knife, release the skin and pull it back.

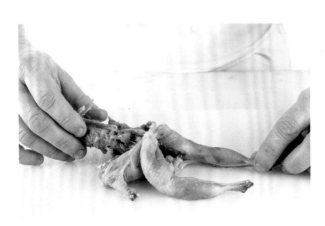

9 • Pull out the entire carcass.

10 • Cut it off.

11 • Remove the leg bones without cutting into the meat.

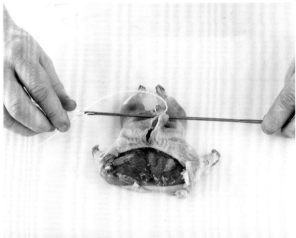

12 • Thread the trussing needle with twine and pass it through the skin just above the legs.

13 • Continue stitching the skin together until you reach the top of the back. Using the pastry bag, pipe your chosen stuffing into the quail.

14 • Fold the loose skin over the neck cavity so the edges meet and enclose the stuffing.

Boning and Stuffing a Quail (continued)

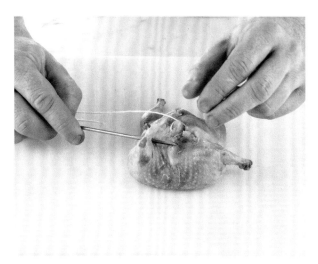

15 • Finish closing up the skin using the needle and twine.

16 • Turn the quail over and pass the twine underneath it. Bring the ends back up and pass them between the body and thighs. Tie a single knot.

17 • Pass the ends of the twine underneath the legs to pull them together with the bone ends crossed.

18 • Secure the legs together by tying a double knot.

Boning a Pigeon

Ingredients

Pigeon

Equipment

Kitchen torch
Dish towel
Poultry shears
Boning knife

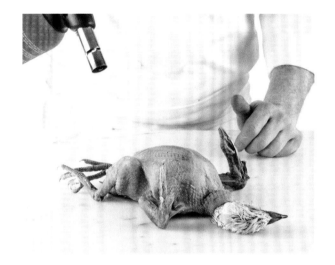

1 • Using the kitchen torch, singe off any remaining feathers.

2 • Wipe the pigeon with the dish towel.

3 • Using the poultry shears, cut off the feet and wings.

Boning a Pigeon (continued)

4 • Place the pigeon breast side down and cut off the head. Using the tip of the boning knife, cut through the skin from the neck to the shoulder blades.

5 • Cut off the neck at the top of the backbone.

6 • Gently pull back the skin at the neck cavity to expose the meat.

7 • Using the knife, cut along the wishbone to release it.

8 • Remove the wishbone with your thumb.

9 • Turn the pigeon over and make a crosswise cut just beneath the oysters. This will serve as a guide for removing the legs.

10 • Make a cut above each leg.

11 • Separate each leg from the body by snapping the bone at the joint.

Boning a Pigeon (continued)

12 • Cut the legs off with the knife.

13 • Using the poultry shears, cut along both sides of the backbone.

14 • Lift the backbone at the neck end and pull it toward the back end.

15 • Pull the backbone off.

16 • Turn the pigeon over and cut out the breast fillets, leaving the base of the wing bones still attached.

17 • Trim the excess fat off the breast fillets.

Preparing a Duck Magret

Ingredients

Boneless duck breast (magret)

Equipment

Boning knife

Chef's knife

1 • Locate the silver skin.

2 • Cut it off using the boning knife.

3 • Make sure you have removed all the silver skin, veins, and connective tissues.

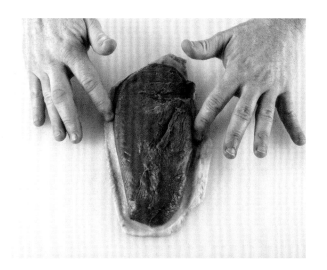

4 • Using your fingers, separate the fat from around the magret flesh.

5 • Trim off the excess fat using the chef's knife.

6 • Using the tip of the knife, score the skin in a crosshatch pattern.

7 • The magret is now ready to be cooked.

GAME

Trussing a Pheasant

Ingredients

Pheasant, trimmed and gutted (see technique p. 97)

Thinly sliced pork fatback (*barde de porc*)

Equipment

Boning knife

Trussing needle

Butcher's twine

1 • Cut a piece of fatback large enough to cover the top of the pheasant. Score a crosshatch pattern into the fatback, without cutting all the way through.

2 • Place the fatback over the breast of the pheasant.

3 • Turn the pheasant over. Thread the trussing needle with twine and push the point of the needle through one side of the fatback at the neck end.

4 • Pass the needle and twine over the back of the pheasant and push the needle through the other side of the fatback.

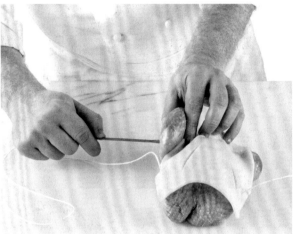

5 • Turn the pheasant over again and push the needle and twine into one thigh.

6 • Push the needle straight through the pheasant and out through the other thigh.

7 • Tie a double knot on the side.

Trussing a Pheasant _(continued)

8 • Push up the pope's (parson's) nose with your thumb.

9 • Pass the needle and twine through the rump end from one side to the other.

10 • Turn the bird over and push the needle and twine through the top, ensuring you include the fatback.

11 • Tie a double knot on the side.

Cutting Up a Hare

Ingredients
Hare, skinned and gutted

Equipment
Boning knife
Chef's knife

CHEFS' NOTES

This method can also be used
to cut up rabbits.

1 • Using the boning knife, cut off the forelegs.

2 • Cut off the hind legs.

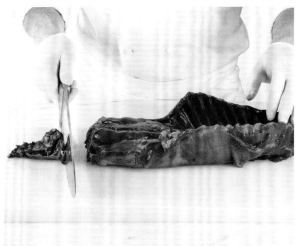

3 • Cut off the tail bones using the chef's knife.

Cutting Up a Hare (continued)

4 • Cut off the part below the shoulders.

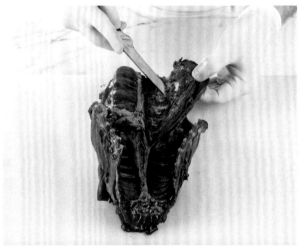

5 • Remove the tenderloins from each side of the backbone.

6 • Turn the hare over and cut along the backbone to separate the loins on either side.

7 • Trim the fat and sinew off the tenderloins and loins.

8 • Separate the top and bottom parts of the shoulder.

9 • Cut each hind leg into 2 pieces at the knee joint, then separate the thighs from the lower part of the legs.

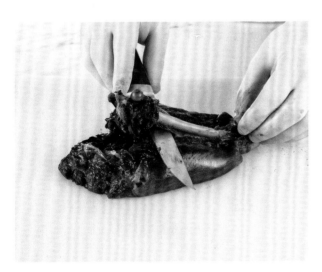

10 • Cut out the thigh bones.

11 • The cuts of hare are now ready for use.

Cutting Venison Steaks (*Pavés*)

Ingredients

Venison tenderloin fillet (*filet de chevreuil*)

Equipment

Boning knife

Chef's knife

1 • Cut off the silver skin using the boning knife.

2 • Trim the sides, cutting off any sinew.

3 • Cut the tenderloin into steaks measuring about 3 in. (8 cm) in length.

Preparing Venison Loins

Ingredients

Bone-in venison saddle (*dos de chevreuil*)

Equipment

Boning knife

1 • Cut along one tenderloin fillet to release it.

2 • Remove the tenderloin.

3 • Repeat on the other side.

Preparing Venison Loins (continued)

4 • Turn the saddle over and cut along the backbone.

5 • Continue cutting to separate the loin (backstrap).

6 • Repeat on the other side.

Marinating Game

Ingredients

2 tenderloins of game meat, cut into pieces

1 carrot, peeled

2 stalks celery

1 onion, peeled

1 tsp (3 g) peppercorns

2 cups (500 ml) red wine

2 bay leaves

Equipment

Chef's knife

Marinating time

Overnight

1 • Place the meat in a large bowl.
Cut the vegetables into ½-in. (1-cm) pieces and add to the bowl.

2 • Add the peppercorns and pour in the wine.

3 • Add the bay leaves. Let marinate overnight in the refrigerator.

RECIPES

BEEF

BOURGIGNON-STYLE BEEF CHEEKS

Joues de bœuf façon bourguignonne

Serves 2

Active time
2 hours

Cooking time
2 hours

Storage
5 days

Equipment
Butcher's twine
Large fine-mesh sieve
5-in. (12-cm) stainless-steel ring

Ingredients

Beef cheeks

1 tbsp (10 g) all-purpose flour

2 beef cheeks, 1¾ lb. (800 g) each

1½ onions

1 carrot

2 cloves garlic

3½ tbsp (50 ml) sunflower oil

3 cups (750 ml) red wine

2 cups (500 ml) brown veal stock (*fond brun de veau*, see recipe p. 16)

1 bouquet garni (leek greens, bay leaf, and thyme)

3 whole cloves

5 juniper berries

Salt and freshly ground pepper

To garnish

4½ oz. (125 g) smoked slab bacon (*poitrine de porc salé*)

Sunflower oil

4½ oz. (125 g) shimeji mushrooms

4½ oz. (125 g) pearl onions, peeled

4 tbsp (2 oz./60 g) butter, divided

2 pinches sugar, divided

9 oz. (250 g) mixed orange and yellow carrots

Salt

To serve

A few sprigs fresh parsley

Oil for deep-frying

Croutons

A few marigold leaves and flowers

3½ tbsp (50 ml) parsley-infused olive oil

PREPARING THE BEEF CHEEKS

Preheat the oven to 350°F (180°C/Gas Mark 4). Place the flour on a baking sheet lined with parchment paper and toast for 10 minutes. Leave the oven on. Trim the fat and silver skin from the beef cheeks (see technique p. 38) and tie them with butcher's twine. Peel and finely chop 1 onion and the carrot. Peel and crush the garlic cloves. Heat the sunflower oil over high heat in a large Dutch oven and brown the beef cheeks on all sides. Add the chopped onion and carrot and the garlic cloves and sweat for a few minutes. Transfer the ingredients to a colander to allow as much excess fat to drain off as possible, then return them to the pan. Using a wooden spoon, stir in the toasted flour. Add the red wine and bring to a boil, stirring continuously. Flambé, then pour in the veal stock. Add the bouquet garni and bring back to a boil, skimming off any foam on the surface. Stick the cloves in the remaining ½ onion and add to the pan with the juniper berries. Cover and cook in the oven for 1½–2 hours, or until the beef cheeks are tender. Strain the cooking liquid through the fine-mesh sieve into a separate saucepan. Reduce the sauce over high heat until it coats the back of a spoon. Adjust the seasonings if necessary.

PREPARING THE GARNISH

Cut the bacon into ½-in. (1-cm) lardons and place them in a saucepan of cold water. Blanch by bringing to a boil, then drain (without cooling the lardons under cold water) and pat dry. Sauté the bacon in a large skillet with a little sunflower oil until golden but not too dry. Drain on paper towels. In the same skillet, cook the mushrooms in the bacon fat until softened but not browned. Season with salt and pepper. Add the bacon and mushrooms to the beef cheek sauce and let simmer for a few minutes. To glaze the pearl onions, place them in a saucepan with ½ in. (1 cm) of water, 2 tbsp (1 oz./30 g) of the butter, and 1 pinch each of sugar and salt. Simmer until the onions have absorbed the liquid and are completely tender, then continue to cook until they are caramelized. To glaze the carrots, peel and rinse them, then cut them lengthwise into approximately 1/16-in. (2-mm) slices, 1¼ in. (3 cm) in width. Place in a skillet with ½ in. (1 cm) of water, the remaining butter, and 1 pinch each of sugar and salt. Simmer until the carrots have absorbed the liquid and are completely tender. Cook until they are glossy but remove from the heat before they caramelize.

TO SERVE

De-stem the parsley, wash the leaves, and pat with paper towels until completely dry. Heat the oil for deep-frying to 284°F (140°C), add the parsley leaves, and fry until crisp. Drain on paper towels. For each serving, arrange the carrot slices around the inside of the 5-in. (12-cm) ring in two rows, overlapping them slightly. Place a beef cheek in the center, then arrange the lardons and pearl onions on top. Scatter with the fried parsley, a few marigold leaves and petals, and the croutons. Remove the ring. Pour sauce around the carrots and drizzle with parsley-infused oil.

FLEMISH BEEF AND BEER STEW

Carbonnade flamande gratinée au pain d'épice

Serves 10

Active time

45 minutes

Cooking time

4½ hours

Resting time

30 minutes

Storage

3 days

Equipment

Mandolin

Food mill or potato ricer

Ingredients

Flemish beef and beer stew

1 lb. 2 oz. (500 g) shallots

10½ oz. (300 g) sweet onions, preferably Cévennes

3 cloves garlic, unpeeled

Scant 2 lb. (850 g) boneless beef shoulder (*macreuse*)

Scant 2 lb. (850 g) boneless beef shank (*jarret de bœuf*)

4 tsp (20 g) salt

10½ oz. (300 g) smoked slab bacon (*lard paysan*)

Scant ½ cup (100 ml) olive oil

1½ packed tbsp (20 g) brown sugar, preferably *vergeoise*

½ cup (120 ml) aged red wine vinegar

3 tbsp (1 oz./30 g) all-purpose flour

1 bottle (330 ml) abbey beer of your choice

4 cups (1 liter) beef jus

⅔ oz. (20 g) spiced bread (*pain d'épice*)

Potato gnocchi

2¼ lb. (1 kg) semi-waxy potatoes, preferably Agria

Coarse sea salt

1¾ cups (7 oz./200 g) 00 (pizza) flour

1 egg

Scant ½ cup (100 ml) olive oil

PREPARING THE FLEMISH BEEF AND BEER STEW

Preheat the oven to 340°F (170°C/Gas Mark 3). Peel and finely chop the shallots and onions. Crush the unpeeled garlic cloves using the flat of a chef's knife blade. Trim the fat off the beef shoulder and shank and cut the meat into approximately 1¾-oz. (50-g) pieces. Season with the 4 tsp (20 g) salt. Cut the bacon into 1-oz. (30-g) lardons, ¼ in. (5 mm) in width, and slowly brown in a Dutch oven to render the fat. Remove the bacon, add the olive oil, and increase the heat. Add the beef and brown on all sides, working in batches if necessary. Remove the meat from the pan and add the shallots, onions, and garlic, then stir in the brown sugar. Cook over low heat until the vegetables are softened and lightly caramelized. Deglaze with the vinegar, then return the meat to the pan and stir in the flour to coat. Pour in the beer and beef jus, and bring to a simmer. Cover, place in the oven, and cook for 3 hours, until the meat is completely tender. Remove the pan from the oven, uncover, and reduce the cooking juices if necessary to thicken. Increase the oven temperature to 400°F (200°C/Gas Mark 6). Using the mandolin, cut the spiced bread into paper thin (1⁄16-in./1-mm) slices. Place on a baking sheet and toast in the oven for 3 minutes, keeping a close eye on them to ensure they do not burn.

PREPARING THE POTATO GNOCCHI

Preheat the oven to 400°F (200°C/Gas Mark 6). Wash and dry the potatoes and put them over a bed of coarse sea salt on a rimmed baking sheet. Bake for about 1½ hours, or until the potatoes are tender throughout; the exact time will depend on their size. While the potatoes are still warm, peel them and pass them through the food mill or potato ricer into a bowl. Sprinkle the flour over the potatoes and add the egg, then combine using your hands, taking care not to overmix. Let the mixture rest for 30 minutes at room temperature. Shape the dough into small balls, about ½ oz. (13 g) each, and roll each one on the tines of a fork to form gnocchi. Poach the gnocchi in boiling salted water for 1 minute (or until they float), then transfer to a large dish and drizzle with the olive oil.

TO SERVE

Serve the stew topped with toasted spiced bread and gnocchi. Pair with abbey beer, if desired.

LAYERED POT-AU-FEU WITH CELERY LEAF SAUCE

Compression de pot-au-feu et bouillon lié aux feuilles de céleri

Serves 2

Active time
1 hour

Cooking time
3 hours 40 minutes

Storage
3 days

Equipment
Fine-mesh sieve

Immersion blender

Steam oven (or steamer)

2 × 2-in. (5-cm) stainless-steel rings, 3 in. (8 cm) deep

2-in. (5-cm) round cookie cutter

Ingredients

Pot-au-feu

1 beef cheek

¼ oxtail

About 4 qt. (4 liters) water

3 juniper berries

1 bay leaf

2 carrots

1 leek, white part only

½ celery root (celeriac)

½ long white turnip (*navet long*) or 2 round turnips

1 onion

3 whole cloves

2 cloves garlic

1 shallot

1 tbsp (15 g) Meaux mustard

1 tbsp finely chopped fresh tarragon

1 tbsp finely chopped fresh parsley

2 green cabbage leaves

Salt and freshly ground pepper

Celery leaf sauce

1 shallot

2 tsp (10 g) butter

Generous ¾ cup (200 ml) pot-au-feu broth (see left)

Scant ½ cup (100 ml) heavy cream, min. 35% fat

2½ oz. (70 g) celery leaves

Salt and freshly ground pepper

Tartines

1 thin slice sandwich bread

3½ tbsp (50 ml) clarified butter

2 hard-boiled quail eggs

1 cornichon

Pickled carrot slices

Pickled mustard seeds

4–6 red shiso leaves

A few chervil sprigs

PREPARING THE POT-AU-FEU

Place the beef cheek and oxtail in a Dutch oven, add enough water to just cover them, and bring to a boil, skimming any foam from the surface. Add the juniper berries and bay leaf. Peel the carrots, leek, celery root, and turnip, and add them all whole to the pan. Peel the onion, cut it in half crosswise, and char the cut side directly over a gas or electric burner (it should be well-blackened to color and flavor the broth). Stick the cloves into the charred onion and add it to the pan. Peel the garlic cloves, crush them using the flat of a chef's knife blade, and add to the pan. Let cook over low heat for 3½ hours, until the meat is completely tender. Remove the beef cheek and oxtail. When they are cool enough to handle, shred the meat and place in a bowl. Peel and finely chop the shallot and place in a bowl with the mustard, tarragon, and parsley. Stir until well combined. Strain the broth through the fine-mesh sieve into a bowl. Cut the cooked carrots, celery root, and turnip into ⅛-in. (3-mm) slices and set aside for assembling the dish. Cook the cabbage leaves in boiling salted water until just tender, drain, refresh under cold water, and set aside for assembly.

PREPARING THE CELERY LEAF SAUCE

Peel and finely chop the shallot and sweat it in a saucepan with the butter. Add the generous ¾ cup (200 ml) pot-au-feu broth and reduce by half over medium heat. Add the cream and allow to thicken slightly, then take the pan off the heat, add the celery leaves and process with the immersion blender until smooth. Strain through the fine-mesh sieve and adjust the seasonings as necessary.

ASSEMBLING THE POT-AU-FEU

Preheat the steam oven, if using, to 185°F (85°C/Gas on lowest setting). Place the stainless-steel rings on a baking sheet lined with parchment paper. Using the 2-in. (5-cm) cookie cutter, cut 2 disks out of the cooked cabbage leaves. Arrange the vegetable slices and shredded meat in well-defined layers in the rings, starting with the celery root and continuing with layers of meat, carrots, meat, and turnip, in that order, trimming the vegetables to fit as you go. Top each stack with a cabbage disk. Cover the rings with plastic wrap and cook in the steam oven, or steamer, for 15 minutes.

TARTINES

Meanwhile, preheat the oven to 325°F (160°C/Gas Mark 3). Remove the crusts from the slice of sandwich bread and cut it into two ¾ × 2¾-in. (2 × 7-cm) rectangles. Brush with the clarified butter and bake between two baking sheets for 8 minutes. Let cool. Peel and quarter the quail eggs and thinly slice the cornichon. Arrange the eggs, cornichon slices, and a few pickled carrot slices and mustard seeds in an attractive pattern over each tartine. Top with red shiso and chervil leaves.

TO SERVE

Carefully place each layered pot-au-feu in the center of a soup bowl and remove the rings. Top each one with a tartine and pour celery sauce around them.

CHEFS' NOTES

In place of the carrot, celery root, and turnip, you can use other, lesser-known vegetables, such as Jerusalem artichoke, black radish, parsnip, parsley root, or chervil root. You could also replace one of the vegetables with truffles or add bone marrow or a slice of pan-seared foie gras.

BEEF TARTARE TARTLETS

Tartelettes de tartare de bœuf

Makes 12, to serve 6

Active time

1½ hours

Cooking time

20 minutes

Chilling time

45 minutes

Equipment

Pasta maker

4-in. (10-cm) round pastry cutter

24 brioche molds, 2¾ in. (7 cm) in diameter

Ingredients

Tartlet shells

Scant ½ cup (3¾ oz./105 g) lightly beaten egg (about 2 eggs)

1⅔ cups (7 oz./200 g) all-purpose flour

¾ tsp (4 g) salt

1 oz. (25 g) lard, cut into pieces

Butter for the molds

Beef tartare

1¼ lb. (600 g) boneless beef rib-eye steak (*entrecôte de bœuf*)

4 salt-cured anchovy fillets

2 shallots

5 sprigs parsley

1¾ oz. (50 g) capers

2 oz. (55 g) cornichons

3 tsp (15 ml) olive oil

Tabasco

Worcestershire sauce

Salt and freshly ground pepper

Shiso tempura

Oil for deep-frying

2 tbsp (20 g) rice flour

3 tbsp (1 oz./30 g) all-purpose flour

1 tbsp (10 g) cornstarch

Generous ½ tsp (3 g) salt

Scant ½ cup (100 ml) ice-cold sparkling water

1 tbsp + 2 tsp (25 g) lightly beaten egg (½ egg)

12 shiso leaves

To serve

12 quail egg yolks

4 salt-cured anchovy fillets, cut into ⅛-in. (4-mm) pieces

PREPARING THE TARTLET SHELLS

Lightly whisk the eggs in a bowl. Sift the flour and salt onto a clean work surface, add the pieces of lard, and rub the two together between your fingertips until the texture is like coarse sand. Make a well in the center and add the eggs. Gradually draw the flour into the well with your fingertips or a bowl scraper, mixing in the eggs, then knead to make a smooth dough. Shape the dough into a ball, cover with plastic wrap, and chill for at least 30 minutes. Preheat the oven to 350°F (180°C/Gas Mark 4). Roll the dough through the pasta maker to a thickness of 1/16 in. (2 mm), place it flat on the countertop, and cut out 12 disks using the 4-in. (10-cm) pastry cutter. Grease 12 of the brioche molds with butter and line them with the dough disks. Stack a second mold on top of each one and place upside down on a baking sheet lined with parchment paper. Chill for 15 minutes, then bake upside down between the two molds for 15 minutes. Carefully turn the shells out of the molds and set aside on paper towels.

PREPARING THE BEEF TARTARE

Cut the beef into ⅛-in. (3-mm) dice and place in a bowl over a bed of ice. Chop the anchovy fillets and peel and finely chop the shallots. Wash and finely chop the parsley, then finely chop the capers and cornichons. Toss the steak with the olive oil and season with salt and pepper. Stir in the capers, cornichons, parsley, and shallots, and season to taste with Tabasco and Worcestershire sauce.

PREPARING THE SHISO TEMPURA

Heat the oil for deep-frying to 320°F (160°C) in a deep pan. Combine the dry ingredients, then sift them together into a medium bowl. Whisk in the sparkling water and egg. Using a paring knife, trim the shiso stems to give them a long pointed tip. Using tongs, dip the leaves in the batter until coated and fry them in batches in the hot oil until they stop producing bubbles. Drain on paper towels.

TO SERVE

Spoon the beef tartare into the tartlet shells, shaping it into a dome. Using the back of the spoon, press down on the top of each dome to create a small hollow. Add 1 quail egg yolk to each one. Scatter over the anchovy pieces and serve with the shiso tempura leaves on the side.

CALIFORNIA-STYLE BURGERS WITH SMOKED BACON

Burgers Californiens au lard fumé

Serves 6

Active time

4 hours

Cooking time

25–30 minutes

Resting time

50 minutes

Rising time

1 hour

Storage

24 hours (buns and/or uncooked burgers)

Equipment

Stand mixer + dough hook

Cast-iron skillet

Wooden sandwich skewers

Ingredients

Buns

²⁄₃ oz. (20 g) fresh yeast, crumbled

¾ cup (180 ml) water at 77°F (25°C)

4²⁄₃ cups (1 lb./490 g) pastry flour (T45), divided

2 tsp (10 g) salt

Generous 2 tbsp (1½ oz./45 g) honey

5 tsp (20 g) sugar

2 tbsp (1¼ oz./35 g) egg yolk (scant 2 yolks)

3 tbsp (45 ml) olive oil

Egg wash and garnish

1 egg yolk

1 egg

1 tsp (5 ml) water

1 pinch salt

White sesame seeds, for sprinkling

Beef patties

2 lb. (900 g) ground beef

4 tbsp (2 oz./60 g) Dijon mustard

1¾ tsp (8 ml) Worcestershire sauce

2 tsp (10 g) salt

2 tsp (5 g) ground pepper

Remoulade sauce

1 egg yolk

1 tbsp (15 g) Dijon mustard

1 tbsp (15 g) wholegrain mustard

1 tsp champagne vinegar, preferably from Reims

²⁄₃ cup (150 ml) grape-seed oil

Salt and freshly ground pepper

To serve

3 tomatoes

Olive oil

12 slices smoked bacon (*ventrèche*)

1 head butter lettuce, divided into leaves

1 red onion

2 avocados

Fleur de sel

Butter, at room temperature

6 slices Comté

Fries (optional)

Salt and freshly ground pepper

BUNS

Place the yeast, water, and 1 scant cup (3¼ oz./90 g) of the pastry flour in the food mixer bowl and beat until well blended. Scrape down the sides of the bowl using a bowl scraper or flexible spatula, then add the rest of the flour to the bowl, without mixing yet. Let rest for 20 minutes at room temperature. Meanwhile, whisk the remaining ingredients together in a separate bowl. After the 20 minutes have passed, add the whisked ingredients to the mixer bowl and knead on low speed for 2 minutes. Scrape down the sides of the bowl and let rest for 20 minutes. Knead on low speed for an additional 8 minutes, then on medium speed for 7 minutes, or until the dough is smooth. Cut the dough into 6 pieces weighing 3½ oz. (100 g) each and shape into loose balls. Let rest for 10 minutes, then shape into taut balls and place on a baking sheet lined with parchment paper. Whisk together the ingredients for the egg wash and brush over the buns. Let rise at room temperature for about 1 hour, or until the buns have doubled in size. Preheat the oven to 350°F (175°C/Gas Mark 4). Brush the buns again with egg wash and sprinkle with sesame seeds. Bake for 12–15 minutes, until puffed and golden brown.

PREPARING THE BEEF PATTIES

Combine the ground beef with the mustard and Worcestershire sauce. Season with the salt and pepper. Divide the mixture into six portions weighing 5¼ oz. (150 g) each and flatten into rounds the same diameter as the buns. Chill until ready to grill.

PREPARING THE REMOULADE SAUCE

Whisk together the egg yolk, mustards, and vinegar in a bowl. Whisking vigorously, gradually add the oil, pouring it into the egg yolk mixture in a thin, steady stream, until the sauce is thick and emulsified. Adjust the seasonings if necessary and reserve in the refrigerator.

TO SERVE

Preheat the oven to 350°F (180°C/Gas Mark 4). Peel and hull the tomatoes and cut them crosswise into ¼-in. (5-mm) slices. Drizzle with olive oil and season with salt and pepper. Cook the bacon in the cast-iron skillet over medium heat until crisp on both sides. Transfer to a rack and wipe the skillet clean with paper towels. Wash and dry the lettuce leaves. Peel the onion, cut it crosswise into 1/16-in. (2-mm) slices and separate the slices into rings. Cut the avocados in half and remove the pits. Scoop out the flesh using a spoon, slice it thinly, and season with fleur de sel. Cut the buns in half, spread a little butter over the cut sides, and toast buttered side down in the skillet. Spread remoulade sauce over the cut sides. Cook the burgers to your liking in the skillet and place them on the bun bases. Top each one with a cheese slice and place in the oven for 3 minutes to melt. Top with 2 slices of bacon, the lettuce leaves, and tomato, avocado, and onion slices. Finish by replacing the bun lids. Spear the burgers with sandwich skewers to hold them together. Serve immediately, with the remaining remoulade sauce on the side and fries, if desired.

SEARED BEEF ROAST WITH MUSTARD RELISH

Paleron snacké, condiment moutarde et sucrine

Serves 10

Active time

30 minutes

Cooking time

4 hours

Storage

2 days

Equipment

Fine-mesh sieve

Ingredients

Beef jus

5¼ oz. (150 g) sweet onions, preferably Cévennes

6 cloves garlic

3½ lb. (1.5 kg) beef brisket (*poitrine de bœuf*)

Olive oil

¼ bunch thyme

1 generous tbsp (10 g) black peppercorns

2 sticks (9 oz./250 g) butter

3 qt. (3 liters) vegetable stock, divided

Shallot and mustard relish

1½ lb. (750 g) shallots

3½ oz. (100 g) beef fat (*graisse de bœuf*)

¼ bunch thyme

1 bay leaf

2 tsp (10 g) salt

3 cups (750 ml) beef jus

3 generous tbsp (1¾ oz./50 g) wholegrain mustard

2 tbsp (30 ml) aged red wine vinegar

¼ bunch parsley, roughly chopped

Charred lettuce

½ bunch scallions

3 medium button mushrooms

20 sun-dried tomatoes

5 heads Little Gem lettuce

Generous ¾ cup (200 ml) olive oil

2 tsp (10 g) salt

Top-blade roast

4½ lb. (2 kg) top-blade roast (*paleron*), trimmed

Scant ½ tsp (2 g) salt

Scant ½ tsp (1 g) cracked pepper

⅔ cup (150 ml) olive oil

¼ bunch thyme

To serve

Fleur de sel

PREPARING THE BEEF JUS

Peel the onions and cut each one into 8 wedges. Roughly crush the garlic cloves, unpeeled, using the flat of a chef's knife blade. Cut the beef into 1½-in. (4-cm) pieces. Heat a little olive oil in a Dutch oven and sear the pieces of beef over medium-high heat until they are pale golden brown. Add the onions, garlic, thyme, peppercorns, and butter. Reduce the heat to low and cook until the meat is deeply browned, basting it with the oil and butter. Remove the beef and vegetables from the pan, pour off the excess fat, then return them to the pan and deglaze with a small ladleful of vegetable stock to release the browned bits sticking to the bottom. Add the remaining stock and simmer for 2 hours. Strain through the fine-mesh sieve into a bowl, letting the beef and aromatics drain for 5 minutes. Reserve at room temperature.

PREPARING THE SHALLOT AND MUSTARD RELISH

While the beef jus is simmering, peel the shallots and thinly slice them lengthwise. Heat the beef fat in a saucepan with the thyme, bay leaf, and salt, and sweat the shallots until softened but not browned. Cover and let cook very gently over the lowest possible heat for 2 hours, stirring occasionally, until meltingly soft. Add the beef jus and reduce until thick and jammy. Remove from the heat, stir in the mustard, vinegar, and parsley, and adjust the seasonings if necessary.

PREPARING THE CHARRED LETTUCE

Wash and cut the scallions diagonally into ¼-in. (5-mm) slices. Wash the button mushrooms and cut them into ¹⁄₁₆-in. (2-mm) slices. Cut the sun-dried tomatoes into ¼-in. (5-mm) strips. Remove any damaged outer leaves from the Little Gem lettuce heads and trim the bases flat. Cut each lettuce in half lengthwise and toss with the olive oil and salt. Sear the lettuce halves in a skillet until lightly charred but still crisp.

PREPARING THE TOP-BLADE ROAST

Cut the meat into 10 long slices, about 1-in. (2-cm) thick and weighing 5 oz. (140 g) each, and season with the salt and cracked pepper. Heat the olive oil and thyme in a skillet and sear the slices of meat (in batches if necessary) over high heat for 2 minutes on each side until they are deeply browned on the outside but still rare inside. Remove the meat, let rest for 2 minutes, then cut through each piece lengthwise to obtain two ½-in. (1-cm) slices.

TO SERVE

Place a Little Gem lettuce half on each plate and arrange mushroom, sun-dried tomato, and scallion slices over the top. Add a quenelle of shallot and mustard relish and 2 slices of meat. Drizzle with beef jus and sprinkle with fleur de sel.

BEEF TONGUE WITH SPICY SAUCE

Langue de bœuf, sauce piquante

Serves 4

Active time
30 minutes

Cooking time
2¼ hours

Chilling time
2 hours

Storage
4 days

Equipment
Fine-mesh sieve
1¼-in. (3-cm) round cookie cutter

Ingredients

Beef tongue
3½–4½ lb. (1.5–2 kg) beef tongue
1 onion
4 whole cloves
2 carrots
1 leek
3 stalks celery
2 bay leaves
½ head garlic

Spicy sauce
1 shallot
3 tbsp (1½ oz./40 g) butter
⅓ cup (1½ oz./40 g) all-purpose flour
4½ tbsp (70 ml) apple cider vinegar
Generous ¾ cup (200 ml) Sauvignon Blanc wine
Generous ¾ cup (200 ml) tomato coulis
Scant ½ cup (100 ml) thickened brown veal stock (*fond brun de veau lié*, see recipe p. 16)
Scant ½ cup (100 ml) beef tongue cooking juices (see above)
1 tbsp (15 g) hot mustard
½ tsp *piment d'Espelette*
Salt and freshly ground pepper

To garnish
2 slices sandwich bread
Scant ½ cup (100 ml) clarified butter, melted
1 bunch chives
8 cornichons
8 quail eggs
8 caper berries with stems
Leaves of ⅛ bunch chervil
A few marigold petals
A few purple basil leaves

PREPARING THE BEEF TONGUE

To blanch the beef tongue, place it in a large saucepan filled with cold water and bring to a boil, then drain and plunge it into cold water. Place the tongue in a large Dutch oven or saucepan. Peel the onion and stud it with the cloves. Peel the carrots. Cut the carrots, leek, and celery into short lengths, and add to the pan with the onion and remaining ingredients. Pour in enough water to cover and cook over low heat for 2 hours (see Chefs' Notes). Drain, trim, and skin the tongue while it is still warm (see technique p. 46), then cut it into eight ¾-in. (2-cm) slices and place them in a clean saucepan. Strain the cooking juices through the fine-mesh sieve and measure out a scant ½ cup (100 ml) for the spicy sauce. Pour a little of the remaining strained liquid over the tongue to prevent it from drying out and to make it easier to reheat when ready to serve.

PREPARING THE SPICY SAUCE

Peel and finely chop the shallot. Heat the butter in a saucepan and fry the shallot over low heat until very soft. Add the flour and cook for 1 minute, stirring continuously. Deglaze with the vinegar and wine, and reduce by half. Add the tomato coulis, veal stock, and cooking juices, and let simmer for 15 minutes. Strain the sauce through the fine-mesh sieve into a bowl and stir in the mustard and *piment d'Espelette*. Adjust the seasonings if necessary. Place the bowl over a pan of barely simmering water to keep the sauce warm.

PREPARING THE GARNISHES

Cut the bread into ¼-in. (5-mm) dice. Heat the clarified butter in a skillet and fry the diced bread until lightly golden. Drain on paper towels. Finely chop the chives and slice the cornichons. Fry the quail eggs for 3 minutes over low heat, until the whites set, then use the cookie cutter to cut them into neat circles around the yolks. Cut the caper berries in half lengthwise.

TO SERVE

Reheat the beef tongue, if necessary, and place 2 slices on each serving plate. Spoon sauce over the meat and drizzle a little around each plate. Arrange the garnishes attractively over the top of the tongue, with a quail egg in the center of each one.

CHEFS' NOTES

To check if the beef tongue is cooked, push the tip of a paring knife into it or, even better, a trussing needle, as the latter will cause less tearing. The meat should be completely tender.

TRIPE WITH CITRUS FRUITS

Gras-double aux agrumes

Serves 10

Active time

1 hour

Cooking time

5 hours

Soaking time

Overnight

Storage

3 days

Equipment

6-in. (15-cm) stainless-steel ring

Ingredients

Tripe

3½ lb. (1.5 kg) ox or beef tripe

3½ tbsp (50 ml) white vinegar

7 oz. (200 g) sweet onions, preferably Cévennes

5¼ oz. (150 g) celery

1¼ cups (300 ml) dry white wine

6 cloves garlic, unpeeled

¼ bunch lemon thyme

4 bay leaves

3½ oz. (100 g) kosher salt

2 generous tbsp (20 g) white peppercorns

Tomato compote and potatoes

7 oz. (200 g) red onions

9 oz. (250 g) carrots

9 oz. (250 g) celery

1½ lb. (750 g) tomatoes on the vine

Scant ½ cup (100 ml) olive oil

2 tsp (10 g) fine sea salt

4 cups (1 liter) vegetable stock

1 lb. 2 oz. (500 g) baby potatoes

2 tbsp (30 ml) aged red wine vinegar

1 generous tbsp (10 g) finely grated lemon zest

To garnish

3½ oz. (100 g) kumquats

1¼ cups (300 ml) water

Scant ½ cup (3¼ oz./90 g) sugar

4 blood oranges

2 pomelos

To serve

Parsley leaves

PREPARING THE TRIPE (1 DAY AHEAD)

Place the tripe in a large bowl with the vinegar. Add ice cubes and enough cold water to cover and soak overnight in the refrigerator. The following day, peel and roughly chop the onions and celery. Drain the tripe and cut it into 1½-in. (4-cm) squares. Place in a Dutch oven with the onions, celery, wine, garlic, lemon thyme, bay leaves, kosher salt, and peppercorns, and cover with cold water. Cover the pan and gently simmer for 4 hours, skimming foam from the surface regularly. Drain the tripe and set aside in a saucepan with a little of the cooking liquid.

PREPARING THE TOMATO COMPOTE AND POTATOES

Peel and finely chop the onions, carrots, and celery. Peel the tomatoes, remove the seeds, and chop finely. Heat the olive oil in a sauté pan with the salt and sweat the onions, carrots, celery, and tomatoes until softened but not browned. Pour in enough vegetable stock to cover and let simmer gently for 30 minutes, adding more stock as needed during cooking. Wash the potatoes, cut them in half, and add to the pan. Continue to cook for an additional 30 minutes, until the compote is thick and the potatoes are tender. Adjust the seasonings if necessary and stir in the vinegar and lemon zest.

PREPARING THE GARNISHES

Reheat the tripe in the saucepan with the cooking liquid. Wash the kumquats and cut them crosswise into slices. Warm the water and sugar in a saucepan until the sugar dissolves, then bring to a boil. Add the kumquat slices and poach for 1 minute in the syrup. Remove and set aside. Supreme the blood oranges and pomelos, holding them over a saucepan to catch the juices. After removing the segments, squeeze all the juice you can out of the membranes into the saucepan. Cut the segments into three or four pieces each and set aside. Reduce the juice until syrupy, then add the tripe.

TO SERVE

For each serving, place the 6-in. (15-cm) stainless-steel ring in the center of a plate and spoon a layer of tomato compote, about ¼ in. (5 mm) deep, into it. Add potatoes and scatter with pieces of tripe, blood orange, pomelo, and kumquat. Garnish with parsley leaves.

LYON-STYLE TRIPE WITH GRIBICHE RELISH

Tablier de sapeur, condiment gribiche

Serves 10

Active time
1 hour

Cooking time
4 hours 40 minutes

Soaking time
Overnight

Marinating time
Overnight

Drying time
1 hour

Storage
24 hours

Equipment
Food processor
Immersion blender
Fine-mesh sieve

Ingredients

Beef tripe
3½ lb. (1.5 kg) beef tripe (*panse de bœuf*)

3½ tbsp (50 ml) white vinegar, for soaking

For boiling the beef tripe:

7 oz. (200 g) sweet onions, preferably Cévennes

5¼ oz. (150 g) celery

1¼ cups (300 ml) dry white wine

6 cloves garlic, unpeeled

¼ bunch lemon thyme

4 bay leaves

3½ oz. (100 g) coarse sea salt

2 generous tbsp (20 g) white peppercorns

For marinating the beef tripe:

¼ bunch parsley

¼ bunch tarragon

¼ bunch chervil

2 tsp (5 g) ground bay leaves

Scant ½ cup (100 ml) lemon juice

3½ tbsp (50 ml) grape-seed oil

3½ tbsp (50 ml) aged red wine vinegar

⅓ cup (3½ oz./100 g) Dijon mustard

3 tbsp (1¾ oz./50 g) Meaux mustard

For breading the beef tripe:

3¾ cups (15¾ oz./450 g) all-purpose flour

5 eggs

6⅔ cups (1½ lb./750 g) dried breadcrumbs

Scant ½ cup (100 ml) grape-seed oil

7 tbsp (3½ oz./100 g) butter

2 tsp (10 g) fine sea salt

2 tsp (5 g) freshly ground pepper

Gribiche relish

¼ bunch chervil

¼ bunch tarragon

¼ bunch parsley

12 lemons

4 cups (1¾ lb./800 g) sugar

Scant ½ cup (100 ml) olive oil

2 eggs

1 oz. (30 g) capers

1 oz. (30 g) cornichons

To serve

Scallions, thinly sliced

Fleur de sel

Parsley-infused oil

SOAKING THE BEEF TRIPE (2 DAYS AHEAD)
Place the tripe in a large bowl with the vinegar. Add ice cubes and enough cold water to cover the tripe. Let soak overnight in the refrigerator.

BOILING THE BEEF TRIPE (1 DAY AHEAD)
The following day, peel and roughly chop the onions. Cut the celery into 1¼-in. (3-cm) pieces. Drain the tripe and cut it into 1½ × 3-in. (4 × 8-cm) rectangles. Place the tripe in a Dutch oven with the onions, celery, wine, garlic, lemon thyme, bay leaves, salt, and peppercorns. Cover with cold water and gently simmer, covered, for 4 hours, skimming foam from the surface regularly. Drain the tripe.

MARINATING THE BEEF TRIPE (1 DAY AHEAD)
Wash and finely chop the herbs and place in a large bowl with the remaining marinade ingredients, whisking to blend. Add the tripe and let marinate overnight in the refrigerator.

PREPARING THE GRIBICHE RELISH
Preheat the oven to 195°F (90°C/Gas on lowest setting). Place the herbs on a baking sheet lined with parchment paper and dry in the oven for 1 hour. Grind to a powder in the food processor. Supreme the lemons over a bowl to obtain 14 oz. (400 g) of segments and catch all the juice. Place the segments and juice in a large saucepan, add the sugar, and cook over low heat until the sugar dissolves and the mixture thickens to a marmalade consistency (about 30 minutes). With the immersion blender running, gradually drizzle in the olive oil until emulsified. Cook the eggs in boiling water for 9 minutes, then let cool and remove the shells. Press the whites and yolks separately through the fine mesh sieve. Finely chop the capers and cornichons.

BREADING AND COOKING THE BEEF TRIPE
Sift the flour into a shallow bowl. Whisk the eggs in a second shallow bowl. Place the breadcrumbs in a third shallow bowl. Drain the tripe. Roll each rectangle in the flour to coat, dip it in the egg, then coat with the bread-crumbs. Repeat this process once more. Heat the oil in a large skillet and fry the tripe until pale golden, then add the butter and continue to cook until deeply golden. Drain on paper towels and season with salt and pepper.

TO SERVE
If necessary, reheat the tripe in the oven preheated to 325°F (160°C/Gas Mark 3) for 5 minutes. Cut into wedges and serve sprinkled with egg, scallions, capers, cornichons, and fleur de sel. Add a spoonful of lemon marmalade and dots of parsley-infused oil. Dust the serving plates with ground herbs and serve immediately.

BEEF HANGER STEAK WITH OYSTERS AND *GUEULANTES* POTATOES

Onglet de bœuf aux huîtres et pommes gueulantes

Serves 6

Active time
1 hour

Cooking time
40 minutes

Chilling time
30 minutes

Storage
24 hours

Equipment
Shallow roasting pan

Steam oven (or steamer)

Butcher's twine, as needed

Instant-read thermometer

Ingredients

Potatoes

3 large waxy potatoes, preferably Bintje (about 3½ lb./1.5 kg)

2 cups (1 lb. 2 oz./500 g) melted clarified butter

Fleur de sel

Freshly ground pepper

Oysters

18 oysters, preferably no. 3

Hanger steak

5¼ oz. (150 g) shallots

1 bunch chives

2 lb. (900 g) beef hanger steak (*onglet de bœuf*)

2 tbsp (30 ml) grape-seed oil

2 tbsp (1 oz./30 g) butter

⅔ cup (150 ml) dry white wine

1⅔ cups (400 ml) brown veal stock (*fond brun de veau*, see recipe p. 16)

Salt and freshly ground pepper

Wilted spinach

2 kg (4½ lb.) fresh spinach

4 cloves garlic

3½ tbsp (50 ml) olive oil

Salt

To serve

12 oyster plant leaves (*Mertensia maritima*)

Small edible flower petals

PREPARING THE POTATOES

Preheat the oven to 325°F (160°C/Gas Mark 3) on the grill setting. Peel and rinse the potatoes, and pat them dry using a clean dish towel. Cut them in half lengthwise, then trim the sides to make an octagonal shape. Do not rinse. Cut the potatoes into 1/8-in. (3-mm) slices without separating them, to maintain the whole potato shape. Place side by side in the roasting pan with the clarified butter, which should come two-thirds up the sides of the pan. Place in the oven, 8–10 in. (20–25 cm) from the grill, and cook for 20 minutes, or until the potatoes are tender and the tops are golden and crisp. Carefully drain the potatoes from the butter and season with fleur de sel and freshly ground pepper.

PREPARING THE OYSTERS

Preheat the steam oven, if using, to 200°F (100°C/Gas Mark 1/4). Place the oysters in the oven, or steamer, for 1–2 minutes, or just until they start to open. Transfer them to the refrigerator.

PREPARING THE HANGER STEAK

Peel and finely chop the shallots. Wash and finely chop the chives. Trim the hanger steaks, then cut them into 6 pieces, each weighing 5¼ oz. (150 g). If necessary, tie them with butcher's twine so they keep their shape. Season with salt and pepper. Warm the oil and butter in a sauté pan over high heat, add the steaks, and sear them until they are browned all over and the internal temperature reaches 122°F–126°F (50°C–52°C). Transfer the steaks to a rack and let rest. Reduce the heat to low, add the shallots to the sauté pan, cover, and cook in the pan juices for 3 minutes. Deglaze with the white wine and reduce until all the liquid has evaporated. Add the stock and reduce until the sauce coats the back of a spoon.

PREPARING THE WILTED SPINACH

Wash and dry the spinach and remove the stems. Peel and finely chop the garlic and sweat it in the olive oil in a large pan until tender. Add the spinach, season with salt, cover, and cook over high heat until the leaves wilt. Do not cook for longer to ensure the spinach retains its green color. Transfer to a colander.

TO SERVE

Remove the oysters from their shells. Reheat the meat, spinach, and potatoes in the oven as needed. At the last minute, reheat the oysters in the reduced sauce and sprinkle with the chives. Spoon a little sauce onto serving plates and add the spinach. Slice the meat and arrange it over the sauce and spinach. Add the oysters and garnish with oyster plant leaves and small flower petals. Serve the potatoes on the side, with a little sauce drizzled around the plate.

OXTAIL CAPPELLETTI WITH CONSOMMÉ

Cappelletti de queue de bœuf avec son consommé

Serves 6

Active time
6 hours

Cooking time
6 hours

Chilling time
Overnight + 3 hours

Storage
2 days

Equipment
Butcher's twine
Fine-mesh sieve
Blender
3½-in. (9-cm) round pastry cutter
Conical sieve lined with muslin
Immersion blender

Ingredients

Braised oxtails
5¼ oz. (150 g) leeks
3 stalks celery
5¼ oz. (150 g) onions
4 whole cloves
3 Roma tomatoes
5¼ oz. (150 g) carrots
5¼ oz. (150 g) turnips
Grape-seed oil
3½ lb. (1.5 kg) oxtails
6 cloves garlic
1 tbsp (10 g) peppercorns
1 bouquet garni (thyme, parsley stems, rosemary, and bay leaf)
Salt

White cappelletti pasta dough
¾ cup + 2 tbsp (3½ oz./100 g) all-purpose flour (T55)
⅔ cup (3½ oz./100 g) fine semolina flour
Scant ½ cup (4 oz./110 g) lightly beaten egg (about 2 eggs)

Green cappelletti pasta dough
2 oz. (55 g) parsley
Scant ¼ cup (2 oz./55 g) lightly beaten egg (about 1 egg)
¾ cup + 2 tbsp (3½ oz./100 g) all-purpose flour (T55)
⅔ cup (3½ oz./100 g) fine semolina flour

Consommé
Scant 5½ cups (1.2 liters) oxtail broth (see left)
1¾ oz. (50 g) carrots
3½ oz. (100 g) leeks
1¾ oz. (50 g) celery
14 oz. (400 g) ground beef
2 tbsp (1 oz./30 g) tomato paste
3 egg whites
2 tsp (5 g) ground black pepper
5 sprigs thyme
2 small sprigs rosemary
1 bay leaf

Morel mushrooms
1 lb. 2 oz. (500 g) morel mushrooms
2½ oz. (70 g) shallots
1 clove garlic
4 sprigs parsley
4 tbsp (2 oz./60 g) butter
Salt and freshly ground pepper

Soubise foam
3 sweet onions, preferably Cévennes
2 oz. (60 g) *lardo di Colonnata* (Italian cured pork fat)
2 bay leaves
1⅔ cups (400 ml) whole milk
Salt and freshly ground pepper

To serve
Pea shoots

PREPARING THE BRAISED OXTAILS (1 DAY AHEAD)

Wash the leeks and celery and tie them together using the butcher's twine. Peel the onions, cut them in half crosswise, and stud them with the cloves. Char the cut sides in a nonstick skillet over high heat until well blackened to add color and flavor to the broth. Wash and hull the tomatoes, then peel and finely chop the carrots and turnips. Warm a little grape-seed oil in a Dutch oven until hot, then add the oxtails and brown on all sides. Pour off the excess fat and deglaze by adding enough cold water to just cover the oxtails. Add all the prepared vegetables, season with salt, and bring to a boil, thoroughly skimming off any foam on the surface. Add the garlic cloves, peppercorns, and bouquet garni and bring to a simmer. Let simmer over medium heat, without letting it come to a full boil, for 4–5 hours, or until the meat is completely tender and falls off the bones. Remove the oxtails from the pan, take the meat off the bones, and place in a bowl. Cover and chill overnight. Strain the broth through the fine-mesh sieve into a second bowl. Cover and chill overnight to allow the fat to rise to the surface of the broth and solidify.

PREPARING THE CAPPELLETTI DOUGHS

To prepare the white cappelletti dough, combine the all-purpose and semolina flours and pour onto a work surface. Make a well in the center. Pour the eggs into the well and mix them into the flour using your fingertips. When the dough comes together in a ball, knead it until it is smooth. Cover with plastic wrap and let rest in the refrigerator for at least 2 hours. To prepare the green cappelletti dough, blanch the parsley in boiling water for 3–4 minutes. Pat dry, transfer to the blender, and process with the egg until smooth. Combine the all-purpose and semolina flours, and pour onto a work surface. Make a well in the center. Pour the parsley-egg mixture into the well and mix into the flour using your fingertips. When the dough comes together in a ball, knead it until it is smooth. Cover with plastic wrap and let rest in the refrigerator for at least 2 hours. On a lightly floured surface, roll each piece of dough to a thickness of about ¼ in. (6 mm). Cut into ¼-in. (6-mm) strips. Place the strips side-by-side on the worktop, alternating the colors, and brush the sides with a little water to stick them together. Cover with plastic wrap and chill for 30 minutes.

PREPARING THE CONSOMMÉ

Lift off the solidified layer of fat on the surface of the broth and pour the broth into a large saucepan. Peel the carrots and wash the leeks and celery. Finely chop all three and combine with the ground beef and tomato paste in a large bowl. Lightly whisk the egg whites until frothy, then stir them into the meat mixture. Add the meat mixture to the saucepan with the broth and bring to a boil, stirring gently. Once boiling, stop stirring: as the meat and egg whites coagulate, they will rise to the top and form a "raft." Add the pepper and thyme, reduce the heat, and let simmer gently for 45 minutes. Strain through the conical sieve lined with muslin into a clean saucepan. Adjust the seasonings, if necessary, then add the rosemary sprigs and bay leaf, and keep warm.

ASSEMBLING THE CAPPELLETTI

Let the oxtail meat come to room temperature. On a lightly floured surface, roll the striped cappelletti dough to a thickness of ¹⁄₁₆ in. (2 mm). Cut out 30 disks using the 3½-in. (9-cm) pastry cutter. Place some oxtail meat in the center of each disk. Dampen the edges of the disks and fold them in half to enclose the meat. Bring the two ends together to create a round hat-like shape, dampening where the ends meet with a tiny amount of water on your fingertip and pinching the ends together to seal. Cover the cappelletti with plastic wrap and chill for 30 minutes.

PREPARING THE MOREL MUSHROOMS

Wipe the morel mushrooms with a damp paper towel and trim the stems using a paring knife. Peel and finely chop the shallots and garlic. Wash, de-stem, and finely chop the parsley. Warm the butter in a sauté pan until foamy, then add the shallots and garlic, and sweat until softened but not browned. Add the morels, cover, and cook for 4–5 minutes, or until tender. Stir in the parsley, season with salt and pepper, and remove from the pan.

PREPARING THE SOUBISE FOAM

Peel and finely chop the onions. Cut the *lardo di Colonnata* into ¼-in. (5-mm) dice and heat in a large skillet to render the fat. Add the onions, a pinch of salt, a little pepper, and the bay leaves. Cover and cook over low heat for 10 minutes, or until the onions are softened and translucent. Add the milk and let simmer for 20 minutes. Remove the bay leaves and transfer the mixture to the blender. Process until smooth, then strain through the fine-mesh sieve into a heatproof bowl. Adjust the seasonings if necessary. Set the bowl over a saucepan of barely simmering water to keep the soubise warm.

TO SERVE

Cook the cappelletti in a pot of boiling salted water for 4 minutes. Meanwhile, reheat the morel mushrooms. Place 5 cappelletti in each shallow serving bowl and add the morel mushrooms. Use the immersion blender to process the soubise sauce into a foam, then spoon it attractively around the cappelletti. Pour a little consommé into each bowl, scatter pea shoots over the top, and serve immediately.

BEEF AND VEGETABLE STIR-FRY WITH RICE NOODLES

Sauté de bœuf, pâtes de riz et légumes

Serves 10

Active time
1 hour

Cooking time
20 minutes

Resting time
30 minutes

Marinating time
20 minutes

Storage
3 days

Equipment
Wok

Ingredients

Rice noodles

3¼ cups (14 oz./400 g) rice flour

1 cup (5¼ oz./150 g) potato starch

Scant ½ cup (1¾ oz./50 g) tapioca starch

2 tsp (10 g) fine sea salt

5 cups (1.2 liters) lukewarm water

3½ tbsp (50 ml) grape-seed oil + more for brushing

Stir-fried beef

1¼ lb. (600 g) boneless beef round steak (*poire de bœuf*)

2 cloves garlic

1½ oz. (40 g) fresh ginger

Scant ½ cup (100 ml) soy sauce

3½ tbsp (50 ml) oyster sauce

1½ tbsp (10 g) cracked pepper

Stir-fried vegetables

7 oz. (200 g) orange carrots

7 oz. (200 g) yellow carrots

½ bunch scallions

3½ oz. (100 g) shimeji mushrooms

3½ oz. (100 g) shiitake mushrooms

3 heads bok choy

½ bunch radishes

3½ oz. (100 g) Brussels sprouts

1 red endive

¼ head romaine lettuce

2 tsp (10 ml) grape-seed oil

4 tsp (20 ml) soy sauce

2 tsp (10 ml) orange juice

To serve

⅔ cup (150 ml) neutral oil

PREPARING THE RICE NOODLES

Combine the dry ingredients in a bowl, then gradually whisk in the water until well blended. Let rest for 30 minutes, then whisk in the oil until smooth. Warm a 10-in. (26-cm) skillet over medium heat and pour a little of the batter into it, tilting the pan so the batter covers the bottom in a very thin (1/16-in./1-mm) layer. Cover and cook for 1 minute, or until translucent. Remove from the pan, place on a cutting board brushed with a little grape-seed oil, and brush the noodle sheet with a little oil, to prevent sticking. Repeat with the remaining batter, placing each noodle sheet on top of the previous one and brushing it with oil. Cut the sheets into strips measuring ¾ in. (1.5 cm) in width, then toss them gently to separate the noodles.

PREPARING THE STIR-FRIED BEEF

Cut the beef into strips measuring ½ in. (1 cm) in width and 2½ in. (6 cm) in length. Peel and finely chop the garlic and ginger. Combine the soy sauce, oyster sauce, garlic, ginger, and pepper, and pour over the beef. Let marinate for at least 20 minutes in the refrigerator.

PREPARING THE STIR-FRIED VEGETABLES

Peel the carrots and cut them in half lengthwise, then cut diagonally into 1/16-in. (2-mm) slices. Wash the scallions, cut diagonally into 1/16-in. (2-mm) slices, and separate the white and green parts. Trim the bases off the shimeji and shiitake mushrooms, then cut the shiitakes into ½-in. (1-cm) slices. Wash the bok choy and cut each one into 4 pieces lengthwise. Wash the radishes and Brussels sprouts and cut them in half lengthwise. Cut the red endive and romaine leaves into feather-like pieces. Place the wok over high heat until very hot, then add the carrots, mushrooms, bok choy, radishes, Brussels sprouts, and the white parts of the scallions and stir-fry until lightly charred in places. Gradually add the oil, followed by the soy sauce and orange juice, stir-frying all the time. Transfer to a bowl and toss in the green parts of the scallions and the red endive and romaine lettuce.

TO SERVE

As soon as the vegetables are cooked, drain the beef, if necessary. Heat the neutral oil in a large skillet over high heat and, when sizzling, stir-fry the beef for 3–4 minutes until browned. Reheat and soften the noodles by immersing them briefly in hot water, then drain. Serve the beef and vegetables over the noodles in shallow bowls.

MOUSSAKA

Serves 4

Active time

1¾ hours

Cooking time

1 hour

Standing time

15 minutes

Storage

4 days

Equipment

8 × 12-in. (20 × 30-cm) baking dish

Ingredients

Ground beef sauce

1 white onion

Scant ½ cup (100 ml) olive oil

1½ lb. (700 g) ground beef

Generous ¾ cup (200 ml) dry white wine

1¾ lb. (800 g) crushed tomatoes

Generous ¾ cup (200 ml) water

3 tbsp dried oregano

3 egg whites

½ bunch flat-leaf parsley, finely chopped

10 mint leaves, finely chopped

½ tsp ground cinnamon

Salt and freshly ground pepper

Eggplant layer

6 eggplants

Olive oil

Salt

Potato layer

6 large potatoes

Olive oil

Salt

Béchamel

3 tbsp (1¾ oz./50 g) butter

Scant ½ cup (1¾ oz./50 g) all-purpose flour

2 cups (500 ml) whole milk

5¼ oz. (150 g) *kefalotyri* (Greek sheep's milk cheese, or use Ossau-Iraty), grated

1 egg yolk

Salt and ground white pepper

To serve (optional)

Salad of your choice

Extra-virgin olive oil

PREPARING THE GROUND BEEF SAUCE

Peel and finely chop the onion. Heat the olive oil in a large Dutch oven and sweat the onion until soft. Add the ground beef and cook until it is browned, stirring regularly with a wooden spoon to break up any lumps of meat. Deglaze with the wine and let reduce. Add the tomatoes, water, and oregano, and let simmer, covered, for 1 hour. Stir the egg whites into the meat all at once, then add the parsley and mint. Cook for an additional 2 minutes, then add the cinnamon and season with salt and pepper.

PREPARING AND COOKING THE EGGPLANTS

Cut the eggplants lengthwise into approximately ½-in. (1-cm) slices. Sprinkle with salt and let stand for about 15 minutes. Rinse off the salt, pat the slices dry, then fry them in a single layer in olive oil in a non-stick skillet over medium-high heat, until the slices are cooked and golden on both sides.

PREPARING AND COOKING THE POTATOES

Peel and wash the potatoes and cut them into approximately ½-in. (1-cm) slices. Fry them in a single layer in olive oil in a non-stick skillet over medium heat, until cooked through and lightly golden.

PREPARING THE BÉCHAMEL

Melt the butter in a large saucepan over low heat, then whisk in the flour to make a roux. Cook for 2 minutes, whisking continuously, then gradually whisk in the milk. Still whisking, bring the milk to a boil and simmer for 5 minutes. Take the pan off the heat, stir in the cheese and egg yolk, and season with salt and pepper.

ASSEMBLING AND BAKING THE MOUSSAKA

Preheat the oven to 400°F (200°C/Gas Mark 6). Arrange the potatoes in a single layer in the baking dish and cover with the ground beef sauce. Arrange the eggplant slices over the ground beef in a single layer. Add the béchamel and smooth into an even layer. Bake for 35 minutes. Let cool slightly, then cut into slices. Serve with a salad of your choice, if desired, dressed with a little extra-virgin olive oil.

VEAL

VEAL BLANQUETTE

Blanquette de veau

Serves 4

Active time

30 minutes

Cooking time

1½ hours

Storage time

4 days

Equipment

Butcher's twine

Fine-mesh sieve

Ingredients

Veal

2 leeks, white parts only

1 onion

3 whole cloves

2 carrots

2 stalks celery

2 cloves garlic

2¾ lb. (1.2 kg) boneless veal flank (*flanchet*), breast (*tendron*), or rib roast (*bas de carré*)

1 bouquet garni (leek greens, thyme, and bay leaf)

About 4 qt. (4 liters) water

Velouté sauce

2 tbsp (1 oz./30 g) butter

3 tbsp (1 oz./30 g) all-purpose flour

2 cups (500 ml) reserved veal broth (see above)

Scant ½ cup (100 ml) crème fraîche

Salt

Mushrooms

4½ oz. (125 g) button mushrooms

Scant ½ cup (100 ml) water

1 pinch ground white pepper

1 tbsp (20 g) butter

Juice of ¼ lemon

Salt

Glazed pearl onions

4½ oz. (125 g) pearl onions

⅔ cup (150 ml) water

1 pinch salt

3 tbsp (1¾ oz./50 g) butter

1 tsp sugar

Glazed mini carrots

8 mini yellow carrots

⅔ cup (150 ml) water

1 pinch salt

3 tbsp (1¾ oz./50 g) butter

1 tsp sugar

To serve

Red-veined sorrel leaves

¼ bunch parsley, finely chopped

Leaves of ⅛ bunch chervil, finely chopped

Cooked long-grain white rice (optional)

PREPARING THE VEAL

Wash the leek whites, cut them in half lengthwise, and tie the pieces together with twine. Peel the onion and stud it with the cloves. Peel the carrots and cut them in half lengthwise. Wash the celery stalks and cut them into 3 or 4 pieces, depending on their length. Roughly crush the garlic using the flat of a chef's knife blade. Cut the meat into large pieces, about 2¾ oz. (80 g) each, allowing 3 pieces per person. Place the meat in a large Dutch oven, cover with the water, and bring to a rolling boil. Skim off any foam on the surface, then add the leek whites, clove-studded onion, carrots, celery, garlic, and bouquet garni. Lower the heat and gently simmer, covered, for about 1 hour, or until the meat is completely tender. Strain the cooking liquid through the fine-mesh sieve and measure out 2 cups (500 ml) for the sauce (store the rest in an airtight container in the refrigerator for up to 3 days for another use). Return the meat to the pot. Set aside the most intact carrots for garnishing.

PREPARING THE VELOUTÉ SAUCE

Melt the butter in a saucepan over low heat, then whisk in the flour to make a roux. Cook for 3 minutes, whisking continuously, until thickened but not colored. Whisk in the reserved broth and cook over low heat for 5 minutes, then whisk in the crème fraîche. Taste and add more salt, if necessary. Pour the velouté into the Dutch oven, cover, and let simmer over low heat for 10 minutes.

PREPARING THE MUSHROOMS

Trim the mushroom stems and submerge the mushrooms briefly in two changes of cold water to wash them. Pour the ⅔ cup (150 ml) water into a large saucepan and add the pepper, butter, and lemon juice. Season with salt and bring to a boil. Add the mushrooms, cover, and cook over high heat for 3 minutes. Remove from the heat and drain.

PREPARING THE GLAZED PEARL ONIONS

Peel the pearl onions and place them in a saucepan with the water, salt, butter, and sugar. Cover with a piece of parchment paper cut to fit snugly inside the pan. Cook over low heat for about 10 minutes, or until the onions are tender, have absorbed all the liquid, and are coated with a glossy butter-sugar glaze.

PREPARING THE GLAZED MINI CARROTS

Peel the carrots and place them in a saucepan with the water, salt, butter, and sugar. Cover with a piece of parchment paper cut to fit snugly inside the pan. Cook over low heat for about 10 minutes, or until the carrots are completely tender, have absorbed all the liquid, and are coated with a glossy butter-sugar glaze.

TO SERVE

Arrange the mushrooms, pearl onions, and carrots attractively over the blanquette and scatter with red-veined sorrel, parsley, and chervil. Accompany with steamed white rice, if desired.

VITELLO TONNATO

Serves 4

Active time

1 hour

Cooking time

25 minutes

Chilling time

2 hours

Storage

4 days

Equipment

Instant-read thermometer

Food processor

Meat slicer or carving knife

3-in. (8-cm) stainless-steel ring

Ingredients

Veal

2 tbsp (30 ml) neutral oil

3 tbsp (1¾ oz./50 g) butter

14 oz. (400 g) veal roast tied with twine (see technique p. 42)

2 cloves garlic

2 sprigs thyme

Salt and freshly ground pepper

Mayonnaise

1 egg yolk

1 tbsp (15 g) Dijon mustard

1 tsp vinegar

⅔ cup (150 ml) grape-seed oil

Salt and freshly ground pepper

Tonnato sauce

2¾ oz. (75 g) oil-packed canned tuna (drained weight)

6 anchovy fillets

1 tbsp salt-packed capers

Finely grated zest and juice of ½ lemon

⅔ cup (5¼ oz./150 g) mayonnaise (see left)

Salt and freshly ground pepper

To garnish

2 slices sandwich bread

Scant ⅓ cup (70 ml) melted clarified butter

1¾ oz. (50 g) Parmesan

1 scallion, green part only

12 caper berries with stems

4 confit or sundried tomatoes

Salt

To serve (optional)

A few small basil sprigs

A few red-veined sorrel leaves

A few purple shiso sprigs

PREPARING THE VEAL

Preheat the oven to 285°F (140°C/Gas Mark 1). Heat the oil and butter in an oven-safe sauté pan and brown the veal on all sides. Add the garlic and thyme sprigs, and baste the meat with the fat. Season with salt and pepper. Place in the oven and roast for about 25 minutes, or until the internal temperature of the veal reaches 133°F (56°C). Transfer the meat to a rack set over a plate to catch any juices, let cool, then chill in the refrigerator for 2 hours.

PREPARING THE MAYONNAISE

Whisk together the egg yolk, mustard, and vinegar, and season with salt and pepper. Whisking continuously, gradually drizzle in the oil in a thin, steady stream until the mixture is pale, thick, and emulsified.

PREPARING THE TONNATO SAUCE

Place the tuna, anchovies, capers, and lemon zest and juice in the food processor and process until smooth. Incorporate the mayonnaise and season with salt and pepper.

PREPARING THE GARNISHES

Cut the sandwich bread into ⅛-in. (3-mm) dice. Heat the clarified butter in a small skillet and, when foaming, fry the diced bread until lightly golden. Drain on paper towels and season with salt. Using a vegetable peeler, shave off small curls of Parmesan. Trim and thinly slice the scallion, drain the caper berries, and cut the confit or sundried tomatoes into small pieces.

TO SERVE

Cut the chilled veal into ¹⁄₁₆-in. (2-mm) slices using the meat slicer or a carving knife. Place the 3-in. (8-cm) ring in the center of a serving plate. Arrange the veal slices attractively around the outside of the ring to make a wreath shape. Remove the ring. Spoon small mounds of tonnato sauce over and around the veal and scatter over the croutons, Parmesan curls, confit or sundried tomatoes, caper berries, and scallion. Garnish with basil, red-veined sorrel leaves, and small sprigs of purple shiso, if desired.

LOMBARDY-STYLE OSSO BUCO

Osso-buco comme en Lombardie

Serves 4

Active time

1 hour

Cooking time

4½ hours

Infusing time

15 minutes

Storage

2 days

Equipment

Fine-mesh sieve

Ingredients

Osso buco

2 sweet onions, preferably Cévennes

1 carrot

1 stalk celery

10½ oz. (300 g) Olivette plum tomatoes (or use Romas)

4 osso buco (slices cut crosswise from veal shank)

¾ cup + 2 tbsp (3½ oz./100 g) all-purpose flour

Scant ⅓ cup (70 ml) grape-seed oil

1 generous tbsp (20 g) tomato paste

1¼ cups (300 ml) white wine

2 cups (500 ml) brown veal stock (*fond brun de veau*, see recipe p. 16)

1 bouquet garni (bay leaf and thyme sprigs)

Salt and freshly ground pepper

Gremolata

1 orange

1 lemon

1 clove garlic

½ bunch parsley

1½ tbsp (25 ml) extra-virgin olive oil

Salt and freshly ground Timut pepper

Creamy polenta

1⅔ cups (400 ml) whole milk

1⅔ cups (400 ml) white poultry stock (*fond blanc de volaille*, see recipe p. 19) + more as needed

2 bay leaves

3 sprigs thyme + extra leaves to garnish

1¼ cups (7 oz./200 g) polenta

2¼ cups (3½ oz./100 g) mascarpone

Salt and freshly ground pepper

PREPARING THE OSSO BUCO

Preheat the oven to 325°F (160°C/Gas Mark 3). Peel and finely chop the onions, carrot, celery, and tomatoes. Cut the skin surrounding the osso buco to prevent them from shrinking too much during cooking and to help the slices keep their shape. Season the meat with salt and pepper, and coat it with flour. Heat the oil in a Dutch oven until shimmering, then add the osso buco and brown them on both sides. Remove the meat and add the onions, carrot, and celery, and sweat until softened but not browned. Stir in the tomato paste, cook for a few minutes, then deglaze with the white wine. Reduce until all the liquid has evaporated, then add the tomatoes, stock, and bouquet garni. Return the meat to the Dutch oven. Cut a piece of parchment paper to fit snugly inside the pan, place it over the ingredients, then put the lid on. Cook in the oven for about 4 hours, or until the meat is completely tender. Remove the meat from the pan and strain the cooking liquid through the fine-mesh sieve into a clean saucepan. Reduce until the sauce coats the back of a spoon, then remove from the heat.

PREPARING THE GREMOLATA

Remove the zest in strips from the orange and lemon using a vegetable peeler. Cut all the bitter white pith off the orange and remove the segments. Cut each segment into triangles with ¾-in. (2-cm) sides and set aside for garnish. Using a small sharp knife, cut away any bitter white pith from the strips of orange and lemon zest and place them in a saucepan of cold water to blanch. Bring to a boil, then drain and plunge the zests into ice water to cool them quickly. Repeat this process twice more. Peel the garlic and remove the germ, then blanch it in the same way as the citrus zests were blanched. Dry the zests and garlic with paper towels, finely chop all three, and combine in a bowl. Wash, dry, and finely chop the parsley and add it to the bowl. Stir in the oil and season with salt and Timut pepper. Reserve in the refrigerator.

PREPARING THE CREAMY POLENTA

Combine the milk and stock in a large saucepan and bring to a boil. Add the bay leaves and thyme sprigs, remove the pan from the heat, cover, and let infuse for 15 minutes. Remove the herbs, add the polenta, and bring to a boil, whisking continuously. Still whisking, cook for 5–10 minutes over low heat, until thick and smooth. Stir in the mascarpone and season with salt and pepper. Adjust the consistency if necessary, cooking for another minute or two.

TO SERVE

Reheat the osso buco in the sauce, basting them frequently. Serve over a bed of polenta, drizzled with sauce and scattered with gremolata, orange pieces, and a few thyme leaves.

VEAL MILANESE

Escalope milanaise

Serves 4

Active time

30 minutes

Cooking time

10 minutes

Storage

24 hours

Equipment

Mallet-style meat pounder

Fine-mesh sieve

Instant-read thermometer

Microplane grater

Ingredients

Veal Milanese

1 lb. (500 g) double-cut, French trimmed veal rib chop (*double côte de veau*)

2 eggs

4 tsp (20 ml) olive oil

1⅔ cups (7 oz./200 g) all-purpose flour

3½ cups (400 g) dried breadcrumbs

Oil for shallow frying

3 tbsp (1¾ oz./50 g) butter, well chilled and diced

Salt and freshly ground pepper

Lemon-caper butter sauce

1 shallot

Leaves of 4 sprigs parsley

1 lemon

5 tbsp (3 oz./80 g) butter, divided

1¾ oz. (50 g) capers in vinegar, drained

2 tsp heavy cream, min. 35% fat

Salt and white pepper

Arugula and cherry tomatoes

9 oz. (250 g) mixed red and yellow cherry tomatoes

7 oz. (200 g) arugula

Extra-virgin olive oil

Salt and freshly ground pepper

Finely grated lemon zest (optional)

Balsamic glaze (optional)

To serve (optional)

Parsley leaves

Lemon wedges

PREPARING THE VEAL MILANESE

Cut through the double-cut veal chop lengthwise between the bones, leaving about ½ in. (1 cm) of meat on either side. Using the meat pounder, flatten the meat between two sheets of plastic wrap, into an elephant-ear shape. Lightly season the meat with salt and pepper. Whisk together the eggs and olive oil, and strain through the fine-mesh sieve into a shallow bowl. Sift the flour into another shallow bowl. Place the breadcrumbs in a third shallow bowl. To bread the veal, coat it in the flour, dip it in the egg mixture, then coat it with the breadcrumbs. Dip the veal in the egg mixture again, followed by the breadcrumbs. Heat the oil for shallow frying to 355°F (180°C) in a wide shallow pan large enough to hold the meat. Place the veal in the oil with the serving side facing downward. Cook for 3 minutes, until golden, then turn the meat over, add the butter, and cook the other side for 3 minutes. Transfer to a rack.

PREPARING THE LEMON-CAPER BUTTER SAUCE

Peel and finely chop the shallot. Wash, dry, and finely chop the parsley. Zest the lemon using the Microplane grater, then juice it. Sweat the shallot in 2 tsp (10 g) butter in a small saucepan until translucent, then add the capers and lemon juice. Bring to a boil and add the cream. Reduce the heat to low, dice in the remaining butter, and gradually whisk it in. Stir in the parsley and adjust the seasonings if necessary.

PREPARING THE ARUGULA AND CHERRY TOMATOES

Wash and dry the tomatoes and arugula, and cut the tomatoes in half. Place the tomatoes and arugula in separate bowls, toss both with olive oil, and season with salt and pepper. Sprinkle the arugula with finely grated lemon zest and drizzle with balsamic glaze, if desired.

TO SERVE

Serve the veal Milanese on a cutting board, garnished with a few parsley leaves and lemon wedges to squeeze over. Serve the sauce and salads in bowls on the side.

VEAL TENDERLOIN WITH BROCCOLI PURÉE AND SPRING VEGETABLES

Filet mignon et purée brocolis, asperges, petits pois, févettes et morilles

Serves 10

Active time

45 minutes

Cooking time

3 hours

Storage

3 days

Equipment

Fine-mesh sieve

Immersion blender

Ingredients

Veal jus

2¼ lb. (1 kg) veal breast

7 oz. (200 g) onions

½ head garlic

Scant ½ cup (100 ml) olive oil

¼ bunch thyme

1¾ sticks (7 oz./200 g) butter

8 cups (2 liters) vegetable stock, divided

Veal tenderloin

3½ lb. (1.5 kg) veal tenderloin

2 tsp (10 g) salt

Generous ¾ cup (200 ml) olive oil

3 cloves garlic, unpeeled

¼ bunch thyme

7 tbsp (3½ oz./100 g) butter, at room temperature and diced

Broccoli purée

2 heads broccoli

1 tbsp (10 g) kosher salt

⅔ cup (150 ml) olive oil

To garnish

2 bunches green asparagus

7 oz. (200 g) peas in their pods

7 oz. (200 g) baby fava beans in their pods

1¾ sticks (7 oz./200 g) butter, divided

10 morel mushrooms

4 cloves garlic, finely chopped

¼ bunch thyme

To serve

Fleur de sel

Baby arugula

PREPARING THE VEAL JUS

Cut the veal breast into 1½-in. (4-cm) cubes. Peel the onions and cut each one into 8 wedges. Roughly crush the garlic using the flat of a chef's knife blade. Heat the olive oil in a large saucepan and sear the meat over medium-high heat until pale golden brown. Add the onions, garlic, thyme, and butter, and continue to cook until the meat is deeply browned, basting it with the butter. Pour off the excess fat and deglaze with 2 cups (500 ml) of the vegetable stock, stirring to release the browned bits stuck to the bottom of the pan. Add the remaining stock and simmer for 1½ hours. Strain the jus through the fine-mesh sieve into a clean saucepan and reduce by half. Reserve at room temperature.

PREPARING THE VEAL TENDERLOIN

Preheat the oven to 140°F (60°C/Gas on lowest setting). Season the veal tenderloin with the salt. Heat the olive oil in an oven-safe skillet and sear the veal over medium-high heat with the garlic and thyme until pale golden brown all over. Add the butter and continue to cook until the meat is deeply browned, basting it regularly. Transfer to the oven and cook for about 1 hour.

PREPARING THE BROCCOLI PURÉE

Cut off the broccoli florets, then peel and finely chop the stems. Fill a large saucepan with water, add the salt, and bring to a boil. Add the broccoli florets and stems, and cook for 8 minutes, or until tender. Drain and return to the pan. While the broccoli is still hot, add the olive oil and process using the immersion blender to make a purée. Adjust the seasonings if necessary.

PREPARING THE GARNISHES

Peel the asparagus stalks and cut off the tough ends on the diagonal. Shell the peas and fava beans. Heat half the butter in a small saucepan and sweat the asparagus, peas, and fava beans in the butter until just tender. Clean the morels and cook them whole in a covered saucepan with the remaining butter, garlic, and thyme for 10 minutes.

TO SERVE

Cut the veal tenderloin into 20 slices. Serve two slices per person and sprinkle them with a little fleur de sel. Drizzle a little veal jus over one side of each plate and spoon a little broccoli purée over it. Arrange the garnishes over the purée, top with baby arugula, and drizzle with a little more jus. Finish with a quenelle of broccoli purée.

BREAST OF VEAL WITH ROSEMARY AND LEMON

Tendrons de veau au citron et romarin

Serves 4

Active time
1 hour

Cooking time
3 hours

Storage
4 days

Equipment
Fine-mesh sieve
Food processor

Ingredients

Breast of veal
1 onion
2 cloves garlic
4 × 9-oz. (250-g) boneless slices of veal cut from the middle of the breast (*tendrons de veau*)
3½ tbsp (50 ml) olive oil
2 cups (500 ml) water
¾-in. (2-cm) piece of fresh ginger, peeled and grated
Peel of 2 salt-preserved lemons
2 sprigs rosemary
Finely grated zest of 1 lemon
1 tsp finely chopped fresh rosemary
Salt and freshly ground pepper

Onion shells
2 white onions
3 tbsp (1¾ oz./50 g) butter

Carrot purée
1 lb. 2 oz. (500 g) carrots
3½ oz. (100 g) potatoes
1½ tsp (8 g) salt
1 tsp ground cumin
Peel of 1 salt-preserved lemon
3½ tbsp (50 ml) olive oil

To serve
⅓ cup (1¾ oz./50 g) toasted blanched almonds
Chives, finely chopped
Pea shoots

PREPARING THE BREAST OF VEAL
Preheat the oven to 350°F (180°C/Gas Mark 4). Peel and finely chop the onion. Crush the unpeeled garlic cloves using the flat of a chef's knife blade. Season the veal with salt and pepper. Heat the olive oil in a Dutch oven and sear the veal over high heat until deeply browned all over. Lower the heat, add the onion, and sweat until softened and lightly browned. Pour in the water and bring to a boil, skimming off any foam on the surface. Add the ginger, preserved lemon peel, garlic, and rosemary sprigs. Cover and braise in the oven for 1½ hours, until the meat is completely tender, then remove it from the pan. Strain the cooking liquid through the fine-mesh sieve into a clean large saucepan and reduce over low heat until it coats the back of a spoon. Place the meat back in the sauce and simmer gently for about 10 minutes to thoroughly glaze it. Adjust the seasonings, if necessary, then stir in the lemon zest and chopped rosemary.

PREPARING THE ONION SHELLS
Preheat the oven to 325°F (160°C/Gas Mark 3). Peel the onions and cut them in half lengthwise. Heat the butter in an oven-safe skillet and brown the onions on the cut sides. Transfer to the oven and roast for about 20 minutes, until the onions are completely tender and charred in places. Remove the center layers and set the shells aside.

PREPARING THE CARROT PURÉE
Peel the carrots and potatoes. Cook them in a large saucepan of boiling salted water until tender. Drain and place in the food processor with the cumin, preserved lemon peel, and olive oil, and process to a smooth purée.

TO SERVE
Place a slice of veal breast on each plate and top with almonds and chives. Add a quenelle of carrot purée and a few half-onion shells to each plate and drizzle over the veal sauce. Garnish with pea shoots and serve immediately.

VEAL PAUPIETTES IN TOMATO SAUCE

Paupiettes de veau à la tomate

Serves 10

Active time
1½ hours

Cooking time
2 hours

Chilling time
20 minutes

Storage
3 days

Equipment
Meat tenderizer

Meat grinder + medium plate

Butcher's twine

Ingredients

Paupiettes

1½ lb. (700 g) veal top round roast (*noix de veau*)

3½ oz. (100 g) thinly sliced pork fatback (*barde de porc*)

1 lb. 2 oz. (500 g) veal breast

5¼ oz. (150 g) shallots

Generous ¾ cup (200 ml) olive oil, divided

10½ oz. (300 g) button mushrooms

¼ bunch parsley

¼ bunch chives

1 egg

2 tsp (10 g) salt

Tomato sauce

7 oz. (200 g) shallots

Generous ¾ cup (200 ml) olive oil, divided

2¼ lb. (1 kg) tomatoes on the vine

3 cloves garlic

¼ bunch thyme

2 bay leaves

2 tsp (10 g) fine sea salt

To garnish

3½ oz. (100 g) red onions

4 cloves garlic

¼ bunch thyme, divided

1⅔ cups (400 ml) olive oil + more as needed

14 oz. (400 g) multicolored cherry tomatoes

10 green Swiss chard leaves

Salt

PREPARING THE PAUPIETTES

Cut the veal top round into 10 equal pieces and, using the meat tenderizer, flatten into scaloppine (see technique p. 52). Cut the fatback into 10 strips measuring 1½ in. (4 cm) in width. Partially trim the fat off the veal breast and pass the meat through the meat grinder fitted with the medium plate. Peel and finely chop the shallots. Heat half the olive oil in a skillet and sweat the shallots. Wash and quarter the mushrooms, slicing them slightly on a diagonal through the cap. Heat the remaining olive oil in a skillet and sauté the mushrooms until golden brown, then drain and chop them finely. Wash and finely chop the parsley and chives. Combine the ground veal breast, shallots, mushrooms, herbs, egg, and salt in a bowl. To shape the paupiettes, divide the filling between the veal scaloppine and wrap the meat around the filling (see technique p. 53, steps 1–3). Wrap the strips of fatback around the paupiettes to hold them together and tie with twine (see steps 6–10).

PREPARING THE TOMATO SAUCE

Peel and finely chop the shallots. Heat half the olive oil in a large skillet and sweat the shallots until softened. Peel the tomatoes, remove the seeds, and chop the flesh finely. Add to the skillet with the garlic, thyme, and bay leaves, and cook over low heat for 30 minutes, until the juices from the tomatoes have evaporated and the sauce is reduced.

COOKING THE PAUPIETTES

Meanwhile, preheat the oven to 325°F (160°C/Gas Mark 3). Heat the remaining olive oil in a separate skillet and brown the paupiettes all over. Transfer the tomato sauce to a Dutch oven and place the paupiettes over it. Cook in the oven for 1 hour, uncovered. After the paupiettes have been cooking for 30 minutes, prepare the garnishes.

PREPARING THE GARNISHES

Peel and quarter the red onions and place on a baking sheet lined with parchment paper. Add 2 cloves garlic, half the thyme, and a drizzle of olive oil, and roast in the oven at 325°F (160°C/Gas Mark 3) with the paupiettes for 25 minutes. Meanwhile, roughly crush the remaining garlic cloves using the flat of a chef's knife blade. Confit the tomatoes in a skillet with the 1⅔ cups (400 ml) olive oil, the crushed garlic, and the remaining thyme until the tomatoes are tender. Cut the chard leaves diagonally into 2¾ × 1¼-in. (7 × 3-cm) strips and toss with a drizzle of olive oil and a pinch of salt.

TO SERVE

Serve the paupiettes with the garnishes arranged attractively alongside.

VEAL SWEETBREAD VOL-AU-VENTS

Vol-au-vent au ris de veau

Serves 6

Active time

2 hours

Cooking time

45 minutes

Chilling time

30 minutes

Soaking time

12 minutes

Infusing time

15 minutes

Storage

24 hours

Equipment

4-in. (10-cm) round pastry cutter

3-in. (8-cm) round pastry cutter

Silicone baking mat

Butcher's twine

Ingredients

Vol-au-vent cases

1 lb. (500 g) puff pastry (store-bought or homemade)

1 egg yolk

Duxelles

1¼ lb. (600 g) button mushrooms

2 oz. (60 g) shallots

1 clove garlic

2 tbsp (1 oz./30 g) butter

1 bouquet garni (thyme and bay leaf)

Scant ½ cup (100 ml) heavy cream, min. 35% fat

Salt

Morel velouté

1 tbsp (20 g) clarified butter

2 tbsp (20 g) all-purpose flour

4 cups (1 liter) white poultry stock (*fond blanc de volaille,* see recipe p. 19)

1 oz. (30 g) dried morel mushrooms

⅓ cup (2¾ oz./80 g) crème fraîche

Salt and freshly ground pepper

To garnish

2 bunches carrots

6 stalks white asparagus

Salt

Veal sweetbreads

2 cups (500 ml) water

2½ tbsp (1½ oz./40 g) salt

1½ lb. (700 g) veal sweetbreads (3 sweetbreads)

½ onion

2 whole cloves

2 cups (500 ml) whole milk

1 bouquet garni (thyme and bay leaf)

5 peppercorns

¾ cup + 2 tbsp (3½ oz./100 g) all-purpose flour

2 tbsp (1 oz./30 g) butter

2 tbsp (30 ml) grape-seed oil

To serve

Shiso microgreens

PREPARING THE VOL-AU-VENT CASES

Roll the pastry to a thickness of $\frac{1}{16}$ in. (2–3 mm) and cut out 12 disks using the 4-in. (10-cm) pastry cutter. Using the 3-in. (8-cm) pastry cutter, cut the centers out of 6 of the pastry disks to make rings. Place the rings on top of the uncut disks, first dampening the undersides of the rings with a little water to fix them in position. Place the cases on a baking sheet lined with parchment paper. Beat the egg yolk and brush it over the tops of the vol-au-vent cases, then chill them for 30 minutes. Preheat the oven to 400°F (200°C/Gas Mark 6). Score the pastry rings at regular intervals using the back of a paring knife, making an attractive pattern all the way around. Place the silicone baking mat over the cases to help the pastry to rise evenly. Bake for 10 minutes at 400°F (200°C/Gas Mark 6), then lower the oven temperature to 325°F (160°C/Gas Mark 3), remove the silicone mat, and continue to bake for an additional 20 minutes. Let cool on a wire rack.

PREPARING THE DUXELLES

Wash and finely chop the button mushrooms. Peel and finely chop the shallots and garlic. Heat the butter with a pinch of salt in a skillet and, when foaming, sweat the shallots and garlic until softened but not browned. Add the mushrooms, bouquet garni, and another pinch of salt. Cut a piece of parchment paper to fit snugly inside the skillet, place it over the mushroom mixture, and cook until the mushrooms are tender and all the liquid has evaporated. Pour in the cream and bring to a boil. Adjust the seasonings if necessary and remove from the heat.

PREPARING THE MOREL VELOUTÉ

Melt the clarified butter in a medium saucepan over low heat to prepare a blond roux. Whisking continuously, sprinkle in the flour and cook until the roux is frothy and very lightly golden. Let cool to room temperature. Place the stock and dried morel mushrooms in a large saucepan, bring to a boil, and reduce by half, until 2 cups (500 ml) of liquid remain. While the stock is still boiling hot, remove the morels, reserving them for garnishing. Gradually whisk half the hot stock into the roux in the saucepan and bring to a boil, whisking continuously. Let boil for 2 minutes, continuing to whisk to prevent any lumps from forming. Whisk in the remaining stock and bring to a boil, then stir in the crème fraiche just before removing from the heat. Adjust the seasoning with salt and pepper if necessary.

PREPARING THE GARNISHES

Peel the carrots and cut them diagonally into 1¼-in. (3-cm) pieces. Cook them in boiling salted water until just tender, then cool them in ice water and drain on paper towels. Peel the asparagus stalks and tie them together with twine. Cook in boiling salted water for 5 minutes, or until completely tender, then cool in ice water and drain on paper towels.

PREPARING THE VEAL SWEETBREADS

Place the water and salt in a large bowl and stir to dissolve, then add a few ice cubes. Submerge the veal sweetbreads in the brine and let them soak for 12 minutes. Peel the onion, stud it with the cloves, and place in a large saucepan with the milk, bouquet garni, and peppercorns. Bring to a boil, remove from the heat, and let infuse for 15 minutes. Drain the sweetbreads and add them to the saucepan with the warm infused milk. Bring to a simmer and cook for 3 minutes. Cool the sweetbreads quickly in a bowl of ice water. Once cooled, place them on a clean dish towel and press down to release any excess liquid. Peel off the membranes and remove any fat and gristle. Cut the sweetbreads into six 3-in. (8-cm) pieces and coat them in flour. Heat the butter and grape-seed oil in a skillet and brown the pieces on both sides. Cook until a trussing needle inserted into the center meets no resistance.

TO SERVE

Preheat the oven to 195°F (90°C/Gas on lowest setting). Cut the centers out of the vol-au-vent cases and set them aside. Fill the vol-au-vent cases with the duxelles, place them on a baking sheet lined with parchment paper, and reheat in the oven for 15 minutes. Meanwhile, in a small saucepan, reheat the garnishes with 4 tbsp of the morel velouté. Place a piece of sweetbread in each vol-au-vent case. Just before serving, place the vol-au-vents on serving plates, with the lids alongside and the carrots, asparagus, and reserved morels arranged attractively on one side of each plate. Fill the vol-au-vents with morel velouté and drizzle a little over the garnishes. Decorate with shiso microgreens and serve immediately.

CALVES' KIDNEYS IN ZITONE TIMBALES WITH MUSTARD SAUCE

Rognons de veau en timbales de zitone, sauce moutarde

Serves 4

Active time
1 hour

Cooking time
About 45 minutes

Chilling time
40 minutes

Storage
24 hours

Equipment
Food processor

Disposable pastry bag

4 × 5-in. (12-cm) stainless-steel rings, ¾ in. (2 cm) deep

Steam oven (or steamer)

Ingredients

Filling

2¾ oz. (75 g) boneless chicken breast, skinned

1 egg white

½ cup (125 ml) heavy cream, min. 35% fat

Salt

Zitone timbales

2 cups (500 ml) white poultry stock (*fond blanc de volaille*, see recipe p. 19), or use salted water

7 oz. (200 g) zitone no. 19 pasta

Butter for greasing

Calves' kidneys in mustard sauce

2 calves' kidneys, external fat removed (see technique p. 60)

3 tbsp (1¾ oz./50 g) butter

2 tbsp (30 ml) sunflower oil

1 shallot

Scant ½ cup (100 ml) cognac

⅔ cup (150 ml) Madeira

⅔ cup (150 ml) thickened brown veal stock (*fond brun de veau lié*, see recipe p. 16)

⅔ cup (150 ml) heavy cream, min. 35% fat

2 tbsp (1 oz./30 g) wholegrain mustard

2 tbsp finely chopped tarragon

Salt and freshly ground pepper

Oyster mushrooms

7 oz. (200 g) oyster mushrooms

Scant ⅓ cup (2½ oz./70 g) melted clarified butter

Salt and freshly ground pepper

To serve

Wholegrain mustard (optional)

Dijon mustard (optional)

Red-veined sorrel

Pea shoots

PREPARING THE FILLING

Cut the chicken breast into approximately 1¼-in. (3-cm) pieces and process with the egg white in the food processor until smooth. Transfer to a bowl and set over a bed of ice. Using a flexible spatula, fold in the cream in three equal quantities, fully incorporating each third before adding the next. Season with a pinch of salt, transfer to the pastry bag, and chill for at least 10 minutes or until using.

PREPARING THE ZITONE TIMBALES

Bring the stock or water to a boil in a large pan, add the zitone, and cook until al dente (about 10 minutes). Drain the pasta and lay the pieces side by side on a clean dish towel so they are touching to make four long strips to fit inside the 5-in. (12-cm) stainless-steel rings. As the pasta cools, the starch will make the pieces stick together. Cover with a second clean dish towel and chill in the refrigerator for 10 minutes. Grease the insides of the stainless-steel rings with butter and place them on a baking sheet lined with parchment paper. Grease the rings with a second layer of butter. Line the rings with the strips of pasta, which should be vertical. Snip the tip off the pastry bag and pipe the filling into the pasta tubes, filling them completely. Cover the rings with plastic wrap and chill for at least 20 minutes.

PREPARING THE CALVES' KIDNEYS IN MUSTARD SAUCE

Cut each kidney in half lengthwise and remove the interior fat and white parts without altering the shape of the kidneys. Season with salt and pepper. Heat the butter and oil in a skillet until very hot, then add the kidneys and sauté for 2–3 minutes, until browned on the outside but still pink in the center. Remove the kidneys from the pan and pour off the excess fat if necessary. Peel and finely chop the shallot and sweat it in the same skillet over low heat until softened but not browned. Add the cognac and flambé, then deglaze with the Madeira and reduce by half. Add the stock and let simmer for a few minutes. Pour in the cream and reduce until the sauce coats the back of a spoon. Stir in the mustard and tarragon, and adjust the seasonings if necessary. Remove from the heat, return the kidneys to the pan, and set aside.

PREPARING THE OYSTER MUSHROOMS

Wash and quarter the mushrooms. Heat the butter in a skillet with a little salt and pepper and sauté the mushrooms for 2 minutes over high heat, until just tender and lightly golden in places.

TO SERVE

Preheat the steam oven, if using, to 185°F (85°C/Gas on lowest setting). Cook the zitone timbales in the steam oven, or steamer, for 10 minutes. Meanwhile, reheat the kidneys in the sauce. Place each timbale in the center of a shallow serving bowl and carefully remove the rings. Arrange the kidneys and oyster mushrooms in the center. Pour a little sauce into the center and around the outside. Top with a spoonful of wholegrain mustard and a few randomly placed dots of Dijon mustard on the kidneys and mushrooms, if desired. Scatter with red-veined sorrel and pea shoots.

VEAL TOP RUMP WITH ZUCCHINI AND CARDOON FRITTERS

Quasi de veau, courgette et cardon frit

Serves 10

Active time
1 hour

Cooking time
About 2–3 hours

Chilling time
10 minutes

Storage
24 hours

Equipment
Fine-mesh sieve
Cast-iron grill pan
Mandolin
Mortar and pestle

Ingredients

Veal jus
7 oz. (200 g) white onions
½ head garlic
2¼ lb. (1 kg) veal breast
Scant ½ cup (100 ml) olive oil
¼ bunch thyme
1¾ sticks (7 oz./200 g) butter, diced, at room temperature
8 cups (2 liters) vegetable stock, divided

To garnish
10 cardoons
1 cup + 2 tbsp (5¼ oz./150 g) all-purpose flour
1 tsp (5 g) salt
1 egg
4 tsp (20 ml) sunflower oil
1 cup (250 ml) water
4 cups (1 liter) olive oil + more as needed
1 lb. 2 oz. (500 g) violin zucchini
1 × 7-oz. (200-g) green zucchini
2 cloves black garlic

Generous 1 cup (5¼ oz./150 g) pine nuts, toasted
⅔ cup (150 ml) hazelnut oil

Veal top rump
3½ lb. (1.5 kg) top rump of veal (*quasi de veau*)
2 tsp (10 g) salt
Scant ½ cup (100 ml) olive oil
5 tbsp (2½ oz./75 g) butter
3 cloves garlic
Leaves of ¼ bunch savory

To serve
Extra-virgin olive oil
20 black garlic cloves
Fleur de sel
Parsley-infused oil
Salt and freshly ground pepper

PREPARING THE VEAL JUS
Peel the onions and cut each one into 8 wedges. Separate the garlic cloves and roughly crush them, unpeeled, using the flat of a chef's knife blade. Cut the veal breast into 1½-in. (4-cm) pieces. Heat the olive oil in a large saucepan and sear the veal until pale golden brown. Add the onions, garlic, thyme, and butter, and continue to cook until the meat is deeply browned, basting it with the oil and butter. Pour off the excess fat and deglaze with 2 cups (500 ml) of the vegetable stock to release the browned bits from the bottom of the pan. Add the remaining stock and simmer, uncovered, for 1½ hours. Strain through the fine-mesh sieve into a clean saucepan and reduce until the jus coats the back of a spoon.

PREPARING THE GARNISHES
Peel the stringy outer layer off the cardoons and cook them in a large pan of boiling salted water for 30 minutes, until tender. Meanwhile, prepare the batter: whisk together the flour, salt, egg, sunflower oil, and water in a large bowl. Drain the cardoons and cut them diagonally into 2-in. (5-cm) pieces. Heat the olive oil in a wide, deep skillet to 360°F (180°C). Dip the cardoon pieces in the batter and deep-fry them until golden. Wash the violin zucchini and cut them in half lengthwise, then cut each half into 2-in. (5-cm) thick pieces. Warm the grill pan over high heat with a little olive oil. Add the violin zucchini pieces and cook until lightly colored. Wash the green zucchini and, using the mandolin, shave half of it lengthwise into ¹⁄₁₆-in. (2-mm) slices. Set the slices aside in ice water until serving. Cut the remaining half into small pieces and, using the pestle, crush them in the mortar with the black garlic, pine nuts, and hazelnut oil.

PREPARING THE VEAL
Preheat the oven to 325°F (160°C/Gas Mark 3). Season the veal with the salt. Heat the olive oil in a skillet and sear the veal until pale golden brown. Add the butter, garlic, and savory, and continue to cook until the meat is deeply browned on all sides, basting it with the oil and butter. Transfer to a Dutch oven and cook in the oven for about 40 minutes–1 hour, or until the meat is done to your liking. Let rest for 10 minutes.

TO SERVE
Drain the violin zucchini slices and toss with a little olive oil, salt, and pepper. Place a generous spoonful of the crushed green zucchini mixture on each plate and top with a slice of violin zucchini, a cardoon fritter cut in two, and a few green zucchini slices. Cut the veal into 10 equal pieces and place one on each plate. Drizzle with veal jus and season with fleur de sel and pepper. Add a few drops of parsley-infused oil and serve immediately.

SPICED HONEY-GLAZED VEAL BREAST

Poitrine de veau confite laquée au miel et aux épices

Serves 6

Active time
1 hour

Cooking time
3¾ hours

Resting time
Overnight

Chilling time
30 minutes

Infusing time
15 minutes

Storage
2 days

Equipment
Microplane grater
Fine-mesh sieve

Ingredients

Braised veal breast
1 orange
1 lime
1½ oz. (40 g) fresh ginger
3 lb. (1.4 kg) bone-in veal breast
Grape-seed oil
1¼ oz. (35 g) yellow curry paste
4 cups (1 liter) coconut milk
3 sprigs thyme
1 bay leaf
Salt and freshly ground pepper

Broccolini and carrots
10½ oz. (300 g) spring carrots with their tops
1 lb. 2 oz. (500 g) broccolini
Salt

Spiced honey glaze
½ cup (6 oz./170 g) honey
½ cup (120 ml) sherry vinegar
Scant ½ cup (100 ml) orange juice
1⅔ cups (400 ml) thickened brown veal stock (*fond brun de veau lié*, see recipe p. 16)
1 cinnamon stick
2 whole cloves
1 tsp (2 g) Sichuan peppercorns
1 orange
1 lime
1 vanilla bean, split lengthwise

To serve
Olive oil
Whole cloves (optional)
Cinnamon sticks (optional)
Star anise pods (optional)

PREPARING THE BRAISED VEAL BREAST (1 DAY AHEAD)

Preheat the oven to 300°F (150°C/Gas Mark 2). Wash the orange and lime and cut them crosswise into approximately ⅛-in. (4-mm) slices. Peel and cut the ginger into ⅛-in. (4-mm) slices. Season the veal breast with salt and pepper. Heat a little grape-seed oil in a Dutch oven and brown the veal all over. Remove the meat from the pan, add the curry paste, and cook for a few minutes, until fragrant. Deglaze with the coconut milk, then return the meat to the pan and add the citrus slices, ginger, thyme, and bay leaf. Season with salt and pepper. Cut a piece of parchment paper to fit snugly inside the pan, place over the ingredients, and put the lid on. Bring to a simmer over medium heat, then transfer to the oven and slowly braise for 3½ hours, turning the meat over twice and cleaning the sides of the pan regularly with a damp brush. Once the meat is completely tender (a knife should enter easily), remove it and take out the bones and cartilage. Cover the boned meat with plastic wrap, shape it into a square, and press to make it compact, placing a weight on top. Let rest overnight in the refrigerator.

PREPARING THE BROCCOLINI AND CARROTS

Peel the carrots and trim off the tops, leaving about ½ in. (1 cm). Blanch the carrots and broccolini in a large pot of boiling salted water until just tender. Drain, then chill for 30 minutes.

PREPARING THE SPICED HONEY GLAZE

Warm the honey in a large saucepan until it turns a deep golden brown color and caramelizes. Deglaze with the vinegar and reduce to a syrup. Stir in the orange juice and reduce again to a syrupy consistency. Add the veal stock and reduce until it is thick but can still be drizzled. Toast the spices in an ungreased skillet until they smell fragrant, then add them to the sauce. Wash and dry the orange and lime and zest them over the sauce using the Microplane grater. Scrape in the vanilla seeds. Remove from the heat and let infuse for 15 minutes. Strain the glaze through the fine-mesh sieve into a bowl.

TO SERVE

Preheat the oven to 340°F (170°C/Gas Mark 3). Remove the plastic wrap from the meat and cut it into 6 equal slices. Carefully place the slices on a baking sheet lined with parchment paper and brush them with the glaze. Reheat in the oven for 15 minutes, then brush the slices with two to three layers of glaze so they are well coated. Reheat the carrots and broccolini in a skillet with a little olive oil. Arrange the meat and garnishes attractively on each serving plate and drizzle over the remaining glaze. Decorate the plate with whole cloves, cinnamon sticks, and star anise pods, if desired.

CALVES' LIVER WITH STUFFED SHALLOTS

Foie de veau et échalote farcie

Serves 10

Active time
45 minutes

Cooking time
2½ hours

Storage
24 hours

Equipment
Fine-mesh sieve

Disposable pastry bag
fitted with a plain tip

Ingredients

Veal jus
2¼ lb. (1 kg) veal breast
7 oz. (200 g) onions
½ head garlic
Scant ½ cup (100 ml)
olive oil
¼ bunch thyme
1¾ sticks (7 oz./200 g)
butter
8 cups (2 liters)
vegetable stock, divided
7 oz. (200 g) lemons
3½ oz. (100 g) capers

Stuffed shallots
2¼ lb. (1 kg) large
banana shallots,
preferably Cuisse
de Poulet du Poitou
½ bunch chives
¼ bunch tarragon
1 bunch scallions
1 tsp (5 g) Dijon mustard

Calves' liver
2 cloves garlic
2¾ lb. (1.2 kg) calves'
liver
2 tsp (10 g) salt
⅔ cup (150 ml) olive oil
2 bay leaves
¼ bunch thyme

To serve
Baby spinach
Pickled mustard seeds

PREPARING THE VEAL JUS

Cut the veal breast into 1½-in. (4-cm) cubes. Peel the onions and cut each one into 8 wedges. Roughly crush the garlic using the flat of a chef's knife blade. Heat the olive oil in a large saucepan and sear the meat over medium-high heat until pale golden brown. Add the onions, garlic, thyme, and butter, and continue to cook until the meat is deeply browned, basting it with the butter. Pour off the excess fat and deglaze with 2 cups (500 ml) of the vegetable stock, stirring to release the browned bits stuck to the bottom. Add the remaining stock and cook at a simmer for 1½ hours. Strain the jus through the fine-mesh sieve into a clean saucepan and reduce by half. Peel the lemons, removing all the bitter white pith. Remove the segments, cut them into ¼-in. (5-mm) dice, and add to the reduced jus along with the capers. Reserve at room temperature.

PREPARING THE STUFFED SHALLOTS

Preheat the oven to 325°F (160°C/Gas Mark 3). Place the unpeeled shallots on a rimmed baking sheet and roast for about 1 hour, or until tender. Wash, dry, and finely chop the chives. Wash and dry the tarragon, remove the stems, and finely chop the leaves. Wash, dry, and finely chop the scallions. When the shallots are tender, take them out of the oven and carefully remove the skins. Gently push out the inside layers, keeping the outside layers intact. Set the outside layers aside and finely chop the inner layers you have removed. Combine the chopped shallots, chives, tarragon, scallions, and mustard in a bowl. Transfer to the pastry bag and pipe into the outside shallot layers. Reshape the shallots so the stuffing is enclosed. Reheat the veal jus in a saucepan and add the stuffed shallots to glaze them.

PREPARING THE CALVES' LIVER

Peel and finely chop the garlic. Cut the calves' liver into 10 thin slices, each weighing 4¼ oz. (120 g). Season with the salt. Heat the olive oil in a skillet and brown the liver over medium-high heat. Add the garlic, bay leaves, and thyme, and continue to cook until the liver is just done to your liking, being careful not to overcook it.

TO SERVE

Place a slice of liver on each serving plate, along with two or three stuffed shallots glazed with jus and several capers. Garnish with pickled mustard seeds and baby spinach.

PORK

ROAST PORK SHOULDER WITH SPRING VEGETABLES

Échine de porc rôti printanier

Serves 8

Active time
1 hour

Cooking time
About 2 hours

Marinating time
30 minutes

Storage
24 hours

Equipment
Leave-in probe thermometer
Fine-mesh sieve
Mandolin

Ingredients

Roast pork shoulder
1 onion
1 carrot
1 stalk celery
1 clove garlic
3½ tbsp (50 ml) grape-seed oil
2¼-lb. (1-kg) boneless pork shoulder (échine de porc), tied into a roast (see technique p. 68)
Salt and freshly ground pepper

Sauce Robert
Pan juices and aromatics from the roast pork shoulder (see above)
Generous ¾ cup (200 ml) dry white wine
Generous ¾ cup (200 ml) brown veal stock (fond brun de veau, see recipe p. 16)
3 tbsp (1¾ oz./50 g) Dijon mustard

Spring vegetables
1 bulb fennel
Juice of ½ lemon
Extra-virgin olive oil
2¼ lb. (1 kg) peas in their pods
10½ oz. (300 g) spring carrots with their tops
14 oz. (400 g) baby turnips
1 bunch French breakfast radishes
1 pinch sugar
2 tbsp (1 oz./30 g) butter
1 bunch scallions
Salt and freshly ground pepper

PREPARING THE ROAST PORK SHOULDER

Preheat the oven to 265°F (130°C/Gas Mark ½–1). Peel the onion, carrot, and celery, and dice them finely. Roughly crush the unpeeled garlic using the flat of a chef's knife blade. Warm the oil in a Dutch oven over high heat for 3 minutes, until shimmering. Season the roast with salt and pepper, place it in the pan, and brown it all over. Remove the meat and add the onion, carrot, celery, and garlic to the pan. Stir to combine, then place the roast on top. Insert the leave-in probe thermometer into the center of the roast, then place in the oven. Lower the oven temperature to 250°F (120°C/Gas Mark ½) and cook until the internal temperature reaches 108°F (42°C). Lower the oven temperature to 195°F (90°C/Gas on lowest setting), turn the roast over, and continue cooking until the internal temperature reaches 162°F (72°C), which should take about 1 hour. Transfer the roast to a rack and cover it with aluminum foil. Reserve the pan juices and aromatics for the sauce Robert.

PREPARING THE SAUCE ROBERT

Place the reserved pan juices and aromatics in a large saucepan and reduce until all the liquid has evaporated. Deglaze with the white wine and reduce by one-third, then add the stock and let simmer for 15 minutes. Strain through the fine-mesh sieve into a clean saucepan and reduce until the sauce coats the back of a spoon. Stir in the mustard.

PREPARING THE SPRING VEGETABLES

Wash the fennel and use the mandolin to cut it into ¹⁄₁₆-in. (2-mm) slices. Toss the slices with the lemon juice and a little olive oil, and let marinate for 30 minutes in the refrigerator. Shell the peas. Wash and peel the remaining vegetables as necessary. Trim the greens off the carrots, turnips, and radishes, leaving about ½ in. (1 cm). Cut the turnips into halves, or quarters if they are large, halve the radishes, and turn the carrots (see instructions for fondant potatoes p. 241). Place all three vegetables in a skillet and add enough water to just cover. Add the sugar, butter, and a pinch of salt, and cook until the sugar and butter melt, all the liquid has evaporated, and the vegetables are glazed. Depending on the size of the vegetables, you may need to add or remove some of the water as they cook. Cut the green parts off the scallions and slice thinly. Cut the white parts in half lengthwise, place them cut side down in a skillet with a little olive oil, and brown them. Blanch the peas in a pan of boiling salted water until just tender. Drain and refresh under cold water.

TO SERVE

Preheat the oven to 265°F (130°C/Gas Mark ½–1). Let the fennel come to room temperature and reheat the vegetables as needed. Reheat the roast in the oven for 25 minutes, glazing it with the sauce. Serve sliced with the vegetables sprinkled with scallion greens. Serve the sauce on the side.

HAY-BRAISED PORK CHOPS WITH CELERY ROOT MILLEFEUILLE

Côtes de cochon roi rose, feuille à feuille de céleri et espuma aux cacahuètes

Serves 4

Active time

2 hours

Cooking time

1 hour

Storage

2 days

Equipment

Steam oven (or steamer)

Mandolin

2 × 3-in. (8-cm) tartlet rings, 1½ in. (4 cm) deep

Whipping siphon + 1 N2O gas cartridge

Instant-read thermometer

Ingredients

Celery root millefeuille

1 celery root (celeriac)

Scant ½ cup (100 ml) melted clarified butter

Scant ¾ cup (3½ oz./100 g) raw peanuts, chopped

Salt

Peanut foam

13 sheets (1 oz./26 g) gelatin (200 Bloom)

1⅔ cups (400 ml) heavy cream, min. 35% fat

Generous ⅓ cup (3½ oz./100 g) smooth peanut butter

Scant ½ cup (4¼ oz./120 g) egg yolk (6 yolks)

Scant ½ cup (110 ml) peanut oil

Salt

Pork chops

3½ oz. (100 g) food-grade hay

2 × 14-oz. (400-g) pork chops, preferably Roi Rose de Touraine

3½ tbsp (50 ml) sunflower oil

5 tbsp (2½ oz./70 g) butter

Salt and freshly ground pepper

To serve

2 tbsp chopped toasted peanuts

2 tbsp parsley powder

⅔ oz. (20 g) pea shoots

Generous ¾ cup (200 ml) pork jus

Salt and freshly ground pepper

PREPARING THE CELERY ROOT MILLEFEUILLE

Preheat the steam oven, if using, to 205°F (95°C/Gas on lowest setting). Peel the celery root and cut it into ⅛-in. (3-mm) slices using the mandolin. Blanch the slices for 3 minutes in boiling water, then cool under cold running water. Pat the celery root dry and lay the slices flat on a sheet of parchment paper. Brush with the clarified butter, season with salt, and scatter the peanuts over. Line the tartlet rings with plastic wrap and place them on a baking sheet lined with parchment paper. Add the celery root in layers, overlapping them as necessary and filling the rings completely. Cover with plastic wrap and cook in the steam oven, or steamer, for 35 minutes.

PREPARING THE PEANUT FOAM

Soak the gelatin in a bowl of cold water until softened. Warm the cream and peanut butter together in a saucepan. When the peanut butter has melted, take the pan off the heat, squeeze the gelatin to remove excess water, and stir it into the cream and peanut butter until dissolved. When the mixture is almost cold, whisk in the egg yolks and peanut oil, and season with salt. Transfer to the whipping siphon, charge it with the cartridge, and place in a bain-marie maintained at 133°F (56°C) until serving.

PREPARING THE HAY-BRAISED PORK CHOPS

Preheat the oven to 300°F (150°C/Gas Mark 2) and place the hay in a Dutch oven. Season the pork chops generously with salt and pepper. Heat the oil in a skillet until hot and sear the chops on both sides until caramelized. Add the butter and baste the chops generously with it. Place the pork chops over the hay in the Dutch oven, cover, and cook in the oven for 20 minutes, or until the internal temperature of the chops reaches 154°F (68°C).

TO SERVE

Remove the bones from the pork chops. Sprinkle the chops and celery root millefeuilles with chopped peanuts and cut them in half. Place half a chop and a half-millefeuille on each serving plate and season with salt and freshly ground pepper. Dispense a mound of foam from the siphon onto each plate and dust with parsley powder. Garnish with the pea shoots and serve immediately, with the pork jus on the side.

HONEY-GLAZED PORCELET HAM

Jambon de porcelet au miel

Serves 4

Active time

2 hours

Cooking time

2 hours

Storage time

3 days

Equipment

Butcher's twine

Instant-read thermometer

Fine-mesh sieve

Ingredients

2½ lb. (1.2 kg) bone-in porcelet (suckling pig) hind shank

Marinade

1¼ cups (300 ml) apple juice

⅓ cup (4¼ oz./120 g) honey

Scant 1 cup (240 ml) apple cider vinegar

1 tbsp (8 g) five-spice powder

10 whole cloves ground to a powder

8 cups (2 liters) white poultry stock (*fond blanc de volaille*, see recipe p. 19)

1 cinnamon stick

Whole cloves

Creamy saffron polenta

⅓ cup (50 g) yellow polenta

2½ cups (600 ml) whole milk + extra as needed

8 saffron threads

Scant ½ cup (100 ml) heavy cream, min. 35% fat

Scant ¾ cup (2½ oz./70 g) grated Parmesan

Asparagus

8 stalks green asparagus

8 stalks white asparagus

3 tbsp (1¾ oz./50 g) butter, melted

To serve

Pea shoots

Parsley-infused oil

Smoked chorizo oil

PREPARING THE PORCELET HAM

Remove the shoulder blade from the pork shank and tie the shank with twine so it keeps its shape during cooking (see similar techniques pp. 88 and 90).

PREPARING THE MARINADE AND COOKING THE HAM

Preheat the oven to 285°F (140°C/Gas Mark 1). Warm the apple juice in a saucepan. In a large Dutch oven, cook the honey and vinegar to a light golden caramel. Deglaze with the warm apple juice, then stir in the five-spice powder, ground cloves, and stock. Add the cinnamon stick. Place the ham in the pan, cover, and cook in the oven for about 1½ hours, or until the internal temperature of the ham reaches 147°F (64°C). As soon as you remove the ham from the oven, score it with a crosshatch pattern using the tip of a paring knife. Stick several whole cloves into the ham, then baste it with cooking juices to glaze. Cover loosely with foil and let sit while you prepare the polenta and asparagus. Strain the remaining juices through the fine-mesh sieve for serving.

PREPARING THE CREAMY SAFFRON POLENTA

Cook the polenta in the milk and saffron in a large saucepan over low heat, following the instructions on the package. Stir in the cream and Parmesan. The polenta should have the consistency of thick unwhipped cream, so add a little extra milk to thin it, if necessary.

PREPARING THE ASPARAGUS

Peel the green and white asparagus stalks and cook them separately in boiling salted water until just tender. Drain and brush with the melted butter immediately before serving.

TO SERVE

Cut the ham into slices and serve with the asparagus, polenta, and strained cooking juices on the side. Top the asparagus with pea shoots and drizzle the polenta with parsley and chorizo oil.

TEXAS-STYLE PORK SPARERIBS

Travers de porc à la Texane

Serves 6

Active time
1 hour

Cooking time
5½ hours

Marinating time
Overnight

Draining time
Overnight

Resting time
30 minutes

Storage
3 days

Equipment
Smoker (optional)
Blender
Fine-mesh sieve

Ingredients

Pork spareribs
1 full rack pork spareribs (5½ lb./2.5 kg)
Scant 2½ tbsp (1¼ oz./36 g) salt
¾ cup (3¼ oz./90 g) smoked sweet paprika
1½ tsp (4 g) ground cayenne pepper
1 tbsp (8 g) *piment d'Espelette*
1 tbsp (8 g) ground cumin
2–3 tbsp (8 g) dried oregano
1 tbsp (9 g) garlic powder
2 tbsp (1 oz./30 g) packed brown sugar
⅔ cup (5¼ oz./150 g) mayonnaise

Barbecue sauce
2½ lb. (1.1 kg) finely chopped tomatoes
⅓ oz. (10 g) lemongrass
½ oz. (15 g) fresh ginger
2¾ oz. (75 g) onions
2 tbsp (1 oz./30 g) butter
1 generous tbsp (25 g) honey
4 tsp (20 g) mustard
3 tbsp (1½ oz./40 g) packed brown sugar
1½ tbsp (25 ml) apple cider vinegar
¼ cup (1 oz./30 g) dry rub for ribs of your choice
2 tsp (10 ml) Worcestershire sauce
Celery salt

Coleslaw
5¼ oz. (150 g) carrots
1 lb. 2 oz. (500 g) green cabbage
¼ bunch parsley
Scant ½ cup (3½ oz./100 g) mayonnaise
4 tsp (20 g) Dijon mustard
Scant ¼ cup (1¾ oz./50 g) sour cream
1 tbsp (15 ml) apple cider vinegar
2 tbsp (15 g) toasted sesame seeds
A drizzle of toasted sesame oil, or to taste
2 tsp superfine sugar
Salt and freshly ground pepper

PREPARING THE PORK SPARERIBS (1 DAY AHEAD)

Trim excess fat off the spareribs, if necessary, and remove the membrane attached to the underside of the ribs. Season the rack on both sides with the salt. Combine all the spices, dried oregano, and garlic powder with the brown sugar, and generously rub the mixture over the rack. Brush the rack with the mayonnaise, making sure it is thoroughly coated. Let marinate overnight in the refrigerator. The following day, preheat the smoker, if using, to 221°F–225°F (105°C–107°C). Alternatively, preheat the oven to 230°F (110°C/Gas Mark ¼). Place the ribs in the smoker, or in a shallow pan if using the oven, and cook for 3 hours. Remove the ribs, place them on a large sheet of aluminum foil, add 3 tbsp water, and wrap the foil around the ribs to make a tightly sealed package. Continue to cook for an additional 1–2 hours, until the meat starts to pull away from the bones. Remove the foil, reserving the juices for the barbecue sauce. Let the ribs sit at room temperature for 30 minutes.

PREPARING THE BARBECUE SAUCE (1 DAY AHEAD)

Place the chopped tomatoes in a colander set over a bowl and let drain overnight in the refrigerator. The following day, thinly slice the lemongrass and peel and chop or grate the ginger. Peel and finely chop the onions and sweat in the butter in a saucepan over low heat for 10 minutes. Add the lemongrass and ginger and continue to sweat for an additional 5 minutes. Add all the remaining ingredients except for the celery salt. Cover and let simmer for 30 minutes. While the sauce is still hot, blend it to a purée with the reserved juices from cooking the ribs and a little celery salt. Strain through the fine-mesh sieve.

PREPARING THE COLESLAW (1 DAY AHEAD)

Peel and julienne the carrots. Wash and shred the cabbage, removing any tough stems. Wash, dry, and finely chop the parsley. Place the carrots, cabbage, and parsley in a large bowl. Whisk the remaining ingredients until combined, then toss with the carrots, cabbage, and parsley until coated. Set aside in the refrigerator until serving.

TO SERVE

Preheat the oven to 340°F (170°C/Gas Mark 3). Place the spareribs on a rimmed baking sheet and reheat in the oven, brushing them at least 3 times with the barbecue sauce. Cut the ribs between the bones and serve with the coleslaw and remaining sauce on the side.

PORK HOCK WITH LENTILS

Jarret de porc aux lentilles

Serves 6

Active time
30 minutes

Cooking time
4 hours

Storage
2 days

Ingredients

Pork hock
1 carrot
1 stalk celery
1 onion
2 cloves garlic
1¾ oz. (50 g) lard
3½ lb. (1.5 kg) pork hock from the hind leg (*jarret arrière de porc*)
About 8 cups (2 liters) white poultry stock (*fond blanc de volaille*, see recipe p. 19)
1 bouquet garni of your choice
Salt and freshly ground pepper

Lentils
2 carrots
2 shallots
2 stalks celery
1 bouquet garni (thyme and bay leaf)
5¼ oz. (150 g) piece cured ham
1⅓ cups (10½ oz./300 g) Beluga lentils, soaked for 4 hours in twice their volume of water
3⅓ cups (800 ml) water
2 cloves garlic, unpeeled
3 tbsp (1¾ oz./50 g) butter
Salt and freshly ground pepper

To serve
1½ tsp (4 g) ground cumin
1 tsp sherry vinegar

PREPARING AND COOKING THE PORK HOCK

Preheat the oven to 285°F (140°C/Gas Mark 1). Peel the carrot, celery, and onion, and chop finely. Peel the garlic cloves, cut them in half, and remove the germs. Melt the lard in a Dutch oven large enough to hold the pork hock. Lightly season the meat with salt and pepper, place it in the pan, and brown it on all sides. Remove, reduce the heat, and add the carrot, celery, onion, and garlic. Cook until softened. Return the pork hock to the pan and pour in the stock. Bring to a boil, then add the bouquet garni. Skim any foam from the surface, cover, and cook in the oven for 2 hours. Turn the meat over, then continue to cook for an additional 1–2 hours, until the meat separates easily from the bones. Remove the hock from the pan. Skim the fat off the surface of the stock, then reduce to a glaze over low heat. If the sauce is too salty, add 1 tsp cornstarch mixed with 2 tsp water, repeating this until the desired balance is reached.

PREPARING AND COOKING THE LENTILS

Peel the carrots, shallots, and celery. Cut one carrot into 3 pieces and one shallot in half lengthwise, keeping the root intact. Cut one celery stalk in half and add the leaves to the bouquet garni. Finely chop the remaining shallot, carrot, and celery, then finely chop the cured ham. Drain the lentils and rinse under cold running water. Place in a large saucepan and add the 3⅓ cups (800 ml) water. Add the vegetables that have been cut into large pieces, the garlic, and the bouquet garni. Bring to a boil, then reduce the heat and let simmer for 20 minutes. When the lentils are tender, season with salt and pepper. Remove from the heat and let cool. Melt the butter in a skillet and add the chopped cured ham. Sauté briefly, then add the finely chopped shallot, carrot, and celery, and cook until softened and lightly browned in places. Season with salt and pepper.

TO SERVE

Preheat the oven to 250°F (130°C/Gas Mark ½). Reheat the pork hock in the oven, glazing it several times with reduced stock until it is heated through and glossy. Add the sautéed vegetables and ham to the pan with the lentils and reheat. Stir in the remaining reduced stock along with the cumin and vinegar. Transfer the lentils to a clean Dutch oven for serving and place the glazed pork hock on top.

CARAMEL PORK

Porc au caramel

Serves 4

Active time
30 minutes

Cooking time
40 minutes

Storage
3 days

Equipment
Rice cooker (optional)

Ingredients

Caramel pork
1½ lb. (700 g) pork belly
½ cup (3½ oz./100 g) brown sugar
Scant ½ cup (100 ml) toasted sesame oil
2 tbsp (30 ml) nuoc mam (Vietnamese fish sauce)
1 cup (250 ml) water
2 tbsp (30 ml) dark soy sauce
1 tbsp (15 g) five-spice powder
Salt and freshly ground pepper

Roasted cashews
1⅓ cups (5¼ oz./150 g) whole cashews

To garnish
1½ cups (10½ oz./300 g) jasmine rice
4 bunches broccolini
1 bunch scallions
1 fresh red chili pepper

To serve
1 tbsp black sesame seeds
1 tbsp white sesame seeds

PREPARING THE CARAMEL PORK
Cut the pork belly into even ¾-in. (2-cm) slices. Season with salt and pepper. Warm the sugar and sesame oil in a large sauté pan over medium heat until the sugar dissolves and caramelizes. Add the pork belly, fish sauce, water, soy sauce, and five-spice powder, and cook, stirring often, until the meat is well glazed. Cover and cook over low heat for 20 minutes.

PREPARING THE ROASTED CASHEWS
Preheat the oven to 300°F (150°C/Gas Mark 2) and line a baking sheet with parchment paper. Spread the cashews over the baking sheet and toast them in the oven for 10 minutes.

PREPARING THE GARNISHES
Cook the rice in a rice cooker or in a saucepan of boiling salted water, according to the instructions on the package. Cook the broccolini in boiling salted water until crisp-tender, then drain and keep warm until serving. Thinly slice the scallions and chili pepper on the diagonal. Roughly chop some of the toasted cashews.

TO SERVE
Fill half of each serving bowl with rice and sprinkle over black sesame seeds. Fill the other half of each bowl with caramel pork and sprinkle over white sesame seeds. Scatter the scallions, chili pepper, and chopped cashews over the pork, then arrange the broccolini attractively in the center of each bowl.

IBÉRICO PORK PLUMA STEAK WITH RAZOR CLAMS AND MISO EGGPLANT

Pluma ibérique aux couteaux et aubergine miso

Serves 4

Active time

2 hours

Cooking time

1½ hours

Pressing time

2 hours

Storage

3 days

Equipment

Fine-mesh sieve

Steam oven (or steamer)

Plancha grill or griddle

Ingredients

Ibérico pork pluma steaks

4 × 5¼-oz. (150-g) Ibérico pork pluma steaks (cut from the end of the loin)

Salt and freshly ground pepper

Mezcal pork jus

2 shallots

3 tbsp (1¾ oz./50 g) butter

1 tsp ground red Kampot pepper

Scant ½ cup (100 ml) mezcal

Generous ¾ cup (200 ml) pork jus (*jus de cochon*, or use veal stock [see recipe p. 16])

Salt and freshly ground pepper

Miso eggplant

2 eggplants

4 tbsp (60 ml) sweet soy sauce

6 tbsp (90 ml) mirin

2 tbsp (1 oz./30 g) brown miso paste

2 tbsp (1½ oz./40 g) honey

2 cups (500 ml) melted clarified butter

Seaweed potatoes

1¼ lb. (600 g) large waxy potatoes

2 stalks lemongrass

3 cloves spring garlic

7 tbsp (3½ oz./100 g) seaweed butter

Razor clams

12 razor clams

1 shallot

1 clove garlic

1 tbsp (20 g) butter

¼ cup (60 ml) dry white wine

2 tbsp finely chopped chervil

To serve

1 tbsp white sesame seeds

Finely grated zest of 1 lime

A few pea shoots

PREPARING THE IBÉRICO PORK PLUMA STEAKS AND MEZCAL PORK JUS

Season the pork steaks with salt and pepper and refrigerate until ready to cook. To prepare the jus, peel and finely chop the shallots. Heat the butter in a medium saucepan and, when foaming, sweat the shallots until softened but not browned. Add the Kampot pepper, then deglaze with the mezcal and flambé. Pour in the pork jus and cook over low heat for 15 minutes. Strain through the fine-mesh sieve and adjust the seasonings if necessary.

PREPARING THE MISO EGGPLANT

Preheat the steam oven, if using, to 185°F (85°C/Gas on lowest setting). Peel the eggplants and cook them in the steam oven, or steamer, for 50 minutes, until they are meltingly tender. Press the eggplants between two rimmed baking sheets with a weight placed on top, and let sit for 2 hours to release excess liquid and flatten the eggplants. In a small saucepan, combine the soy sauce, mirin, miso paste, and honey for the glaze. Bring to a boil, then remove from the heat. Heat the clarified butter in a large skillet and brown the eggplants on both sides. Add the glaze and cook until both sides of the eggplants are coated with it. Remove from the heat.

PREPARING THE SEAWEED POTATOES

Preheat the oven to 300°F (150°C/Gas Mark 2). Peel the potatoes, then cut and turn them to form 1½-in. (4-cm) ovals (see instructions for fondant potatoes p. 241). To cook the potatoes *en papillote*, place them with the lemongrass, garlic, and seaweed butter on a sheet of parchment paper and wrap the paper around them, sealing the edges to make a tightly sealed package. Bake for about 25 minutes, or until the potatoes are tender when pierced with the tip of a knife.

PREPARING THE RAZOR CLAMS

Rinse the razor clams thoroughly. Peel and finely chop the shallot and garlic. Heat the butter in a sauté pan and, when foaming, sweat the shallot until softened but not browned. Add the wine, razor clams, and garlic, then cover and cook for 4 minutes, or until the clam shells have opened. Remove the clams from their shells, cut off the crystalline style, and cut each clam into four or five pieces. Reheat them in a saucepan with a small amount of the cooking liquid, then add the chopped chervil.

TO SERVE

Just before serving, cut the eggplants crosswise into 4 thick sticks and sprinkle with the sesame seeds and lime zest. Arrange attractively on serving plates with the seaweed potatoes and a drizzle of the jus. Heat the plancha grill or griddle over high heat. When it is very hot, add the pluma steaks and cook them for 3 minutes on both sides, leaving them slightly pink in the center. Let rest on a rack for 2–3 minutes, then place on the plates, top with the razor clams, and serve immediately.

PORK CHEEK-STUFFED CABBAGE

Joues de porc façon choux farcis

Serves 6

Active time
1 hour

Cooking time
2½ hours

Chilling time
Overnight + 1 hour

Marinating time
1 hour

Soaking time
30 minutes

Storage
2 days

Equipment
Fine-mesh sieve

Round-bottomed bowl,
7 in. (18 cm) in diameter

Butcher's twine

8-in. (20-cm) square
earthenware baking dish

Ingredients

Braised pork cheeks

2 onions

2 cloves garlic

14 oz. (400 g) celery
root (celeriac)

7 pork cheeks

2 tbsp (30 ml) grape-
seed oil

Generous ¾ cup
(200 ml) dry white wine

2 cups (500 ml) brown
veal stock (*fond brun
de veau*, see recipe p. 16)

1 bouquet garni (thyme
and bay leaf)

Salt and freshly ground
pepper

Stuffed cabbage

1¾ lb. (800 g) boneless
pork shoulder (*échine
de porc*)

2½ tsp (13 g) salt

¾ tsp (2 g) ground black
pepper

4 cups (1 liter) water

3½ tbsp (50 ml) white
vinegar

10½ oz. (300 g) caul fat

1 oz. (30 g) dried horn-
of-plenty mushrooms

2 heads green cabbage

2 sweet onions,
preferably Cévennes

3 cloves garlic

10½ oz. (300 g) smoked
slab bacon (*poitrine
fumée*)

4 tbsp (2 oz./60 g)
butter

½ bunch parsley, finely
chopped

1 oz. (30 g) sandwich
bread, crusts removed

2 tbsp (30 ml) whole
milk

2 eggs

7 oz. (200 g) pork rind
(*couenne de porc*)

Salt and freshly ground
pepper

PREPARING THE BRAISED PORK CHEEKS (1 DAY AHEAD)

Peel and finely chop the onions and garlic. Peel the celery root and cut it into ½-in. (1-cm) dice. Remove the silver skin from the pork cheeks and season them with salt and pepper. Heat the grape-seed oil in a medium Dutch oven, add the pork cheeks, and brown them on all sides. Remove the meat, add the onions and garlic, and cook until caramelized. Deglaze with the white wine and cook until all the liquid has evaporated. Pour in the veal stock and add the pork cheeks, celery root, and bouquet garni. Cover and let simmer for 1½ hours, or until the meat is completely tender. Every 30 minutes, clean the sides of the pan with a brush moistened with water and scrape the bottom of the pan using a spatula, to ensure nothing is sticking to it. Remove the pork cheeks from the pan and strain the cooking liquid through the fine-mesh sieve to remove the aromatics. Reserve the cooking liquid and pork cheeks in an airtight container in the refrigerator overnight.

PREPARING THE STUFFED CABBAGE

Season the pork shoulder with the ½ tsp (13 g) salt and ¾ tsp (2 g) pepper, then chop the meat using a knife. Let marinate in the refrigerator for 1 hour. Pour the water and vinegar into a bowl, add the caul fat, and let soak for 30 minutes. Rehydrate the dried mushrooms in a little warm water, then drain and finely chop. Remove the green outer leaves from the cabbages, wash them, and set them aside. Remove the white inner leaves, wash them, and remove the stems. Blanch the green leaves in salted boiling water, then plunge them into cold water to stop the cooking. Dry the leaves with a clean dish towel, then flatten them. Cut small disks out of one of the larger green leaves for serving. Peel and finely chop the onions and garlic, then finely chop the white cabbage leaves. Cut the smoked bacon into ¾ × 1½-in. (2 × 4-cm) lardons, place in a saucepan of cold water, and bring to a boil. Drain, transfer to a bowl of cold water to cool, and then drain and dry on paper towels. Heat the butter in a skillet, cook the lardons over medium heat until browned, then remove them. Add the garlic and onions to the skillet and cook in the fat from the bacon until browned. Add the finely chopped white cabbage leaves, season with salt and pepper, cover, and cook for 5 minutes, then remove the lid and cook until all the liquid has evaporated. Add half the lardons, the rehydrated and drained mushrooms, and the parsley. Adjust the seasonings if necessary. Spread this mixture in a thin layer over a baking sheet, press plastic wrap over the surface, and place in the refrigerator to cool quickly. Meanwhile, preheat the oven to 325°F (160°C/Gas Mark 3). Soak the sandwich bread in the milk. Place the chopped, seasoned pork shoulder in a large bowl, add the eggs and soaked bread, and stir to combine. Stir in the cooked cabbage mixture once it has cooled completely. Drain and wring the caul fat to remove excess water. Line the inside of the 7-in. (18-cm) round-bottomed bowl with two layers of caul fat, leaving at least 1½ in. (4 cm) overhanging to cover the stuffed cabbage. Line with green cabbage leaves, then fill halfway with the stuffing mixture. Place 1 pork cheek in the center, then cover with the remaining stuffing. Fold the cabbage leaves over the filling and cover completely with the overhanging caul fat. Carefully remove the stuffed cabbage from the bowl and shape it into a sphere. Tie the twine at regular intervals around the stuffed cabbage to resemble the ridges on a melon. Place in an 8-in. (20-cm) square earthenware baking dish with the cooking liquid from the pork cheeks. Cover with the pork rind and cook in the oven for 1 hour, basting it regularly with the juices.

TO SERVE

In a large saucepan, reheat the remaining pork cheeks in the cooking juices. Remove them and cut them in half. Carefully place the stuffed cabbage in the saucepan and glaze with the juices. Drizzle a little of the cooking juices over a serving plate and place the stuffed cabbage, twine removed, in the center. Cut into 6 servings and arrange the pieces of pork cheek around the cabbage, alternating them with cabbage leaf disks topped with a lardon.

CRISPY PORK BELLY WITH HONEY-ROASTED PARSNIPS

Poitrine de porc et panais au miel

Serves 10

Active time
30 minutes

Cooking time
6 hours 10 minutes

Chilling time
Overnight

Storage
3 days

Equipment
Food processor
Fine-mesh sieve
Mortar and pestle

Ingredients

Pork belly
4½ lb. (2 kg) pork belly (*poitrine de porc*)
3½ oz. (100 g) fresh ginger
3 cloves garlic
1¾ oz. (50 g) lemongrass
Scant ½ cup (100 ml) soy sauce
2 tsp (10 ml) annatto (achiote) oil
Scant ¼ cup (1¾ oz./50 g) salt

Pork jus
2¼ lb. (1 kg) pork belly (*poitrine de porc*)
7 oz. (200 g) onions
½ head garlic
Scant ½ cup (100 ml) olive oil
¼ bunch thyme
1¾ sticks (7 oz./200 g) butter, diced, at room temperature
8 cups (2 liters) vegetable stock, divided

Sesame-cumin powder
¾ cup (2¾ oz./75 g) cumin seeds
3 tbsp (25 g) white sesame seeds
Scant ½ cup (1¾ oz./50 g) ground chili pepper
1 tsp (5 g) salt

Honey-roasted parsnips
10 small parsnips
Generous ½ cup (7 oz./200 g) honey
1 tsp (5 g) salt

To serve
2 tsp (10 ml) neutral oil
Fleur de sel

PREPARING THE PORK BELLY (1 DAY AHEAD)
Preheat the oven to 250°F (130°C/Gas Mark ½). Prepare the pork belly without removing the skin (see technique p. 70). Prick the skin all over using a metal skewer. Peel the ginger and garlic cloves. Prepare a marinade by placing the ginger, garlic, lemongrass, soy sauce, and annatto oil in the food processor. Pulse until the ginger, lemongrass, and garlic are finely chopped and incorporated with the other ingredients. Pour the marinade over the pork belly flesh only, place skin side up in a roasting pan, and slowly roast in the oven for 4 hours. Remove from the oven, then wipe the skin, rub the salt over it, and reserve overnight, uncovered, in the refrigerator.

PREPARING THE PORK JUS
Cut the pork belly into 1½-in. (4-cm) dice. Peel the onions and cut each one into 8 wedges. Separate the garlic cloves and roughly crush them, unpeeled, using the flat of a chef's knife blade. Heat the olive oil in a large saucepan and sear the meat until pale golden brown. Add the onions, garlic, thyme, and butter, and continue to cook until the meat is deeply browned, basting it with foaming butter. Pour off the excess fat and deglaze with 2 cups (500 ml) of the vegetable stock, scraping the bottom of the pan with a spoon to release the browned bits sticking to it. Add the remaining stock and cook at a simmer, uncovered, for 1½ hours. Strain through the fine-mesh sieve into a clean saucepan and reduce until the jus coats the back of a spoon.

PREPARING THE SESAME-CUMIN-CHILI POWDER
Preheat the oven to 300°F (150°C/Gas Mark 2). Spread the cumin and sesame seeds over a baking sheet lined with parchment paper and toast in the oven for 5 minutes. Transfer the seeds to the mortar and add the chili pepper and salt. Pound to a coarse powder using the pestle, leaving a few sesame seeds intact.

PREPARING THE HONEY-ROASTED PARSNIPS
Preheat the oven to 350°F (180°C/Gas Mark 4) and line a baking sheet with parchment paper. Wash the parsnips, cut them in half lengthwise, and place cut side up on the baking sheet. Pour the honey over them to coat. Roast for 10 minutes, until lightly caramelized. Turn the parsnips over and continue to roast for an additional 10 minutes, until tender.

TO CRISP THE PORK BELLY RIND
Increase the oven to 430°F (220°C/Gas Mark 7). Scrape the salt from the pork belly skin as well as the fat released from the skin. Brush with the neutral oil and bake for 15 minutes, or until the rind crackles and becomes crispy.

TO SERVE
Cut the pork belly into slices and sprinkle with fleur de sel. Serve with the honey-roasted parsnips dusted with sesame-cumin-chili powder.

ALSATIAN MEAT AND POTATO CASSEROLE

Baeckeoffe

Serves 10

Active time

1½ hours

Cooking time

4 hours

Marinating time

Overnight

Storage

3 days

Equipment

Mandolin

5-qt. (5-liter) rectangular casserole dish with a lid (18 × 10½ in./46 × 27 cm, 6 in./15 cm deep)

Ingredients

Marinade

3 white onions

2 carrots

3 stalks celery

2 leeks, white parts only (use the green parts in the bouquet garni)

½ head garlic

3 cups (750 ml) white wine

1 bouquet garni (parsley stems, bay leaf, and leek greens from above)

2 whole cloves

Salt and freshly ground pepper

Meats

1½ lb. (700 g) boneless lamb shoulder (*épaule d'agneau*)

1½ lb. (700 g) pork belly (*poitrine de porc*)

1½ lb. (700 g) boneless beef top-blade roast (*paleron de bœuf*)

1 pig's trotter

Potato layers

5½ lb. (2.5 kg) waxy potatoes, preferably Charlotte

PREPARING THE MARINADE (1 DAY AHEAD)

Peel the onions, carrots, celery, and leeks. Chop or slice the onions and cut the carrots, celery, and leeks diagonally into 2-in. (5-cm) pieces. Separate the garlic cloves and roughly crush them, unpeeled, using the flat of a chef's knife blade. Place all the vegetables in a large bowl and add the wine, bouquet garni, and cloves. Season with salt and pepper.

PREPARING THE MEATS (1 DAY AHEAD)

Cut the lamb, pork belly, and beef into 3½-oz. (100-g) pieces and quarter the pig's trotter. Place all the meats in the bowl with the marinade and let marinate overnight in the refrigerator. The following day, drain the meat and reserve the marinade.

COOKING THE CASSEROLE

Preheat the oven to 325°F (160°C/Gas Mark 3). Wash and peel the potatoes and, using the mandolin, cut them crosswise into ¼-in. (5-mm) slices. Line the base of the baking dish with a layer of potato slices, overlapping them slightly, then add a layer of meat and a little marinade. Repeat the layers with the remaining ingredients, finishing with potatoes. Cover and cook in the oven for 4 hours. Remove the lid 20 minutes before the end of the baking time to brown the potatoes.

TO SERVE

Serve the casserole as soon as it comes out of the oven.

PORK TENDERLOIN WITH COCKLES

Filet mignon de porc aux coques

Serves 4

Active time
1 hour

Cooking time
2½ hours

Soaking time
1 hour

Storage
3 days

Equipment
Fine-mesh sieve
Mortar and pestle
Butcher's twine
Instant-read
thermometer
Food processor

Ingredients

**Pork jus with
Madagascar pepper**
1 onion
3 shallots
5 cloves garlic
1 lb. (500 g) pork ribs
(or trimmings)
2½ tbsp (40 ml) peanut
oil
4 tbsp (2 oz./60 g)
butter
Kosher salt or coarse
sea salt
¼ cup (60 ml) mezcal
1 tsp Madagascar
peppercorns

Cockles
1 lb. (500 g) cockles
1 shallot
2 tbsp (30 ml) olive oil
1 clove garlic, unpeeled
Generous ¾ cup
(200 ml) Sauvignon
Blanc
Salt

Pork tenderloin
1 pork tenderloin
10 slices smoked bacon
3½ tbsp (50 ml) olive oil

Roasted carrots
1¼ lb. (600 g) baby
carrots, with bright
green tops
2 tbsp (1½ oz./40 g)
honey
3½ tbsp (50 ml) olive oil
1 tbsp (8 g) ground
cumin
1 tsp *piment d'Espelette*
Salt

Green cabbage purée
10 green cabbage leaves
Olive oil
Finely grated zest
of 1 lime
Salt and ground white
pepper

Carrot top tempura
½ cup (2 oz./60 g)
all-purpose flour
2 tbsp (30 ml) blond
beer
2 tbsp (30 ml) sparkling
water
½ tsp (2 g) baking
powder
½ tsp ground cumin
8 carrot tops (see above)
Oil for deep-frying
Salt

To serve
3½ tbsp (50 ml)
herb-infused oil

PREPARING THE PORK JUS WITH MADAGASCAR PEPPER

Peel and finely chop the onion, shallots, and garlic. Cut the pork ribs (or trimmings) into ¾-in. (2-cm) pieces. Heat the oil and butter with a little salt in a Dutch oven over low heat and cook the ribs (or trimmings) for at least 35 minutes, until they caramelize and flavorful brown bits stick to the bottom of the pan. Add the onion, shallots, and garlic, and cook until softened. Drain the pork and vegetables and pour off the excess fat, then return them to the pan. Add enough water to just cover. Cook at a simmer for 35–45 minutes, regularly skimming any foam from the surface. Strain through the fine-mesh sieve into a clean saucepan, add the mezcal, and reduce the jus until it coats the back of a spoon. Remove from the heat. Using the mortar and pestle, pound the peppercorns until coarsely ground. Stir the pepper into the jus and let infuse for 15 minutes, then strain again through the fine-mesh sieve.

PREPARING THE COCKLES

To remove the sand from the cockles, soak them in a bowl of salted water for about 20 minutes, then drain and repeat this process twice more.

PREPARING THE PORK TENDERLOIN

Preheat the oven to 285°F (140°C/Gas Mark 1). Remove the silver skin from the tenderloin, then wrap the bacon slices around it and tie it with twine (see technique p. 68). Heat the oil in an oven-safe skillet and brown the pork on all sides. Transfer the pan to the oven and roast the pork until the internal temperature reaches 153°F (67°C)—allow about 25 minutes per lb. or 500 g of meat. Cover the meat loosely with aluminum foil and let it rest before serving.

PREPARING THE ROASTED CARROTS

Preheat the oven to 350°F (180°C/Gas Mark 4). Remove the tops from the carrots and set 8 of the best ones aside for the carrot top tempura. Peel the carrots and place in a roasting pan. Toss with the honey, olive oil, cumin, *piment d'Espelette*, and a little salt, and roast for about 30 minutes, turning the carrots over regularly, until they are tender and browned in places. The exact time will depend on their size.

PREPARING THE GREEN CABBAGE PURÉE

Wash the cabbage leaves and cook them in boiling water for 10 minutes. Drain, reserving some of the cooking water, and plunge the leaves into ice water to stop the cooking. Squeeze out the excess water from the leaves and finely chop in the food processor. Add a little of the reserved cooking liquid and process to a purée. With the motor running, drizzle in a little olive oil until the purée is completely smooth. Adjust the seasonings if necessary. Let the purée cool briefly in the refrigerator, then stir in the lime zest.

COOKING THE COCKLES

Peel and finely chop the shallot. Heat the olive oil in a sauté pan and sweat the shallot until softened. Add the garlic, followed by the cockles. Deglaze with the white wine, cover, and cook over high heat for 5 minutes, until the shells open. Remove the cockles from the pan and shell them, reserving a few shells for decoration.

PREPARING THE CARROT TOP TEMPURA

Whisk together the flour, beer, sparkling water, baking powder, and cumin in a bowl. Heat the oil for deep-frying in a deep pan to 325°F (160°C). Using tongs, dip the carrot tops one at a time into the tempura batter and deep-fry them in batches until lightly golden. Drain on paper towels and season with salt.

TO SERVE

Reheat the pork jus and the cabbage purée. Drizzle herb-infused oil over half of each serving plate and jus over the other half. Cut the tenderloin into 1¼-in. (3-cm) slices and arrange them attractively over the jus and oil with the cabbage purée, cockles, roasted carrots, and carrot top tempura.

PIGS' TROTTER AND SQUID SAUSAGES WITH MASHED POTATOES

Saucisses de pieds de cochon aux encornets, pomme purée

Serves 4

Active time
1½ hours

Cooking time
2½ hours

Chilling time
Overnight

Storage
3 days

Equipment
Kitchen torch
Fine-mesh sieve
Manual sausage stuffer or a sausage-filling funnel
Butcher's twine
Food mill or potato ricer
Drum sifter with a #25 mesh

Ingredients

Pickled red onions
1 red onion
¾ cup (175 ml) tarragon vinegar
¼ cup (60 ml) white wine
Scant ⅓ cup (2 oz./60 g) superfine sugar
1 pinch fine sea salt

Pigs' trotter and squid sausages
3 pigs' trotters
(see Chefs' Notes)
1 carrot
1 onion
3½ oz. (100 g) celery
½ head garlic
4 tbsp (2 oz./60 g) butter
Generous ¾ cup (200 ml) white wine
Generous ¾ cup (200 ml) port wine
Generous ¾ cup (200 ml) white poultry stock (*fond blanc de volaille*, see recipe p. 19)

3 whole cloves
5 black peppercorns
1 tbsp (10 g) kosher salt
14 oz. (400 g) squid, cleaned
3½ tbsp (50 ml) olive oil
1 tbsp (15 g) Dijon mustard
2 tbsp finely chopped mixed herbs (tarragon, chives, and parsley)
3 hog casings, cleaned

Mashed potatoes
1 lb. 2 oz. (500 g) Ratte or Yukon Gold potatoes
1 tbsp (10 g) coarse gray sea salt
1 stick + 2 tsp (4½ oz./125 g) butter, diced
⅔ cup (150 ml) whole milk

To serve
Butter
Neutral oil
1 clove garlic, unpeeled
A few sprigs thyme
Pickled mustard seeds
A few red-veined sorrel leaves
1 oz. (30 g) mesclun greens, tossed with vinaigrette of your choice

PREPARING THE PICKLED RED ONIONS (1 DAY AHEAD)

Peel the red onion and cut it into approximately ¼-in. (5-mm) slices. Halve or quarter the slices and place in a shallow dish. Combine the vinegar, wine, and sugar in a saucepan, season with a pinch of salt, and bring to a boil, stirring to dissolve the sugar. Pour the hot liquid over the onion, cool, and refrigerate overnight.

PREPARING THE PIGS' TROTTER AND SQUID SAUSAGES

Using the kitchen torch, singe off any remaining hairs on the trotters. Place the trotters in a large pan of cold water, bring to a boil, and blanch for 10 minutes. Meanwhile, peel and finely chop the carrot, onion, and celery. Divide the garlic into cloves, then peel and finely chop them. Heat the butter in a second large saucepan and, when foaming, sweat the carrot, onion, celery, and garlic for 5 minutes. Drain the pigs' trotters, place them over the vegetables in the pan, and deglaze with the white wine. Add the port wine and stock and bring to a boil, skimming any foam from the surface. Add the cloves, peppercorns, and kosher salt, reduce the heat, and let simmer for about 2 hours, or until the trotters are completely tender. Lift out the trotters and place on a plate. Strain the cooking liquid through the fine-mesh sieve into a clean saucepan and reduce until syrupy. Reserve for serving. Finely chop the squid. Warm the olive oil over high heat in a skillet and quickly sauté the squid until just cooked through. Remove the bones from the trotters and roughly chop the meat. Place the meat in a bowl with the mustard, herbs, and squid. Slide one end of the clean casing onto the filling tube of the sausage stuffer (or sausage-filling funnel). Crank the stuffer to fill the casing, holding it to ensure even distribution and avoid air bubbles. To shape the sausage links, pinch the filled casing at about 5-in. (12-cm) intervals and twist two or three times. Tie each end with pieces of twine.

PREPARING THE MASHED POTATOES

Wash the potatoes thoroughly, place them in a saucepan, cover with cold water, and add the salt. Bring to a simmer, cover, and let cook for 25–30 minutes, or until the potatoes are completely tender. Drain the potatoes. While they are still warm, peel them and pass them through the food mill back into the saucepan. Stirring with a spatula, dry the mashed potato out over low heat, then gradually stir in the butter until melted and incorporated. Meanwhile, bring the milk to a boil in a separate saucepan. Whisking vigorously, pour the milk into the potatoes in a thin, steady stream while it is still very hot. Continue whisking until the milk has been completely absorbed. Pass the mashed potatoes through the drum sifter and warm again over low heat, whisking continuously.

TO SERVE

Heat a little butter and oil in a skillet and fry the sausages with the garlic clove and thyme, until the sausages are evenly browned all over. Divide the mashed potatoes between 4 serving plates and place a sausage on top. Garnish with pickled red onions and mustard seeds, and a few red-veined sorrel leaves. Spoon a little of the reduced pigs' trotter cooking liquid over the mashed potatoes and drizzle more around the plate. Finish with the mesclun greens salad on the side of the plate.

CHEFS' NOTES

You can use already cooked pigs' trotters
from your local butcher, if available.

LAMB

LAMB TAGINE

Tajine d'agneau

Serves 10

Active time

1¼ hours

Cooking time

2 hours

Storage

2 days

Equipment

Fine-mesh sieve

Butcher's twine

Ingredients

Tagine base

10½ oz. (300 g) onions

1–2 bone-in lamb shoulders, weighing 4½ lb. (2 kg) in total

¼ tsp (1 g) fine sea salt

Scant ½ cup (100 ml) olive oil

2 tsp (5 g) ground ginger

2 tsp (5 g) ground turmeric

2 tsp (5 g) ground cumin

2 tsp (5 g) ground coriander

2 tsp (5 g) ground cinnamon

1¾ tsp (5 g) black peppercorns

6 cups (1.5 liters) vegetable stock

To garnish

10 baby purple artichokes (*artichauts poivrade*)

2 onions

Scant ½ cup (100 ml) olive oil

1 tsp (5 g) salt

2 cups (500 ml) vegetable stock

2 preserved lemons

⅓ oz. (10 g) raw almonds

To serve

3½ oz. (100 g) Taggiasche olives

PREPARING THE TAGINE BASE

Preheat the oven to 350°F (180°C/Gas Mark 4). Peel and thinly slice the onions. Bone, roll, and tie the lamb shoulders into roasts (see technique p. 90). Season with the ¼ tsp (1 g) salt. Heat the olive oil in a Dutch oven and brown the meat all over. Remove it, add the onions and spices, and lower the heat. Sweat until the onions are softened but not browned. Return the lamb to the pan and add the vegetable stock. Cover and braise in the oven for 1½ hours, or until the lamb is completely tender. Remove it from the pan and strain the cooking liquid through the fine-mesh sieve into a clean saucepan. Reduce until the sauce coats the back of a spoon. Untie the lamb shoulders, cut into pieces, and reserve the meat in the sauce.

PREPARING THE GARNISHES

Trim the artichokes down to the hearts and cut them in half. Peel the onions, cut each one into 8 wedges, and separate the layers into "petals." Heat half the olive oil with the salt in a large saucepan and sweat the artichokes until softened. Add 250 ml (1 cup) of the vegetable stock and simmer for 5 minutes, or until just tender. Remove the artichokes and repeat with the onion petals. Remove the peel from the preserved lemons and cut it into diamond shapes, 1¼ in. (3 cm) in length. Cut the almonds into quarters lengthwise.

TO SERVE

Pour the sauce into 10 shallow serving bowls and place a few pieces of meat in the center. Arrange the artichokes, onions, preserved lemon peel, almonds, and olives over the top.

LAMB SHANKS WITH VEGETABLE TIAN

Souris d'agneau et tian de légumes

Serves 6

Active time
1 hour

Cooking time
3¼ hours

Chilling time
7 hours

Storage
2 days

Equipment
Fine-mesh sieve
Mandolin
12 × 8-in. (30 × 20-cm) baking dish

Ingredients

Lamb shanks
2 onions
6 cloves garlic
14 oz. (400 g) Roma tomatoes
6 lamb shanks (*souris d'agneau*)
Scant 1 cup (3½ oz./100 g) all-purpose flour
Olive oil
10 saffron threads
Generous 1 tbsp (10 g) ras el hanout
1 bouquet garni (bay leaves, thyme, and rosemary)
6 cups (1.5 liters) water
Salt and freshly ground pepper

Vegetable tian
6 scallions
4 cloves garlic
Olive oil
1 green zucchini
1 yellow zucchini
1 long thin eggplant
6 Olivette tomatoes (or use Roma)
6 sprigs thyme, cut into pieces
Salt and freshly ground pepper

To garnish
Rosemary sprigs

PREPARING THE LAMB SHANKS (1 DAY AHEAD)

Preheat the oven to 295°F (145°C/Gas Mark 2). Peel and finely chop the onions and garlic. Peel and hull the tomatoes and remove the seeds. Place the seeds in a colander and allow the excess liquid from them to drain into a bowl—it will be used for cooking later. Cut the tomatoes into ¾-in. (2-cm) dice. Lightly season the lamb shanks with salt and pepper and dredge them in the flour to coat, shaking off any excess. Warm a little olive oil in a Dutch oven over high heat, then add the lamb shanks and sear until they are browned and caramelized on all sides. Remove the shanks from the pan, reduce the heat, and add the onions and garlic. Cook until they are translucent and any liquid from them has evaporated completely. Crumble in the saffron threads, add the ras el hanout, and cook for 2 minutes. Return the lamb shanks to the pan and add the tomatoes, the juice strained from their seeds, and the bouquet garni. Add as much of the water as needed to just cover the ingredients and bring to a boil, skimming off any foam on the surface. Cut a piece of parchment paper to fit snugly inside the pan and place it over the ingredients, flush with the surface. Cover and cook in the oven for 2½–3 hours, cleaning the sides of the pan regularly with a damp brush. When the meat starts to pull away from the bones, remove the shanks from the pan. Let them cool, then let rest in the refrigerator for at least 7 hours. Strain the cooking liquid through the fine-mesh sieve into a bowl and set aside.

PREPARING THE VEGETABLE TIAN

Preheat the oven to 330°F (165°C/Gas Mark 3). Peel and finely chop the scallions and garlic. Heat a little olive oil in a saucepan, add the onions and garlic, cover the pan, and cook over low heat until meltingly soft. Wash the green zucchini, yellow zucchini, eggplant, and tomatoes and cut them into 1⁄16–⅛-in. (2–3-mm) slices using the mandolin. Spread the onion compote over the base of the 12 × 8-in. (30 × 20-cm) baking dish and arrange the vegetable slices over it in attractive rows, overlapping them and positioning them at an angle. Drizzle with olive oil, season with salt and pepper, and scatter the thyme over the top. Cover and bake for 45 minutes.

TO SERVE

Preheat the oven to 285°F (140°C/Gas Mark 1). Place the shanks in a baking dish, add the strained sauce, and reheat them, basting regularly with the strained sauce. Serve the lamb shanks hot, in their sauce, garnished with rosemary sprigs. Serve the tian on the side.

LAMB CHOPS WITH PAN-GRILLED VEGETABLES

Côtelettes d'agneau et légumes grillés

Serves 10

Active time
30 minutes

Cooking time
1 hour 50 minutes

Resting time
10 minutes

Storage
24 hours

Equipment
Fine-mesh sieve

Mandolin

Cast-iron ridged grill pan

1½-in. (4-cm) round cookie cutter

Ingredients

Lamb jus

7 oz. (200 g) onions

½ head garlic

2¼ lb. (1 kg) lamb trimmings (purchase from your butcher)

Scant ½ cup (100 ml) olive oil

¼ bunch thyme

1¾ sticks (7 oz./200 g) butter

8 cups (2 liters) vegetable stock, divided

To garnish

3 zucchini

2 eggplants

2 tsp (10 g) salt

⅔ cup (150 ml) olive oil

15 confit Torino or Roma tomatoes

10 slices chorizo

15 salt-cured anchovy filets

4 fresh bay leaves

Confit or roasted garlic cloves (optional)

Lamb chops

20 French-trimmed rib lamb chops

1 tsp (5 g) salt

4 cloves garlic

Scant ½ cup (100 ml) olive oil

¼ bunch rosemary

¼ bunch thyme

PREPARING THE LAMB JUS

Peel the onions and cut each one into 8 wedges. Separate the garlic cloves and roughly crush them, unpeeled, using the flat of a chef's knife blade. Cut the lamb trimmings into 1½-in. (4-cm) pieces. Heat the olive oil in a large saucepan and sear the trimmings until pale golden brown. Add the onions, garlic, thyme, and butter, and continue to cook until the meat is deeply browned. The lamb trimmings will render a lot of fat, so when they are browned, thoroughly drain the contents of the pan to remove the excess fat, then return the meat to the pan. Deglaze with 2 cups (500 ml) of the vegetable stock to release the browned bits from the bottom of the pan. Add the remaining stock and simmer, uncovered, for 1½ hours. Strain the jus through the fine-mesh sieve into a clean saucepan and reduce by half. Reserve at room temperature.

PREPARING THE GARNISHES

Wash and trim the zucchini and eggplants and cut them into ¼-in. (7-mm) slices using the mandolin. Season with the salt. Warm the olive oil in the cast-iron grill pan over high heat until hot, then sear the zucchini and eggplant, in batches if necessary, until tender and scorched with grill marks on both sides. Cut the tomatoes into ¼-in. (7-mm) slices. Using the cookie cutter, cut 1½-in. (4-cm) circles out of the grilled vegetable and tomato slices. Cut each chorizo slice diagonally into two ¾-in. (2-cm) diamond-shaped strips. Cut the anchovies diagonally into ¾-in. (2-cm) pieces. Cut the bay leaves into strips, ¾ in. (2 cm) long and 1/16 in. (2 mm) wide. Cut the confit or roasted garlic cloves into halves or quarters, if using.

PREPARING THE LAMB CHOPS

Preheat the oven to 140°F (60°C/Gas on lowest setting) for resting the lamb chops when they are cooked. Season the chops with the salt. Crush the unpeeled garlic using the flat of a chef's knife blade. Heat the olive oil in a shallow heavy pan and sear the chops on both sides, in batches, with the garlic, rosemary, and thyme until browned but still pink inside. Transfer the chops to a large plate as they brown and let them rest in the oven for at least 10 minutes before serving.

TO SERVE

Drizzle a little lamb jus over each serving plate and place 2 lamb chops on top. Arrange the eggplant, zucchini, and tomato slices alongside the chops and scatter over the chorizo, anchovies, bay leaves, and garlic, if using. Drizzle over a little more jus and serve immediately.

SPICED CONFIT LEG OF LAMB WITH MOGETTE BEAN RAGOUT

Gigot d'agneau confit aux épices, mogettes

Serves 8

Active time
2½ hours

Cooking time
2¾ hours

Chilling time
At least 3 hours
(preferably overnight)

Storage
3 days

Equipment
Fine-mesh sieve

Steam oven (or steamer)

Ingredients

Lamb
1 leg of lamb
1 tbsp (8 g) ground cumin
1 tbsp (6 g) ras el hanout
1 tbsp (8 g) *pimentón de la Vera*
Scant ½ cup (100 ml) olive oil
2 white onions
1 head garlic
About 3 qt. (3 liters) lamb stock (*fond d'agneau*)

Mogette bean ragout
1 carrot
½ head garlic
1 onion
3 whole cloves
4½ lb. (2 kg) dried Mogette white beans, soaked overnight
About 4 qt. (4 liters) water
2 tbsp finely chopped fresh parsley

To serve
20 slices *lardo di Colonnata* (Italian cured pork fat)
8 whole piquillo peppers
A few Thai basil sprigs
A few leek sprouts

PREPARING THE LAMB

Preheat the oven to 340°F (170°C/Gas Mark 3). Rub the leg of lamb with the cumin, ras el hanout, and *pimentón*. Heat the olive oil in a large Dutch oven and slowly caramelize the meat on all sides. Peel and thinly slice the onions and add them to the pan, along with the garlic separated into cloves. Cover, place in the oven, and cook for 30 minutes. Pour in the lamb stock and continue to cook, covered, for at least 2 hours, or until the meat is tender, basting it regularly with the pan juices. When the lamb is cool enough to touch but still warm, carefully remove the bone using a chef's knife. Roll the meat tightly in plastic wrap, shaping it into a cylinder with a diameter of 2½–3 in. (6–8 cm). When cool, chill for at least 3 hours (preferably overnight). Strain the pan juices through the fine-mesh sieve into a saucepan and reduce to a glaze, skimming any excess fat from the surface. Adjust the seasonings if necessary.

PREPARING THE MOGETTE BEAN RAGOUT

Peel and finely chop the carrot and garlic. Peel the onion and cut it in half. Finely chop one half and stick the cloves in the other half. Place the carrot, garlic, and onion in a large Dutch oven. Drain the beans and add to the pan, then pour in the 4 qt. (4 liters) water. Cook over low heat until the beans are tender (about 40 minutes–1 hour; follow the package instructions). Drain the beans and stir them together with the parsley and half the lamb juices.

TO SERVE

If using a steam oven, preheat it to 185°F (85°C/Gas on lowest setting). Cut the lamb cylinder into approximately 1¼-in. (3-cm) slices and reheat in the steam oven, or steamer, for 10 minutes. Submerge the lamb slices in the remaining pan juices to glaze them. Serve family-style in an attractive pan, such as a copper casserole. Place the bean ragout in the pan, then top with the *lardo di Colonnata*, piquillo peppers, and glazed lamb slices. Garnish with a few Thai basil sprigs and leek sprouts.

PERSIAN-STYLE LAMB SKEWERS

Brochettes d'agneau à la persane

Serves 6

Active time

1 hour

Cooking time

About 1 hour

Marinating time

At least 3 hours
(preferably overnight)

Chilling time

2 hours–overnight
(for the lamb skewers)

2 hours (for the dip)

Soaking time

30 minutes

Infusing time

10 minutes

Storage

2 days

Equipment

12 metal skewers

Mortar and pestle

Grill

Ingredients

Marinated lamb skewers

1 onion

1 zucchini

1 red bell pepper

2¼ lb. (1 kg) boneless leg
of lamb

3 tsp (16 g) salt

Generous 3 tbsp (23 g)
ground sumac

1½ tsp (4 g) ground
black pepper

Juice of 1 large lemon

2 tbsp (30 ml) olive oil

Generous ¾ cup
(7 oz./200 g) Greek
yogurt

Mast-o-khiar yogurt dip

⅓ bunch mint

1 cucumber

2 cloves garlic

1 pinch salt

2 cups (1 lb./500 g)
Greek yogurt

2½ tbsp (40 ml)
extra-virgin olive oil

Juice of 1 lemon

Salt and freshly ground
pepper

Tahdig rice

1½ cups
(10½ oz./300 g) basmati
rice

2 tsp salt

15 saffron threads

½ tsp (2 g) superfine
sugar

1½ tbsp (25 ml) boiling
water

8 cups (2 liters) water +
more for soaking the rice

2½ tbsp (40 ml) olive oil

Salt and freshly ground
pepper

To serve

½ cup (2 oz./60 g)
walnut halves

3 tbsp (20 g) zaatar

Mint sprigs

PREPARING THE MARINATED LAMB SKEWERS (PREFERABLY 1–2 DAYS AHEAD)

Peel the onion and wash the zucchini and pepper. Halve the pepper and remove the seeds. Cut all three vegetables into 1¼-in. (3-cm) cubes. Trim the fat off the lamb and cut the meat into 1¼-in. (3-cm) cubes. Combine all the remaining ingredients in a bowl to make a marinade. Massage the marinade into the meat and chill it for at least 3 hours, or preferably overnight. Thread the skewers, alternating the cubes of meat and vegetables and using about 2¾ oz. (75 g) of meat per skewer. Reserve in the refrigerator for at least 2 hours, or overnight.

PREPARING THE MAST-O-KHIAR YOGURT DIP

Wash and finely chop the mint. Wash the cucumber and cut it, unpeeled, into ¼-in. (5-mm) dice. Peel and crush the garlic. Combine all the ingredients in a bowl and season with salt and pepper. Keep chilled for 2 hours in the refrigerator.

PREPARING THE TAHDIG RICE

Rinse the rice in three changes of cold water to remove as much starch as possible. Place the rice in a bowl with twice its volume of water and the 2 tsp salt, and let soak for 30 minutes. Place the saffron threads and sugar in the mortar and pound to a fine powder using the pestle. Place in a bowl, add the 1½ tbsp (25 ml) boiling water, and let infuse for 10 minutes. Bring the 8 cups (2 liters) water to a boil in a large saucepan with a little salt. Drain the rice, add it to the pan, and let cook for 5 minutes, or until al dente. Drain the rice and rinse it under cold running water. Stir half the rice into the infused saffron. Pour the olive oil into a heavy-bottomed or nonstick saucepan, then add the saffron rice, followed by the plain white rice, to form two layers. Using the handle of a wooden spoon, poke 5 holes in the rice all the way to the bottom of the pan to allow steam to escape. Cover tightly with a dish towel and lid and cook over medium heat for 10–15 minutes, or until the rice is hot and is crisp at the bottom. Remove the dish towel and lid, place a large plate over the pan, and carefully flip it over to turn the rice out onto the plate, with the crisp, golden layer on top.

TO SERVE

Preheat the oven to 250°F (130°C/Gas Mark ½). Spread the walnuts over a baking sheet lined with parchment paper and toast them in the oven for 30 minutes. Remove from the baking sheet, let cool completely, then chop and sprinkle them over the yogurt dip. Preheat the grill until very hot and grill the skewers for 3–4 minutes on each side. Sprinkle the rice and lamb skewers with zaatar. Cut the rice into 6 servings, garnish the lamb with mint sprigs, and serve with the dip on the side.

SPRING LAMB STEW

Navarin

Serves 10

Active time
45 minutes

Cooking time
2¾ hours

Storage
3 days

Equipment
Fine-mesh sieve

Ingredients
3½ lb. (1.5 kg) bone-in lamb shoulder

Lamb broth
1 small (3½ oz./100 g) onion

5¼ oz. (150 g) carrots

5¼ oz. (150 g) leeks

2¼ lb. (1 kg) lamb bones and trimmings from the shoulder

About 8 cups (2 liters) water

4 sprigs thyme

1 sprig rosemary

4 cloves garlic, unpeeled

Lamb shoulder stew
¾ lb. (350 g) sweet onions, preferably Cévennes

6 cloves garlic, unpeeled

Meat from boned lamb shoulder (see above)

2 tsp (10 g) salt

Scant ½ cup (100 ml) olive oil

3 tbsp (1½ oz./40 g) butter

2½ tsp (10 g) sugar

⅓ cup (1½ oz./40 g) all-purpose flour

18 oz. (500 g) crushed tomatoes

Scant ½ cup (3½ oz./100 g) tomato paste

2 cups (500 ml) lamb broth (see above)

1 bouquet garni (¼ of the parsley stems, the green part from 1 leek, and 2 bay leaves, tied together with butcher's twine)

Salt and freshly ground pepper

To garnish
10½ oz. (300 g) celery

10½ oz. (300 g) fingerling potatoes, preferably La Ratte

1 bunch scallions

4 baby leeks

4 cups (1 liter) lamb broth (see left)

Kosher salt

Scant ½ cup (100 ml) olive oil

7 oz. (200 g) sugar snap peas in their pods

4 tomatoes on the vine

PREPARING THE LAMB SHOULDER

Bone the lamb shoulder (see technique p. 88), reserving the bones and trimmings for the broth. Set the meat aside at room temperature.

PREPARING THE LAMB BROTH

Peel and cut the onion in half crosswise and char the cut sides in an ungreased skillet. Wash and peel the carrots. Wash the leeks. Cut both vegetables lengthwise into two pieces. Place the lamb bones and trimmings in a large saucepan, add the water, and bring to a boil, skimming any foam from the surface. Add the thyme, rosemary, and garlic, and simmer, uncovered, for 2 hours. Adjust the seasoning, if necessary. Strain through the fine-mesh sieve into a bowl and reserve at room temperature. You should have about 6 cups (1.5 liters) of broth, to be divided between the stew and the garnishes.

COOKING THE LAMB STEW

Preheat the oven to 325°F (160°C/Gas Mark 3). Peel and thinly slice the onions and roughly crush the garlic cloves using the flat of a chef's knife blade. Cut the lamb meat into 1¾-oz. (50-g) pieces and season with the salt. Heat the olive oil, butter, and sugar in a sauté pan and brown the pieces of meat on all sides over high heat, removing them from the pan as they brown. Lower the heat, add the onions, and sweat until softened but not browned. Pour off the excess fat, sprinkle in the flour, and stir until the onions are coated. Add the crushed tomatoes, tomato paste, garlic, and browned pieces of lamb. Pour in the lamb broth and add the bouquet garni. Cut a piece of parchment paper to fit snugly inside the pan and place it over the ingredients, flush with the surface. Cook in the oven for 45 minutes, until the meat is completely tender. Remove the meat from the pan, strain the cooking liquid through the fine-mesh sieve into a clean saucepan and reduce by half. Place the meat in the saucepan with the sauce, stir to coat, and adjust the seasoning if necessary.

PREPARING THE GARNISHES

Wash and peel the celery and cut it diagonally into 2¾-in. (7-cm) pieces. Wash the potatoes and cut them crosswise into ½-in. (1-cm) slices. Wash and trim the scallions and cut them in half crosswise. Wash the leeks and cut off the roots and the tough green parts. Cook these vegetables separately in the lamb broth seasoned with kosher salt. Place the celery, potatoes, and scallions in a separate saucepan with a little lamb broth over low heat to keep them warm. Remove the outer layers of the leeks and cut the hearts into 2¾-in. (7-cm) pieces. Drizzle the olive oil over all the cooked vegetables. Open the pea pods on one side. Peel the tomatoes using hot water, remove the seeds, and cut each one into 6 pieces.

TO SERVE

Serve the meat, garnishes, and sauce together in an attractive serving dish.

STUFFED SADDLE OF LAMB WITH FONDANT POTATOES

Selle d'agneau farcie, pommes fondantes

Serves 6

Active time

1½ hours

Cooking time

4½ –5½ hours

Soaking time

30 minutes

Resting time

20 minutes

Chilling time

30 minutes

Storage

24 hours

Equipment

Mallet-style meat pounder

Butcher's twine

Cleaver

Fine-mesh sieve

Blender

Immersion blender

Instant-read thermometer

8½-in. (22-cm) square baking dish, 2 in. (5 cm) deep

Ingredients

Stuffed saddle of lamb

4 cups (1 liter) water

3½ tbsp (50 ml) white vinegar

7 oz. (200 g) caul fat

2 shallots

3 cloves garlic

2¼ lb. (1 kg) fresh spinach

10½ oz. (300 g) chanterelle or oyster mushrooms

6 tbsp (3 oz./90 g) butter, divided

½ cup (1¾ oz./50 g) grated Parmesan

1 saddle of lamb

Grape-seed oil

5 sprigs thyme

Salt and freshly ground pepper

Lamb jus

1¾ oz. (50 g) onion

1¾ oz. (50 g) celery

1¾ oz. (50 g) carrots

2 cloves garlic

About 1 lb. (500 g) lamb bones and trimmings (from the saddle)

3 tbsp (1¾ oz./50 g) butter

4 cups (1 liter) water, divided

1 bouquet garni (thyme and bay leaf)

2 tsp (10 g) tomato paste

Scant 3 tsp (7 g) ground black pepper

Fondant potatoes

18 waxy potatoes, weighing 1¾ oz. (50 g) each

7 tbsp (3½ oz./100 g) butter, diced

8 cups (2 liters) white poultry stock (*fond blanc de volaille*, see recipe p. 19) or water

Salt

Garlic cream sauce

6 cloves garlic

1¼ cups (300 ml) heavy cream, min. 35% fat

2 bay leaves

Salt

Parsley coulis

7 oz. (200 g) fresh parsley

4 cups (1 liter) water

Salt

PREPARING THE STUFFED SADDLE OF LAMB

Combine the water and vinegar in a bowl, add the caul fat, and let soak for 30 minutes. Peel and finely chop the shallots and 2 of the garlic cloves. Peel and crush the third garlic clove using the flat of a chef's knife blade. Wash the spinach and remove the stems. Clean the mushrooms. Heat 3 tbsp (1¾ oz./50 g) butter in a large skillet and sauté the mushrooms until softened and lightly browned, then remove from the pan. Add the chopped shallots and garlic to the pan and cook in the same butter until softened but not browned. Add the spinach and cook until wilted. Transfer the spinach mixture to a colander and place a weight on top to press out as much liquid as possible. Cut the mushrooms into 1/16-in. (2-mm) dice and season with salt and pepper. Finely chop the spinach mixture and incorporate the Parmesan. Adjust the seasonings if necessary. Prepare the saddle of lamb (see technique p. 84), taking care not to pierce the skin and saving the bones and trimmings for the jus. Cut the saddle in half lengthwise, without cutting the flank off each loin. Score the flanks with a crosshatch pattern and flatten them using the meat pounder. Season the saddle with salt and pepper. On each half of the saddle, arrange the spinach and mushroom mixtures side by side between the loin and the flank, then roll each one up tightly, making sure the tenderloin is well centered. Drain and wring the caul fat to remove excess water, cut it into two pieces, and wrap the stuffed saddle rolls individually. Tie each one like a roast (see technique p. 42). Keep chilled until ready to cook.

PREPARING THE LAMB JUS

Wash and peel the onion, celery, carrots, and garlic, as necessary, and chop them all finely. Using the cleaver, chop the lamb bones into small pieces and cut the fat off the meat trimmings with a knife. Melt the butter in a large saucepan over medium heat and cook the bones and meat trimmings for 15 minutes. Add the onion, celery, carrots, and garlic, and scrape the browned bits off the bottom of the pan using a spatula. Cook until the vegetables are caramelized. Deglaze with 2/3 cup (150 ml) water, reduce until all the liquid has evaporated, then repeat this process once more. Add the remaining water, bouquet garni, tomato paste, and pepper, and let simmer for 3–4 hours. Strain the cooking juices through the fine-mesh sieve into a clean saucepan and reduce to a glaze that coats the back of a spoon.

COOKING THE STUFFED SADDLE OF LAMB

Preheat the oven to 350°F (175°C/Gas Mark 4). Warm a little grape-seed oil in a cast-iron skillet over medium-high heat until very hot, add the stuffed saddle rolls, and fry until caramelized on all sides. Add the remaining 3 tbsp (1½ oz./40 g) butter, thyme, and crushed garlic. Baste the rolls with the butter until the butter browns and has a nutty aroma. Place the rolls on a rack over a rimmed baking sheet and roast in the oven until the internal temperature reaches 122°F (50°C). Remove from the oven and let rest for 20 minutes, or until the internal temperature rises to 135°F (57°C).

PREPARING THE FONDANT POTATOES

Preheat the oven to 340°F (170°C/Gas Mark 3). Wash and peel the potatoes and place them in a bowl of water to prevent browning. Using a small, sharp knife, turn the potatoes by trimming the edges from top to bottom toward you, rotating the potato as you do so, to taper the ends and obtain oblong shapes. Arrange the potatoes in the 8½-in. (22-cm) baking dish—they should fit snugly. Dot the butter over the top and season with salt. Pour in enough stock or water to come two-thirds up the sides of the dish and bake for 45 minutes–1 hour, drizzling them with the cooking liquid every 10 minutes. Bake until they are golden brown and the tip of a paring knife enters with no resistance.

PREPARING THE GARLIC CREAM SAUCE

Peel the garlic and remove the germs. To blanch the cloves, place them in a saucepan of cold water and bring to a boil, then drain and cool by running cold water over them. Repeat this process twice more. Drain the garlic, place it in a saucepan with the cream and bay leaves, and cook at a gentle simmer for 15 minutes. Remove the bay leaves and purée the garlic and cream using the immersion blender. Strain through the fine-mesh sieve and season with salt.

PREPARING THE PARSLEY COULIS

Wash the parsley and remove the stems. Blanch the leaves in a saucepan of boiling salted water for 3–4 minutes, then plunge them into ice water. Drain the leaves and place in the blender. Adding the water gradually, blend until you obtain a smooth coulis. Season with salt.

TO SERVE

Reheat the components as needed. Spoon the lamb jus, garlic cream sauce, and parsley coulis onto 6 serving plates and lightly swirl the three together. Slice the stuffed saddle rolls and arrange the slices on the plates, on top of the sauce, with the fondant potatoes alongside.

LAMB NOISETTES

Noisettes d'agneau

Serves 10

Active time

1½ hours

Cooking time

2 hours

Resting time

10 minutes

Storage

3 days

Equipment

Fine-mesh sieve

Grill

Mortar and pestle

Ingredients

Lamb jus

7 oz. (200 g) onions

½ head garlic

2¼ lb. (1 kg) lamb trimmings (purchase from your butcher)

Scant ½ cup (100 ml) olive oil

¼ bunch thyme

1¾ sticks (7 oz./200 g) butter, diced, at room temperature

8 cups (2 liters) vegetable stock, divided

Lamb noisettes

1¼ lb. (600 g) lamb noisettes (*noisettes d'agneau*)

2 tsp (10 g) fine sea salt

3 cloves garlic

Scant ½ cup (100 ml) olive oil

3 tbsp (1¾ oz./50 g) butter

2 sprigs thyme

Vegetables

1 bunch radishes

⅔ cup (150 ml) olive oil, divided

7 tbsp (3½ oz./100 g) butter, divided

2 cloves garlic, peeled and divided

8 sprigs thyme, divided

3½ tbsp (50 ml) red wine vinegar

1 bunch scallions

20 stalks white asparagus

2 tsp (10 g) salt

5¼ oz. (150 g) peas

To garnish

2 stalks white asparagus

1¾ oz. (50 g) shelled peas

2½ tbsp (40 ml) extra-virgin olive oil

Salt and freshly ground pepper

To serve

2 tsp (10 ml) extra-virgin olive oil

Fleur de sel and freshly ground pepper

PREPARING THE LAMB JUS

Peel the onions and cut each one into 8 wedges. Separate the garlic cloves and roughly crush them, unpeeled, using the flat of a chef's knife blade. Cut the lamb trimmings into 1½-in. (4-cm) pieces. Heat the olive oil in a large saucepan and sear the lamb pieces until pale golden brown. Add the onions, garlic, thyme, and butter, and continue to cook until the meat is deeply browned, basting it with the oil and butter. Pour off the excess fat and deglaze with 2 cups (500 ml) of the vegetable stock to release the browned bits from the bottom of the pan. Add the remaining stock and simmer, uncovered, for 1½ hours. Strain through the fine-mesh sieve into a clean saucepan and reduce until the jus coats the back of a spoon.

PREPARING THE LAMB NOISETTES

Season the noisettes with the salt. Crush the unpeeled garlic using the flat of a chef's knife blade. In a very hot skillet with the olive oil, sear the noisettes for 3 minutes on both sides, until deeply browned. Reduce the heat to medium and add the butter, garlic, and thyme. When the butter has browned and has a nutty aroma, continue to cook the meat for 5 minutes, basting it with the butter. Remove the meat from the pan and let it rest for 10 minutes on a rack.

PREPARING THE VEGETABLES

Wash the radishes and cut them in half lengthwise. Heat half the olive oil and half the butter in a skillet with 1 clove garlic and 4 sprigs thyme, and sweat the radishes, basting them with the oil and butter. Deglaze with the vinegar and reduce until the radishes are glazed. Wash the scallions, trim the ends so they are 3 in. (8 cm) long, and cut them in half lengthwise. Cut off the asparagus tips 2½ in. (6 cm) from the end, then trim the bases so the bottom parts are the same length. Blanch the scallions and asparagus in boiling water with the salt added until just tender. Color the scallions lightly in a little butter. Heat the remaining olive oil and butter in a saucepan and cook the peas with the remaining garlic and thyme.

PREPARING THE GARNISHES

Wash the asparagus and trim the bases. Using a vegetable peeler, shave off 20 wafer-thin strips. Roughly chop the remaining asparagus, place in the mortar with the peas, and pound to a coarse purée using the pestle. Mix in the olive oil, pound again, and season with salt and pepper.

TO SERVE

Preheat the oven to 350°F (180°C/Gas Mark 4). Reheat the meat for 2 minutes in the oven, and the vegetables, if necessary. Right before serving, toss the asparagus shavings with the 2 tsp (10 ml) olive oil. Cut the lamb noisettes into 30 slices. Drizzle serving plates with lamb jus, place 3 lamb slices on each plate, and sprinkle with fleur de sel and pepper. Arrange the vegetables over a bed of the asparagus-pea purée and top with the shaved asparagus.

RACK OF LAMB WITH A PARSLEY CRUST AND BUCKWHEAT RISOTTO

Carré d'agneau en croûte d'herbes et risotto de blé noir

Serves 4

Active time
1½ hours

Cooking time
30 minutes

Freezing time
30 minutes

Resting time
20 minutes

Storage
24 hours

Equipment
Food processor

Butcher's twine, if needed

Instant-read thermometer

3-in. (8-cm) stainless-steel ring

Ingredients

Parsley crust
1¾ oz. (50 g) sandwich bread

1¾ oz. (50 g) parsley

1 clove garlic, peeled

5 tbsp (3 oz./80 g) butter, diced and softened

Salt

Rack of lamb
1 rack of lamb with 8 ribs (*carré d'agneau*)

4 tsp (20 ml) grape-seed oil

Salt and freshly ground pepper

Buckwheat risotto
¼ bunch parsley

1 sweet onion, preferably Cévennes

2½ tbsp (40 ml) olive oil

1¾ cups (10½ oz./300 g) buckwheat

Scant ½ cup (100 ml) dry white wine

1 bouquet garni (thyme and bay leaf)

Scant 2½ cups (600 ml) water or white poultry stock (*fond blanc de volaille*, see recipe p. 19)

3 tbsp (1¾ oz./50 g) butter, diced, at room temperature

Scant ¾ cup (2½ oz./70 g) grated Parmesan

To serve
Lamb jus

Extra-virgin olive oil

Fleur de sel

Daikon radish sprouts

PREPARING THE PARSLEY CRUST

Place the bread, parsley, and garlic in the food processor with a pinch of salt. Pulse until finely chopped. Transfer to a bowl, add the butter, and mix together until well combined. Spread the mixture to a thickness of ⅛ in. (3 mm) between two sheets of parchment paper. Place on a baking sheet and freeze flat for 30 minutes.

PREPARING THE RACK OF LAMB

Preheat the oven to 340°F (170°C/Gas Mark 3). French trim the rack of lamb (see technique p 76), tying it with twine if necessary. Season with salt and pepper. Heat the grape-seed oil in an oven-safe sauté pan and brown the lamb on all sides. Place the frozen parsley crust over the lamb and roast in the oven for 12–15 minutes, or until the internal temperature of the meat reaches 126°F (52°C). Transfer the lamb to a rack set over a rimmed baking sheet to catch the juices and let rest for at least 20 minutes.

PREPARING THE BUCKWHEAT RISOTTO

While the lamb is resting, prepare the risotto. Wash and finely chop the parsley. Peel and finely chop the onion. Heat the olive oil in a sauté pan over low heat and sweat the onion for 10 minutes. Add the buckwheat and cook for an additional 2 minutes. Deglaze with the white wine and let cook until all the wine has evaporated. Add the bouquet garni, then add the water or stock one ladleful at a time, waiting until the buckwheat absorbs the liquid before adding the next. Cook until the buckwheat has the al dente texture of risotto rice. Remove from the heat and stir in the butter, followed by the Parmesan and parsley. Adjust the seasonings, if necessary.

TO SERVE

Drizzle a little lamb jus over each plate. Place the 3-in. (8-cm) ring on a plate, spoon in some of the buckwheat risotto, then remove the ring to form a perfect circle; repeat on the other plates. Carefully separate the lamb chops using a very sharp knife to avoid damaging the parsley crust. Serve 2 lamb chops per person, drizzled with a little olive oil and sprinkled with fleur de sel. Garnish with a few daikon radish sprouts and serve immediately.

KOFTAS

Kefta

Serves 10

Active time

1 hour

Cooking time

35 minutes

Resting time

30 minutes

Standing time

10 minutes

Storage

3 days

Equipment

Meat grinder + grinding plate with medium-sized holes

Kitchen torch

Food processor

Cast-iron ridged grill pan

20 × 8-in. (20-cm) metal skewers

Ingredients

Koftas

2¼ lb. (1 kg) bone-in saddle of lamb (or use 1 lb. 2 oz./500 g ground lamb, 10% fat)

5¼ oz. (150 g) tomatoes

3½ oz. (100 g) onions

1 bunch parsley

2 tsp (10 g) salt

1 tsp (3 g) ground cumin

1 tsp (3 g) ground coriander

1 tsp (3 g) sweet paprika

Bell pepper sauce

5 red bell peppers

1 red onion

3 cloves garlic

⅔ cup (150 ml) olive oil

2 tsp (10 g) salt

Tahini sauce

5¼ oz. (150 g) tahini

Scant ½ cup (100 ml) lemon juice

Scant ½ cup (100 ml) water

Salt

Salad

Neutral oil for frying

3½ oz. (100 g) cooked chickpeas

9 oz. (250 g) baby spinach

½ bunch parsley

20 confit tomatoes

1 pomegranate

2 red bell peppers

Scant ½ cup (100 ml) extra-virgin olive oil

Salt

To serve

A few scallions, thinly sliced

White sesame seeds

PREPARING THE KOFTAS

If you are grinding the meat, bone the saddle of lamb (see technique p. 84) and trim off some of the fat (you need to keep a 10% fat-to-muscle ratio). Peel, seed, and finely chop the tomatoes. Peel and finely chop the onions. Wash and dry the parsley, remove the stems, and finely chop the leaves. Pass the lamb twice through the meat grinder fitted with the medium grinding plate, then combine it with the tomatoes, onions, parsley, and the other remaining ingredients in a bowl. Let rest for 30 minutes in the refrigerator.

PREPARING THE BELL PEPPER SAUCE

Char the bell peppers all over using the kitchen torch, then place them in a covered bowl and let stand for 10 minutes to make peeling easier. Peel, seed, and finely chop the peppers. Peel and finely chop the onion and garlic. Heat the olive oil with the salt in a saucepan and sweat the peppers, onion, and garlic until softened. Continue to cook gently for 30 minutes over low heat until reduced to a thick purée. Transfer to the food processor and process until smooth. Adjust the seasonings if necessary.

PREPARING THE TAHINI SAUCE

Whisk together the tahini, lemon juice, and water in a bowl until evenly combined. Season with salt.

PREPARING THE SALAD

Heat a little neutral oil in a skillet and fry the chickpeas until golden, stirring regularly. Wash and dry the baby spinach and parsley, and remove the stems from the spinach. Cut the confit tomatoes in half and remove the seeds. Cut open the pomegranate and take out the arils. Peel and seed the bell peppers, then cut them into strips measuring ¾ in. (2 cm) in length and ⅛ in. (3 mm) in width. Place the ingredients in a large bowl. Just before serving, toss with the olive oil and season with salt.

COOKING THE KOFTAS

Heat the ridged grill pan until very hot. Shape 5¼ oz. (50 g) of the kofta mixture into a cylinder around each skewer, pressing down gently to ensure it holds together. Grill the skewers in the ridged grill pan for 5 minutes on each side, until the koftas are cooked and scorched with grill marks.

TO SERVE

Serve the koftas while hot, sprinkled with sliced scallions and sesame seeds, and accompanied by the bell pepper and tahini sauces. Serve the salad on the side.

POULTRY

ROAST CHICKEN WITH PASTA GRATIN AND SAUCE DIABLE

Poulet rôti, gratin de macaroni et sauce diable

Serves 4

Active time
1½–2 hours

Cooking time
1¾–2 hours

Chilling time
1 hour

Standing time
At least 30 minutes

Freezing time
30 minutes

Storage
24 hours

Equipment
Trussing needle
Butcher's twine
Fine-mesh sieve
Silicone baking mat
Disposable pastry bag fitted with a plain ¼-in. (6-mm) round tip

Ingredients

Roast chicken
1¾ oz. (50 g) carrots
1¾ oz. (50 g) celery
3½ oz. (100 g) onions
2¾-lb. (1.2-kg) chicken, dressed, gutted, and trussed with a needle (see techniques pp. 94, 97, and 103)
Grape-seed oil
1 lemon, halved
8 sprigs thyme
Scant ½ cup (100 ml) water
1 cup (250 ml) brown veal stock (*fond brun de veau*, see recipe p. 16)
1 bouquet garni (thyme and bay leaf)

Sauce diable
⅛ bunch tarragon
⅛ bunch chervil
1½ oz. (40 g) shallots
Scant 1 tbsp (7 g) cracked black pepper
Scant ½ cup (100 ml) dry white wine
3½ tbsp (50 ml) champagne vinegar, preferably from Reims
Roast chicken pan juices (see left)
1 tbsp (20 g) butter

Mushroom-stuffed pasta
1¾ lb. (800 g) zitone no. 19 pasta
14 oz. (400 g) king trumpet (king oyster) mushrooms
1¾ oz. (50 g) shallots
½ bunch chives
3 tbsp (1¾ oz./50 g) butter
1 clove garlic, unpeeled
Scant ½ cup (100 ml) white wine
Scant ½ cup (1½ oz./40 g) grated Parmesan
Salt and freshly ground pepper

Gratin topping
1 cup (9 oz./250 g) mascarpone
1 egg yolk
2½ cups (9 oz./250 g) grated Parmesan

Sautéed king trumpet mushrooms
3½ oz. (100 g) king trumpet (king oyster) mushrooms
Olive oil
Salt and freshly ground pepper

To garnish
Chervil leaves

PREPARING THE ROAST CHICKEN

Preheat the oven to 350°F (180°C/Gas Mark 4). Peel and wash the carrots, celery, and onions, if necessary, and finely chop all three. Brush the chicken with grape-seed oil, season with salt and pepper, and place the lemon halves in the cavity. Set the chicken on its side in a roasting pan and roast for 45–60 minutes, basting regularly: 15–20 minutes on each side and a final 15–20 minutes on its back. To test for doneness, pierce the thickest part of the thigh with the tip of a pointed knife; the chicken is done when the juices run clear. Remove the chicken from the pan, then place the carrots, celery, onions, and thyme in the pan and roast for 15 minutes. Pour off the excess fat from the pan and deglaze with the water. Transfer the contents of the pan to a saucepan, add the veal stock and bouquet garni, and let simmer for 30 minutes. Strain through the fine-mesh sieve and set aside for the sauce diable.

PREPARING THE SAUCE DIABLE

Wash the tarragon and chervil, remove the leaves and set them aside, and tie the stems together to make a bouquet garni. Blanch the tarragon leaves in boiling water for 5 seconds, then drain and run cold water over them to cool. Dry them in a clean dish towel. Finely chop the chervil and tarragon leaves. Peel and finely chop the shallots and cook in a small saucepan with the cracked pepper, wine, and vinegar until all the liquid has evaporated. Stir in the reserved pan juices along with the butter and herbs, adding a little more vinegar to sharpen the flavor, if necessary.

PREPARING THE MUSHROOM-STUFFED PASTA

Cook the pasta in a large saucepan of boiling salted water for 7 minutes. Drain without rinsing. Lay the still warm pasta in a single layer on the silicone baking mat, lining up the pieces side by side so they stick together. Cover with a damp dish towel and chill for 30 minutes. Wash the mushrooms and cut them into very small dice. Peel and finely chop the shallots. Wash and finely chop the chives. Heat the butter in a skillet and sweat the shallots and garlic until softened, then deglaze with the wine and reduce by two-thirds. Add the mushrooms and cook until all their liquid has evaporated. Stir in the Parmesan and chives, and season with salt and pepper. Chill for 30 minutes, then transfer the mixture to the pastry bag and pipe it into the pasta tubes. Cut the pasta into 5 × 1¾-in. (12 × 4.5-cm) rectangles and stack two rectangles together per serving. Place on a baking sheet lined with parchment paper.

PREPARING THE GRATIN TOPPING

Combine the mascarpone, egg yolk, and Parmesan in a bowl. Spread the mixture to a thickness of ⅛ in. (3 mm) between two sheets of parchment paper. Let set in the freezer for 30 minutes, then cut into 5 × 1¾-in. (12 × 4.5-cm) rectangles and place them over the pasta rectangles. Let sit at room temperature for at least 30 minutes before baking. Preheat the oven to 480°F (250°C/Gas Mark 9). Bake the pasta rectangles for 3 minutes, then rotate the baking sheet and bake for an additional 2 minutes, until golden.

PREPARING THE SAUTÉED KING TRUMPET MUSHROOMS

Cut the mushrooms in half and score the cut sides with a crosshatch pattern. Heat a little olive oil in a skillet and sauté the mushrooms until golden. Season with salt and pepper.

TO SERVE

Serve the roast chicken with the pasta gratin and sautéed mushrooms on the side, scattered with a few chervil leaves. Serve the sauce diable separately in a sauceboat.

SPICED DUCK AND RED KURI SQUASH PARMENTIER

Parmentier de canard au potimarron et cinq-épices

Serves 4

Active time
1 hour

Cooking time
2 hours

Storage
3 days

Equipment
Fine-mesh sieve
Food processor

Ingredients

Duck confit
2 onions
1¾ oz. (50 g) fresh ginger
1 stalk lemongrass
2 cloves garlic
3 duck legs
3½ oz. (100 g) duck fat
1 tbsp (8 g) five-spice powder
About 8 cups (2 liters) white poultry stock (*fond blanc de volaille,* see recipe p. 19)
1 bunch cilantro, finely chopped
Salt and freshly ground pepper

Red kuri squash purée
1 red kuri squash
5 tbsp (3 oz./80 g) butter
4 tbsp (60 ml) maple syrup
Generous ¾ cup (200 ml) water
Salt

Cooked red kuri squash
2 tsp (10 g) duck fat
4 slices red kuri squash, peeled

To serve
1¾ cups (7 oz./200 g) dried breadcrumbs
1 cup (3½ oz./100 g) grated Parmesan
Scant 3 tbsp (20 g) pumpkin seeds
1 small basil sprig

PREPARING THE DUCK CONFIT

Preheat the oven to 350°F (180°C/Gas Mark 4). Peel and finely chop the onions, peel and grate the ginger, and cut the lemongrass into large pieces. Peel and crush the garlic cloves. Cut the duck legs into 2 pieces at the joints and brown them in the duck fat in a Dutch oven. Add the onions, garlic, ginger, and lemongrass, cover, and sweat over low heat. Season with salt, pepper, and the five-spice powder. Add the stock (it should just cover the ingredients) and bring to a boil, skimming any foam from the surface. Cover and cook in the oven for 1½ hours, or until the meat pulls away from the bones. Drain the legs, remove the bones, and shred the meat. Strain the sauce through the fine-mesh sieve into a saucepan and reduce until syrupy. Add the shredded meat and cilantro to the sauce, cover, and let simmer over low heat for 5 minutes. Adjust the seasonings, if necessary.

PREPARING THE RED KURI SQUASH PURÉE

Cut the squash in half from top to bottom and scoop out the seeds using a spoon. Peel the squash and cut it into ¾-in. (2-cm) dice. Melt the butter in a saucepan, add the squash, cover the pan, and sweat until softened but not browned. Add the maple syrup and water, cover, and cook over low heat for about 20 minutes, until the squash is tender. Drain the squash, reserving the cooking liquid. Place the squash in the food processor and purée to a consistency of your liking, adding a little cooking liquid to thin it as needed.

PREPARING THE COOKED RED KURI SQUASH

Preheat the oven to 350°F (180°C/Gas Mark 4). Melt the duck fat in an oven-safe pan and cook the squash over low heat until softened. Transfer to the oven and roast for a few minutes, or until completely tender and browned in places.

TO SERVE

Preheat the oven to 350°F (180°C/Gas Mark 4). Spread the duck confit over the base of a baking dish and cover with red kuri squash purée. Sprinkle over the breadcrumbs and Parmesan and bake for 20 minutes, or until golden. Arrange the cooked squash slices on the top and sprinkle with pumpkin seeds. Garnish with the basil sprig.

STUFFED QUAILS

Cailles farcies

Serves 10

Active time
1¼ hours

Cooking time
2½ hours

Storage
2 days

Equipment
Poultry shears
Trussing needle
Butcher's twine
Fine-mesh sieve
Instant-read thermometer
Disposable pastry bag

Ingredients

Quails
10 quails

Quail jus
7 oz. (200 g) white onions
½ head garlic
Carcasses from 10 quails (see above; about 2¼ lb./1 kg)
Scant ½ cup (100 ml) olive oil
¼ bunch thyme
1¾ sticks (7 oz./200 g) butter
8 cups (2 liters) vegetable stock, divided

Stuffing
Scant ½ cup (1¾ oz./50 g) slivered almonds
3½ oz. (100 g) white onions
3½ tbsp (50 ml) olive oil
2 cups (14 oz./400 g) long-grain white rice
Scant 2½ cups (600 ml) vegetable stock
2 preserved lemons
1½ lb. (750 g) soft dried apricots
10 confit tomatoes
Scant ½ cup (1¾ oz./50 g) shelled pistachios
Generous ½ teaspoon (3 g) fine sea salt

Glazed radicchio
4 heads radicchio
2 tsp (10 g) fine sea salt
Scant ½ cup (100 ml) olive oil
⅔ cup (150 ml) balsamic vinegar

PREPARING THE QUAILS AND THE QUAIL JUS

Bone the quails using the poultry shears, trussing needle, and butcher's twine so they are ready for stuffing (see technique pp. 120–123, steps 1–12). Reserve the carcasses for the jus. To prepare the jus, peel the onions and cut each one into 8 wedges. Separate the garlic cloves and roughly crush them, unpeeled, using the flat of a chef's knife blade. Cut the quail carcasses into approximately 1½-in. (4-cm) pieces. Heat the olive oil in a large saucepan and sear the carcasses until pale golden brown. Add the onions, garlic, thyme, and butter, and continue to cook until the carcasses are deeply browned. Pour off the excess fat and deglaze with 2 cups (500 ml) of the stock to release the browned bits from the bottom of the pan. Add the remaining stock and simmer for 1½ hours. Strain the jus through the fine-mesh sieve into a clean saucepan and reduce until it coats the back of a spoon. Set aside at room temperature.

PREPARING THE STUFFING

Preheat the oven to 285°F (140°C/Gas Mark 1). Spread the almonds over a baking sheet lined with parchment paper and toast in the oven for 10 minutes. Peel and finely chop the onions. Heat a little oil in a sauté pan and sweat the onions until softened but not browned. Stir in the rice and cook until the grains are translucent. Pour in the stock, heat it to 355°F (180°C), and let the rice cook at this temperature for 18 minutes. Remove from the heat. Cut the preserved lemons, dried apricots, and confit tomatoes into ⅛-in. (3-mm) dice and combine with the rice. Stir in the almonds, pistachios, and salt.

STUFFING AND ROASTING THE QUAILS

Preheat the oven to 250°F (130°C/Gas Mark ½). Spoon the stuffing into the pastry bag, snip off the tip, and fill the quails with the stuffing. Truss the quails using the trussing needle threaded with twine (see technique pp. 123–124, steps 13–18). Place the quails in a shallow ovenproof dish and roast in the oven for 30 minutes.

PREPARING AND GLAZING THE RADICCHIO

Wash the radicchio and cut each head crosswise into 1¼-in. (3-cm) slices. Secure the rounds with twine, so they will hold their shape while cooking, and season with the salt. Heat the olive oil in a skillet and sear the radicchio until softened and browned. Add the balsamic vinegar and cook until glazed, basting the radicchio with the oil and balsamic. Remove from the pan and discard the twine.

TO SERVE

Reheat the jus and place the quails in it to coat them. Drizzle a little jus on each plate and serve one quail per person, with the radicchio slices opened to resemble flowers.

CHICKEN IN A POT

Poule au pot

Serves 4

Active time

2 hours

Cooking time

About 2 hours

Storage

3 days

Ingredients

Chicken

4–5-lb. (1.8–2.2-kg) chicken

8 orange carrots

8 small yellow carrots, with tops

4 turnips

2 rutabagas

2 leeks

1 stalk celery

1 onion, peeled and studded with 2 whole cloves

1 tbsp (10 g) kosher salt

8 green cabbage leaves

Rice

1²/₃ cups (400 ml) chicken broth (see above)

1 cup (7 oz./200 g) long grain rice

Suprême sauce

2 tbsp (1 oz./30 g) butter

3 tbsp (1 oz./30 g) all-purpose flour

2 cups (500 ml) chicken broth (see above)

²/₃ cup (150 ml) crème fraîche

Salt and freshly ground pepper

To serve

10 celery leaves, preferably yellow

A few sprigs micro purple shiso

PREPARING THE CHICKEN

Place the chicken in a Dutch oven and add enough cold water to just cover it. Bring to a boil, carefully skimming all the foam from the surface. Peel the carrots, turnips, and rutabagas, and cut them into large pieces, quarters, or halves, depending on their size. Wash and trim the leeks and celery and cut them into large pieces. Once the chicken cooking liquid is clear, add the chopped vegetables, clove-studded onion, and salt. Cover and cook for 1¹/₂ hours, or until the chicken and vegetables are completely tender. Cook the cabbage leaves in a separate saucepan of boiling water until tender, then set them aside until serving.

PREPARING THE RICE

Measure out 1²/₃ cups (400 ml) of the broth from cooking the chicken. Cover the Dutch oven with a lid so the chicken and vegetables stay hot. Bring the measured broth to a boil in a medium saucepan, stir in the rice, and cook for 20 minutes.

PREPARING THE SUPRÊME SAUCE

Melt the butter in a large saucepan over low heat, then whisk in the flour to make a roux. Cook for 2 minutes, whisking continuously, then gradually whisk in the 2 cups (500 ml) broth reserved from cooking the chicken, until the sauce is well blended and smooth. Bring to a boil, stir in the crème fraîche, and adjust the seasonings if necessary.

TO SERVE

Remove the chicken from the Dutch oven and cut it into pieces. Chop the cabbage leaves. Spoon the chicken and vegetables over the rice with the remaining broth in the Dutch oven and scatter celery leaves and purple shiso sprigs over the top. Serve the suprême sauce on the side.

ROAST DUCKLING BREAST WITH BEETS

Filet de canette rôtie et déclinaisons de betteraves

Serves 4

Active time
1 hour

Cooking time
About 2 hours

Storage
24 hours

Equipment
Food processor
Instant-read thermometer

Ingredients

Beets *en papillote*
2 bunches mini red beets, greens removed
2 yellow beets, greens removed
7 tbsp (3½ oz./100 g) butter
4 cloves garlic
2 sprigs thyme

Red beet purée
14 oz. (400 g) red beets
1 red onion
5 tbsp (2½ oz./70 g) butter
2 tbsp (1 oz./30 g) brown sugar
Salt and white pepper

Beet jus
⅔ cup (150 ml) beet juice
2 tbsp (30 ml) red wine vinegar
Generous ¾ cup (200 ml) poultry jus
Salt

Roast duckling
4 duckling breasts

To serve
4 purple shiso leaves, torn into pieces
12 red-veined sorrel leaves

PREPARING THE BEETS EN PAPILLOTE AND RED BEET PURÉE

Preheat the oven to 340°F (170°C/Gas Mark 3). To prepare the beets *en papillote*, wash the red and yellow beets, leaving them unpeeled. Prepare two parchment paper parcels: one for the red beets and one for the yellow. Divide the butter, garlic, and thyme between the parcels and fold over the parchment edges to seal them tightly. Place in the oven. Cook the red beets for 45 minutes and the yellow beets for 1½ hours. To make the beet purée, peel and thinly slice the red beets and red onion. Heat the butter and brown sugar in a Dutch oven and, when melted, sweat the beets and onion until softened. Remove from the heat and add enough water to just cover. Cut out a circle of parchment paper to fit snugly inside the Dutch oven and place over the vegetables. Cover the pan and cook in the oven for 1 hour, or until the beets are completely tender. Drain the excess liquid, if necessary, then transfer the beets and onion to the food processor and process to a purée. Season with salt and white pepper.

PREPARING THE BEET JUS

Combine the beet juice and vinegar in a saucepan and reduce by half over low heat. Add the poultry jus and reduce again until syrupy. Adjust the seasonings, if necessary.

PREPARING AND COOKING THE DUCKLING BREASTS

Preheat the oven to 325°F (160°C/Gas Mark 3). Remove the silver skin from the duckling breasts, trim the excess fat off the sides, and score the skin in a crosshatch pattern (see technique p. 130). Brown the breasts on both sides in an oven-safe skillet, then finish cooking them in the oven for about 15 minutes, or until the internal temperature reaches 118°F (48°C).

TO SERVE

Peel the beets *en papillote* and cut the yellow beets into wedges. Cut each duckling breast on the diagonal into 3 pieces. Arrange all the components attractively on serving plates and garnish with a few shiso and red-veined sorrel leaves.

STUFFED TURKEY

Dinde farcie

Serves 8

Active time
1 hour

Cooking time
About 6½ hours

Chilling time
30 minutes

Marinating time
15 minutes

Storage
2 days

Equipment
Food processor
Disposable pastry bag
Trussing needle
Butcher's twine
Instant-read thermometer

Ingredients

Stuffing
5¼ oz. (150 g) button mushrooms
1½ oz. (40 g) horn-of-plenty mushrooms
Olive oil
2 tbsp (1 oz./30 g) butter
2 oz. (60 g) crustless sandwich bread
¼ cup (60 ml) whole milk
10½ oz. (300 g) boneless chicken or turkey breast, preferably organic, well chilled
2½ tsp (13 g) salt + more as needed
¾ tsp (2 g) ground pepper + more as needed
1 egg
Scant 1½ cups (340 ml) heavy cream, min. 35% fat, well chilled

Roast turkey
7–7¾-lb. (3.2–3.5-kg) turkey
3½ oz. (100 g) goose fat
Salt and freshly ground pepper

To garnish and serve
1 lb. (500 g) sweet potatoes
10½ oz. (300 g) Brussels sprouts
2 tbsp (30 ml) maple syrup
4 tsp (20 ml) soy sauce
1 clove garlic, finely chopped
2½ tsp (6 g) ground cumin
3½ tbsp (50 ml) olive oil
2 Golden Delicious apples
3 tbsp (1½ oz./40 g) butter

PREPARING THE STUFFING

Wash, trim, and quarter the button mushrooms. Wash the horn-of-plenty mushrooms. Heat a little olive oil in a skillet and, when hot, add the button mushrooms and sauté until softened and lightly browned. Season lightly with salt and freshly ground pepper. Drain the mushrooms, add the butter to the skillet and, when foaming, return the button mushrooms to it and sear until evenly browned. Add the horn-of-plenty mushrooms and sauté for a few minutes. Let cool, then chill in the refrigerator. Soak the bread in the milk in a bowl. Cut the chicken or turkey breast, which should be well chilled, into strips and place in the food processor. Add the 2½ tsp (13 g) salt and ¾ tsp (2 g) ground pepper, and roughly chop on low speed until the chicken has the texture of ground meat. Drain the soaked bread and add it to the food processor along with the egg, then process for about 30 seconds to blend. With the motor running, gradually pour in the cream down the feeder tube and process until smooth. Transfer to a large bowl and stir in the sautéed mushrooms. Chill until needed.

PREPARING AND COOKING THE ROAST TURKEY

Dress and gut the turkey (see techniques pp. 94 and 97). Preheat the oven to 250°F (130°C/Gas Mark ½). Transfer the stuffing to the pastry bag, snip off the tip of the bag, and pipe the stuffing into the turkey. Truss the turkey using the trussing needle threaded with butcher's twine (see technique p. 103). Place it breast side up in a Dutch oven and add enough water to come up to the top of the leg (about 1½–2½ in./4–6 cm high). Spread the goose fat over the breast of the bird, cover, and roast in the oven for 2½ hours. Remove the lid and roast uncovered for an additional 3 hours, basting every 30 minutes. Cook until the temperature of the stuffing reaches 154°F (68°C) in the center.

PREPARING THE GARNISHES

Preheat the oven to 325°F (160°C/Gas Mark 3). Peel the sweet potatoes and cut them into ¾-in. (2-cm) dice. Wash the Brussels sprouts and cut them in half lengthwise. Combine the maple syrup, soy sauce, garlic, cumin, and olive oil in a large bowl. Toss the sweet potatoes and Brussels sprouts in the marinade to coat and let marinate for 15 minutes. Transfer to a baking dish, cover, and bake for 45 minutes. Meanwhile, peel and core the apples and cut them into ¼-in. (6-mm) dice. Sauté in a skillet with the butter until they start to soften and are lightly browned in places, then mix with the Brussels sprouts and sweet potatoes.

TO SERVE

Carve the turkey, allowing a piece of stuffed breast and a portion of leg meat per serving. Arrange the garnishes attractively on each plate, with the pan juices drizzled around.

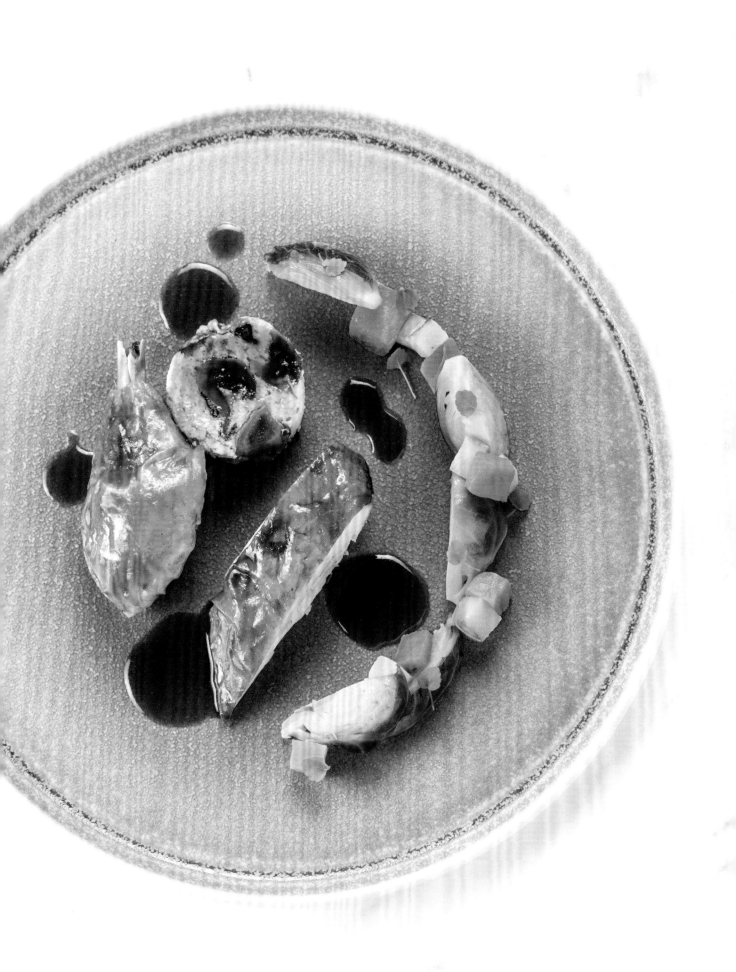

SMOOTH LIVER PÂTÉ

Gâteau de foie

Serves 10

Active time

1 hour

Cooking time

2¼ hours

Storage

3 days

Equipment

8-in. (20-cm) round terrine dish, 3 in. (8 cm) deep, with a lid

Meat grinder + grinding plate with medium-sized holes

Food mill

Fine-mesh sieve

Ingredients

Poultry livers

1 tbsp (20 g) butter for greasing

1 lb. 2 oz. (500 g) poultry livers

5¼ oz. (150 g) pork fatback (*lard gras*)

3½ oz. (100 g) shallots

3½ oz. (100 g) onions

2 cloves garlic

Leaves of ¼ bunch thyme

1¾ oz. (50 g) bread with crusts removed (*mie de pain*), torn into pieces

⅔ cup (150 ml) heavy cream, min. 35% fat

¾ tsp (2 g) ground nutmeg

3½ tbsp (50 ml) cognac

4 eggs

Salt

Tomato sauce topping

1¾ oz. (50 g) white onions

3½ oz. (100 g) carrots

⅓ oz. (10 g) garlic

3½ oz. (100 g) celery

Scant ½ cup (100 ml) olive oil

¾ lb. (350 g) tomatoes on the vine

1 tsp (5 g) fine sea salt

¾ tsp (2 g) ground white pepper

To serve

Baguettes or crusty bread

PREPARING THE POULTRY LIVERS

Preheat the oven to 300°F (150°C/Gas Mark 2). Grease the terrine dish with the butter. Trim any sinew off the livers and remove the veins. Cut the fatback into small pieces. Peel and finely chop the shallots, onions, and garlic. Finely chop the thyme leaves. Combine the bread, cream, and nutmeg in a large bowl. Cook the shallot with the fatback over medium heat in a Dutch oven until the shallot is very soft but not colored and the fatback is browned. Add the onions and garlic, cover the pan, and sweat until softened. Uncover the pan, add the liver, and cook until lightly colored. Deglaze with the cognac and flambé. Season with salt, then pass everything together through the meat grinder fitted with the medium grinding plate. Incorporate the eggs into the mixture one by one, then transfer to the baking dish and spread into an even layer. Cover the dish and cook in a bain-marie in the oven for 45 minutes.

PREPARING THE TOMATO SAUCE TOPPING

Peel and finely chop the onions, carrots, and garlic. Wash and finely chop the celery. Heat the olive oil in a large saucepan and sweat the vegetables over low heat until softened but not browned. Wash, hull, and quarter the tomatoes, add to the pan, and season with the salt and pepper. Let simmer, uncovered, for 1½ hours over low heat. Pass the sauce through the food mill, then strain it through the fine-mesh sieve into a clean saucepan. Reduce over low heat until the sauce has thickened to a coating consistency. Spread a very thin (1/16-in./2-mm) layer of the sauce over the liver pâté while it is still warm.

TO SERVE

Cut into slices and serve with baguettes or crusty bread.

BASQUE-STYLE CHICKEN WITH OCTOPUS

Cuisse de poulet basquaise et poulpe

Serves 4

Active time
1½ hours

Cooking time
3 hours

Chilling time
2 hours

Storage
3 days

Equipment
Butcher's twine

Ingredients

Octopus
1 onion
1 head garlic
1 bunch fresh oregano
2 bunches bay leaves
1 tsp coriander seeds
1 whole octopus, weighing 6½ lb. (3 kg)
Kosher salt or coarse sea salt, as needed

Basque-style chicken
28 oz. (850 g) canned diced tomatoes, or 2¼ lb. (1 kg) fresh tomatoes in season
3 red onions
2 cloves garlic
3 green bell peppers
3 red bell peppers
3 yellow bell peppers
4 chicken legs
5 tbsp (80 ml) olive oil
1 tbsp (8 g) *piment d'Espelette*
1 cup (250 ml) dry white wine
Fine sea salt

To serve
Olive oil
5 slices cured ham, preferably *jambon de Bayonne*
1 tbsp finely chopped parsley
2 tbsp thinly sliced scallions (green parts only)

PREPARING THE OCTOPUS

Peel the onion and cut the head of garlic in half crosswise. Tie the oregano and bay leaves together with twine to make a bouquet garni. Fill a large casserole with cold water, adding 2 tsp (10 g) of kosher or coarse sea salt per 4 cups (1 liter) of water. Add the onion, garlic, coriander seeds, and bouquet garni, and bring to a boil over medium heat. If you wish, let the broth simmer for 20 minutes to concentrate the flavor. Place the octopus in the broth and let simmer for 1–1½ hours. Regularly check for doneness using the tip of a paring knife. The octopus is ready when the knife glides in easily. Drain, cool, then chill the octopus for about 2 hours.

PREPARING THE BASQUE-STYLE CHICKEN

If you are using fresh tomatoes, peel, seed, and chop them. Peel and thinly slice the red onions. Peel and crush the garlic cloves. Peel the bell peppers and cut them into approximately ¼-in. (5-mm) slices. Cut the chicken legs in two at the joints. Heat the olive oil in a Dutch oven over medium-high heat. Add the chicken and brown on all sides, working in batches, if necessary. Remove the chicken and set it aside. Sweat the onions in the same pan over low heat. Add the bell peppers and garlic, cover, and cook for 3 minutes, then remove the lid and continue to cook for an additional 5 minutes. Add the tomatoes and *piment d'Espelette*, cover, and cook for 10 minutes, stirring occasionally. Pour in the wine and let simmer for 5 minutes, then return the chicken to the pan, cover, and cook for about 20 minutes, or until the chicken is cooked through and tender. Adjust the seasonings if necessary and let simmer for an additional 5 minutes.

TO SERVE

Cut the tentacles off the octopus and sauté them in a large skillet with olive oil until browned and crisp on the outside. In a separate skillet, fry the ham in a little olive oil, if desired; alternatively, you can leave it uncooked. Just before serving, stir the parsley into the chicken. Arrange the octopus tentacles and ham over the top and sprinkle with the scallions.

CHICKEN NUGGETS

Nuggets de poulet

Serves 6

Active time
1 hour

Cooking time
About 20 minutes

Soaking time
10 minutes

Freezing time
2½ hours

Chilling time
2 hours

Storage
2 weeks in the freezer

Equipment
Steam oven (or steamer)

Instant-read thermometer

Food processor

Fine-mesh sieve

Disposable pastry bag fitted with a plain ½-in. (1-cm) tip

2 × 15-cavity silicone half-sphere molds, diameter 1½ in. (3.5 cm)

Deep fryer

Ingredients

Chicken breasts

1 lb. 2 oz. (500 g) skinless, boneless chicken breasts

Scant ½ cup (3½ oz./100 g) fine sea salt

4 cups (1 liter) water

4 sprigs thyme

1 bay leaf

Chicken farce

9 oz. (250 g) skinless, boneless chicken breasts

1½ tsp (7 g) salt

¾ tsp (2 g) ground white pepper

¾ tsp (2 g) *piment d'Espelette*

Generous ¾ cup (200 ml) heavy cream, min. 35% fat, well chilled

Cornflake coating

1⅔ cups (7 oz./200 g) all-purpose flour

2 tsp (5 g) paprika

1 tsp (5 g) salt

1⅓ cups (10½ oz./300 g) lightly beaten egg (6 eggs)

4 tsp (20 ml) neutral oil

14 oz. (400 g) cornflakes

Salt

Honey-mustard sauce

1 cup (9 oz./250 g) mayonnaise

½ cup (4½ oz./125 g) barbecue sauce

2 tbsp (1½ oz./40 g) honey

2 tbsp (1 oz./30 g) Dijon mustard

2 tbsp (1 oz./30 g) wholegrain mustard

Salt and freshly ground pepper

To cook and serve

8 cups (2 liters) canola oil, for deep frying

Honey-mustard sauce (see above)

Lamb's lettuce salad (optional)

PREPARING THE CHICKEN BREASTS

If using a steam oven, preheat it to 175°F (80°C/Gas on lowest setting). Trim the veins and membranes from the chicken breasts. Dissolve the salt in the water in a large bowl to make a brine, add the chicken, and let it soak for 10 minutes. Drain and pat dry. Place the chicken breasts on a sheet of plastic wrap, top with the thyme and bay leaf, and cover tightly with the plastic wrap. Cook in the steam oven, or steamer, until the internal temperature reaches 149°F (65°C). Let the chicken cool for a few minutes, then unwrap, remove the herbs, and cut the chicken into cubes weighing about ¼ oz. (7 g) each. Freeze for 30 minutes to allow the chicken to firm up.

PREPARING THE CHICKEN FARCE

Cut the chicken breasts for the farce into large dice (about 1¼ in./3 cm) and toss with the salt, white pepper, and *piment d'Espelette* until coated. Let rest in the refrigerator for 1 hour, then process until very finely chopped in the food processor. With the motor running, mix in the cream, pouring it down the feeder tube. Push through the fine-mesh sieve to obtain a smooth texture and transfer to the pastry bag.

ASSEMBLING THE CHICKEN NUGGETS

Snip the tip off the bag and pipe chicken farce into the cavities of the half-sphere molds. Nestle a chicken cube in the center of each one. Smooth the surface using a spatula and freeze for 1 hour to allow the farce to harden. Reserve the remaining farce in the refrigerator. Turn the frozen half-spheres out of the molds, then pipe the remaining farce into the cavities to fill them by two-thirds. Place the frozen half-spheres on top, to form complete spheres. Freeze for 1 hour.

PREPARING THE CORNFLAKE COATING

Combine the flour, paprika, and 1 tsp (5 g) salt in a bowl. In a second bowl, whisk together the eggs, oil, and a pinch of salt. Using the end of a rolling pin, crush the cornflakes to a fine powder in a third bowl. Roll each farce sphere in the flour mixture, then dip in the egg mixture to coat. Roll in the crushed cornflakes, dip in the egg again, then finish with a second coating of cornflakes. Chill for 1 hour.

PREPARING THE HONEY-MUSTARD SAUCE

Whisk together all the ingredients until well blended. Keep in the refrigerator until serving.

TO COOK AND SERVE

Heat the oil for deep-frying to 350°F (180°C). Deep-fry the nuggets for 3 minutes, or until they are golden brown and the internal temperature is over 150°F (65°C). Serve the nuggets in a shallow bowl with the honey-mustard sauce on the side and a salad of lamb's lettuce, if desired.

CHICKEN LIVERS WITH MOLE SAUCE

Foie de volaille et sauce mole

Serves 10

Active time
1½ hours

Cooking time
1¼ hours

Storage
24 hours

Equipment
Immersion blender
Fine-mesh sieve
Mandolin

Ingredients

Mole sauce

½ cup (1¾ oz./50 g) walnut halves

⅓ cup (1¾ oz./50 g) raw almonds

2½ tbsp (25 g) sesame seeds

⅓ cup (1¾ oz./50 g) raw peanuts

3 dried ancho chili peppers

1½ tsp (3 g) ground cloves

1 tsp (3 g) ground cinnamon

7 oz. (200 g) tomatoes

7 oz. (200 g) onions

½ oz. (15 g) unpeeled garlic cloves

2 oz. (60 g) day-old baguette

3½ tbsp (50 ml) whole milk

Scant ½ cup (100 ml) vegetable stock

¼ oz. (8 g) dark chocolate, 70% cacao

Cauliflower

2 heads cauliflower

1¾ sticks (7 oz./200 g) butter

2 tsp (10 g) fine sea salt

Chicken livers

30 chicken livers

2 tsp (10 g) fine sea salt

2 tsp (5 g) freshly ground pepper

¾ cup + 2 tbsp (3½ oz./100 g) all-purpose flour

Scant ½ cup (100 ml) olive oil

1 stick + 2 tbsp (5¼ oz./150 g) butter

PREPARING THE MOLE SAUCE

Preheat the oven to 285°F (140°C/Gas Mark 1). Spread the walnuts, almonds, sesame seeds, and peanuts over a baking sheet lined with parchment paper and toast in the oven for 15 minutes. Remove the nuts and sesame seeds, then do the same with the chili peppers, cloves, and cinnamon. Remove and increase the oven temperature to 400°F (200°C/Gas Mark 6). Wash the tomatoes and cut them in half crosswise. Cut the unpeeled onions into quarters. Place the tomatoes, onions, and garlic on a baking sheet lined with parchment paper and roast in the oven for 40 minutes. Soak the bread in the milk. Transfer all the ingredients except the vegetable stock and chocolate to a large saucepan and purée until smooth using the immersion blender. Add the vegetable stock and bring to a simmer. Strain through the fine-mesh sieve into a clean saucepan, add the chocolate, and, when the chocolate has melted, reduce to a glaze. Adjust the seasonings, if necessary.

PREPARING THE CAULIFLOWER

Wash the cauliflower and remove about 20 florets weighing 1 oz. (30 g) each. Heat half the butter in a large saucepan until it browns and has a nutty aroma. Add the 20 florets and pan-roast for 15 minutes over low heat, or until just tender. Meanwhile, using the mandolin, shave off several 1/16-in. (1-mm) raw cauliflower "flakes" and set aside for serving. Separate the remaining cauliflower into florets and blanch them three times to remove any bitterness. To do this, drop the florets into a saucepan of boiling salted water, bring back to a boil, then drain and cool under cold water. Heat the remaining butter in a large saucepan and cook the florets until tender and golden. Process to a coarse purée using the immersion blender and season with salt and pepper.

PREPARING THE CHICKEN LIVERS

Separate the livers into halves and remove the veins. Season the livers with the salt and pepper and coat them with flour. Warm the oil and butter in a skillet over medium-high heat until the butter foams. Add the livers and cook until browned and crisp on the outside but still pink inside.

TO SERVE

Arrange 3 livers on each serving plate, along with a little mole sauce and a bed of cauliflower purée topped with pan-roasted florets and raw cauliflower shavings.

CHICKEN CORDON BLEU

Serves 10

Active time

30 minutes

Cooking time

11 minutes

Storage

3 days

Equipment

Mallet-style meat pounder

Ingredients

Mesclun greens

1 head baby chicory

1¾ oz. (50 g) baby orache or spinach greens

1¾ oz. (50 g) baby mizuna greens

⅓ oz. (10 g) red-veined sorrel leaves

Vinaigrette

Generous ½ teaspoon (3 g) fine sea salt

2 tbsp (30 ml) aged red wine vinegar

1½ tsp (3 g) freshly ground white pepper

Scant ½ cup (100 ml) extra-virgin olive oil

Cordon bleu

5 large slices cooked ham

7 oz. (200 g) Cantal

10 boneless chicken breasts

2 cups (9 oz./250 g) all-purpose flour

2 tsp (10 g) salt

6 eggs

4½ cups (1 lb. 2 oz./500 g) dried white breadcrumbs

Scant ½ cup (100 ml) olive oil

3 tbsp (1¾ oz./50 g) butter

PREPARING THE MESCLUN GREENS

Cut the chicory into 1½-in. (4-cm) pieces and remove the stems from the baby greens. Wash and drain the greens and sorrel leaves and set them aside.

PREPARING THE VINAIGRETTE

Dissolve the salt in the vinegar in a bowl, then add the white pepper. Gradually whisk in the olive oil until emulsified.

PREPARING THE CORDON BLEU

Preheat the oven to 350°F (180°C/Gas Mark 4). Cut the ham slices in half lengthwise. Cut 20 slices of Cantal that are about the same size as the half-slices of ham. Trim any excess fat off the chicken breasts and butterfly them. Using the meat pounder, flatten them between two sheets of plastic wrap until they are twice their original size. Place one slice of Cantal over one-half of each chicken breast, followed by a piece of ham and a second slice of Cantal. Close each chicken breast by folding the uncovered half over the covered half so the edges meet. Combine the flour and salt in a shallow dish, whisk the eggs in a second dish, and place the breadcrumbs in a third dish. Roll each cordon bleu in the flour, dip in the egg, and coat in the breadcrumbs. Dip in the egg a second time, then in the breadcrumbs again until well coated. Heat the olive oil in a large oven-safe skillet and brown the cordon bleu for 3 minutes on each side. Add the butter, wait for it to foam, then fry for an additional 3 minutes on each side, basting regularly. Transfer the skillet to the oven and finish cooking the cordon bleu for 5 minutes. Drain on paper towels.

TO SERVE

Combine the greens in a large bowl and toss with the vinaigrette just before serving, to avoid the leaves going soggy. Place each cordon bleu on a serving plate with a little salad alongside.

DUCK CONFIT WITH CHERRY AND POMEGRANATE GASTRIQUE

Confit de canard, gastrique de cerises et grenade

Serves 4

Active time
1½ hours

Cooking time
3 hours

Chilling time
4 hours

Storage
3 days

Equipment
Mandolin
5½-in. (14-cm) round cake pan, 1½ in. (4 cm) deep
Fine-mesh sieve

Ingredients

Duck confit
4 duck legs
7 oz. (200 g) coarse gray Guérande sea salt
2 cloves garlic
2 bay leaves
4 cups (1 liter) duck fat
Freshly ground pepper

Eggplant purée with tahini
6 eggplants
1 white onion
2 cloves garlic
3½ tbsp (50 ml) olive oil
Generous ¾ cup (200 ml) vegetable stock
2 tbsp (1 oz./30 g) tahini
Salt and freshly ground pepper

Potato millefeuille
1 lb. 2 oz. (500 g) potatoes
Scant ⅓ cup (70 ml) clarified butter, melted
Salt and freshly ground pepper

Cherry and pomegranate gastrique
⅓ cup (2½ oz./70 g) sugar
Scant ⅓ cup (70 ml) Banyuls red wine vinegar
Generous ¾ cup (200 ml) pomegranate juice
7 oz. (200 g) pitted fresh cherries
Generous ¾ cup (200 ml) brown poultry stock (*fond brun de volaille*, see recipe and Chefs' Notes p. 19)
Salt and freshly ground pepper

To serve
4 large shiso leaves
1 scallion, julienned
⅛ bunch chervil
Purple basil
A few red-veined sorrel shoots

PREPARING THE DUCK CONFIT
Rub the duck legs with the coarse salt and place them in a baking dish with the garlic and bay leaves. Cover with plastic wrap and chill for 4 hours. Preheat the oven to 300°F (150°C/Gas Mark 2). Rinse the duck legs under cold water to remove the salt, then dry them well. Place them in a Dutch oven and pour over the duck fat. Cover and cook in the oven for about 2 hours, or until the duck legs are tender.

PREPARING THE EGGPLANT PURÉE WITH TAHINI
Wash and peel the eggplants and cut them into small dice. Peel and finely chop the onion and garlic, and sweat them in a saucepan with the olive oil. Season with salt and add the eggplant and vegetable stock. Cover and cook for 10–15 minutes, until the vegetables are tender. Mash the mixture using a fork, then stir in the tahini. Adjust the seasonings, adding more salt and pepper, if necessary.

PREPARING THE POTATO MILLEFEUILLE
Preheat the oven to 350°F (180°C/Gas Mark 4). Peel the potatoes and cut them into 1/16-in. (2-mm) slices using the mandolin. Arrange potato slices over the base of the cake pan in a single layer, without overlapping them. Brush with clarified butter and season with salt and pepper. Repeat the layers until all the potato slices have been used. Cover with parchment paper and bake for 35 minutes, until the potatoes are tender and lightly golden. Remove from the oven and place a plate on top of the potatoes to press them down as they cool.

PREPARING THE CHERRY AND POMEGRANATE GASTRIQUE
Heat the sugar and vinegar together in a small saucepan until the sugar dissolves. Bring to a boil. Continue to boil until the syrup is caramelized and a deep amber color, stopping before it burns. Deglaze with the pomegranate juice and cherries and reduce by half, then add the stock and reduce for 5 minutes. Strain through the fine-mesh sieve, pressing down to extract maximum flavor. Cook for longer to thicken the sauce, if desired, and adjust the seasonings, if necessary.

TO SERVE
Reheat the duck legs in the Dutch oven, then transfer them to a shallow pan and place under the broiler briefly to crisp the skin. Divide the eggplant purée between 4 serving dishes, place the duck legs on the purée, and add a large shiso leaf alongside. Top the duck legs with the scallion julienne and serve with a slice of potato millefeuille sprinkled with chervil, purple basil, and red-veined sorrel shoots. Pour the cherry and pomegranate gastrique around the duck.

PRESSED CHICKEN WITH SQUASH AND PEAR TERRINE

Poulet sous presse

Serves 4

Active time
1 hour

Cooking time
2¾ hours + 20 minutes reheating

Chilling time
Overnight

Storage
24 hours for the chicken
3 days for the terrine

Equipment
Mandolin
12 × 4 ½-in. (30 × 11-cm) terrine mold, 2¾ in. (7 cm) deep
Food processor

Ingredients

Squash and pear terrine
½ butternut squash
½ red kuri squash
3 Boule d'Or turnips
1 firm pear, preferably Williams
⅓ cup (75 ml) coconut oil
Cilantro, chopped
Salt

Celery root purée
14 oz. (400 g) celery root (celeriac)
2 cups (500 ml) whole milk
2 bay leaves
3 tbsp (1¾ oz./50 g) butter, diced, at room temperature
Salt and freshly ground pepper

Pressed chicken
3-lb. (1.4-kg) chicken, dressed, gutted, and cut into 4 pieces (see techniques pp. 94, 97, and 108)
Grape-seed oil
Salt and freshly ground pepper

To serve
Small basil sprigs or celery leaves (optional)

PREPARING THE SQUASH AND PEAR TERRINE (1 DAY AHEAD)

Preheat the oven to 285°F (140°C/Gas Mark 1). Rinse and peel the squashes, turnips, and pear, and remove the seeds and core from the squash and pear. Cut them all into ⅛-in. (3-mm) slices using the mandolin. Set aside the longest slices for the top of the terrine. Grease the terrine mold with a little coconut oil and line the base with a piece of parchment paper. Arrange squash, turnip, and pear slices in an even layer in the base of the mold, overlapping the slices so there are no gaps between them. Season with salt and pepper, sprinkle over a little chopped cilantro, and brush with a thin layer of coconut oil. Repeat layering the slices until you have filled the mold, finishing with the longest slices to make the terrine easier to turn out of the mold. Cover and bake for 2 hours at 285°F (140°C/Gas Mark 1), then increase the oven temperature to 325°F (160°C/Gas Mark 3) and bake for an additional 15 minutes. Place a weight on top of the terrine and chill overnight.

PREPARING THE CELERY ROOT PURÉE

Peel the celery root and cut it into ¾-in. (2-cm) dice. Place in a saucepan with the milk and bay leaves, and let simmer for 20 minutes, or until completely tender. Remove the bay leaves and transfer the celery root to the food processor. Add the butter and process to a coarse purée. With the motor running, gradually pour in the milk down the feeder tube to make a smooth purée. Season with salt and pepper.

COOKING AND PRESSING THE CHICKEN

Bone the chicken legs without piercing the skin (see technique p. 116). Remove the veins from the meat and French trim the chicken wing. Season the chicken all over with salt and pepper. Cut a piece of parchment paper into a circle with the same diameter as a skillet large enough to hold all the chicken pieces. Warm a little grape-seed oil over medium heat in the skillet. Add the chicken pieces, skin-side down, cover with the parchment paper circle, and place a weight on top, such as a terrine mold or a flat-bottomed bowl. Fry for 10 minutes, until the chicken is cooked through and the skin is crisp and golden, adjusting the heat if necessary. Set aside on a rack, skin-side up.

TO SERVE

Preheat the oven to 250°F (130°C/Gas Mark ½). Place the terrine in the oven and reheat for 20 minutes. During the last 10 minutes, place the chicken in the oven to reheat it, if necessary. Reheat the celery root purée. Turn the terrine out of the mold and cut it into 1¼-in. (3-cm) slices. Spread some purée over each serving plate, making an elegant arc. Place chicken pieces in the center and add a slice of terrine. Garnish with a few small basil sprigs or celery leaves, if desired.

TURKEY GIZZARD RAGOUT WITH TAGLIATELLE

Ragoût de gésiers aux noix et tagliatelles

Serves 4

Active time
1 hour

Cooking time
1½ hours

Chilling time
1 hour

Storage
3 days

Equipment
Stand mixer + dough hook
Pasta maker
Fine-mesh sieve

Ingredients

Tagliatelle
2¼ cups (10 oz./280 g) Italian flour (00)
2 eggs
4 egg yolks

Turkey gizzard ragout
1¾ lb. (800 g) turkey gizzards (*gésiers de dinde*)
1 onion
3½ tbsp (50 ml) sunflower oil
¼ bunch savory
Scant ½ cup (100 ml) Madeira
4 cups (1 liter) white poultry stock (*fond blanc de volaille*, see recipe p. 19) + more as needed
3 tbsp (1½ oz./45 g) walnut mustard

To serve
2 oz. (60 g) toasted walnuts, finely chopped
2 oz. (60 g) truffles, julienned (optional)
1 scallion, thinly sliced
A few chives, cut into pieces
A few red sorrel leaves

PREPARING THE TAGLIATELLE

Place all the tagliatelle ingredients in the bowl of the stand mixer and knead on medium speed for 5 minutes to make a smooth dough. Shape the dough into a ball, cover with plastic wrap, and let rest in the refrigerator for 1 hour. Using the pasta maker, gradually roll out the dough, passing it through each thickness setting twice until you reach the sixth, thinnest level. Cut the dough into strips measuring ½ in. (1 cm) in width and reserve in the refrigerator.

PREPARING THE TURKEY GIZZARD RAGOUT

Preheat the oven to 350°F (180°C/Gas Mark 4). Wash the gizzards and thoroughly pat them dry using paper towels. Peel and finely chop the onion. Warm the oil in a Dutch oven until shimmering, then add the gizzards and sear until browned. Add the onion and savory sprigs, and sweat over low heat until the onion is softened but not browned. Pour the contents of the pan into a colander over a bowl to remove the excess fat, then return the gizzards, onion, and savory to the pan. Add the Madeira, reduce by half over low heat, then add the poultry stock. Cover and cook in the oven for 1½ hours. Strain the cooking liquid through the fine-mesh sieve into a clean large saucepan and reduce until it coats the back of a spoon. Stir in the mustard, then place the gizzards and onion in the sauce and let simmer over low heat. Adjust the seasonings and consistency if necessary. If the sauce is too thick, add a little extra stock. If it is too thin, reduce it to the desired consistency over low heat.

TO SERVE

Cook the tagliatelle in boiling salted water for 3 minutes. Drain and toss with enough of the reduced sauce to ensure the tagliatelle is well coated. For each serving, twirl the noodles into a nest in the center of the plate and top with the gizzard ragout, toasted chopped walnuts, and julienned truffles, if using. Garnish with scallion slices, chives, and red sorrel leaves. Serve immediately.

CHICKEN AND FOIE GRAS TERRINE

Pressé de volaille

Serves 10

Active time

1¼ hours

Cooking time

1¾ hours

Chilling time

Overnight (for the terrine)

At least 6 hours (for the pickled vegetables)

Storage

3 days

Equipment

Meat pounder

Steam oven (optional)

6-in. (16-cm) square baking frame, 1½ in. (4 cm) deep

Instant-read thermometer

3 × 2-cup (500-ml) jars

Ingredients

Chicken and foie gras terrine

6 baby leeks

1 lb. 2 oz. (500 g) boneless chicken breasts, skinned

5¼ oz. (150 g) foie gras

Butter for greasing

Salt

Pickled vegetables

½ bunch red radishes

1¾ oz. (50 g) red onions

1 cluster shimeji mushrooms

½ cup (125 ml) apple cider vinegar

Scant ⅓ cup (2 oz./60 g) sugar

1 cup (250 ml) water

½ tsp (3 g) fennel seeds

¹⁄₁₀ oz. (3 g) cardamom pods

¹⁄₁₀ oz. (3 g) star anise pods

¹⁄₁₀ oz. (3 g) long pepper

Vinaigrette

Scant ½ cup (100 ml) chicken jus

3½ tbsp (50 ml) aged white wine vinegar

4 tsp (20 g) Dijon mustard

⅔ cup (150 ml) olive oil

To serve

1 oz. (30 g) mizuna

4 tsp (20 ml) olive oil

Fleur de sel

Piment d'Espelette

PREPARING THE CHICKEN AND FOIE GRAS TERRINE (1 DAY AHEAD)

Preheat the oven to 400°F (200°C/Gas Mark 6). Wash the leeks and place them on a baking sheet. Roast in the oven until they are charred in places and tender throughout (about 15 minutes). Cool, then remove the charred outer layers and any other layers necessary to ensure all the leeks have the same diameter. Trim any excess fat off the chicken breasts and butterfly them. Using the meat pounder, flatten them to a thickness of ¼ in. (7 mm) between two sheets of plastic wrap. Season with salt. Cut the foie gras into ½-in. (1.5-cm) slices and season with salt. Preheat the steam oven, if using, to 200°F (100°C/Gas Mark ¼) with 20% steam. Alternatively, preheat a conventional oven to the same temperature and prepare a pan of boiling water to place in the oven when you cook the terrine. Lightly grease the baking frame with butter and place it on a baking sheet lined with parchment paper. Line the base with half the chicken breasts and top with the foie gras slices, placed side by side in a single layer. Arrange the leeks over the foie gras, spacing them evenly apart. Finish with a layer of the remaining chicken breasts. Place in the oven. If not using a steam oven, place the pan of boiling water beneath the terrine. Cook for about 1½ hours, or until the internal temperature reaches 149°F (65°C). Let cool to room temperature, then place a piece of parchment paper and a weight on the top. Reserve overnight in the refrigerator.

PREPARING THE PICKLED VEGETABLES (1 DAY AHEAD)

Wash the radishes, cut them in half, cut off the green tops, and place in one of the jars. Peel and slice the red onions (not too thinly) and add to the same jar. Trim the mushrooms and place in the second jar. Warm the vinegar, sugar, water, fennel seeds, cardamom, star anise, and long pepper in a saucepan until the sugar dissolves, then bring to a boil. Pour into the jars, adding equal amounts to each one. Let cool to room temperature, close the jars, and reserve in the refrigerator for at least 6 hours.

VINAIGRETTE

Reduce the chicken jus in a small saucepan over low heat until it coats the back of a spoon. Whisk in the wine vinegar and mustard and let cool to room temperature. Gradually whisk in the olive oil to emulsify. Reserve in the refrigerator until serving.

TO SERVE

Wash and dry the mizuna, remove the stems, and toss with the olive oil. Remove the weight and parchment paper from the terrine, unmold, and cut into ½-in. (1.5-cm) slices. Serve cold with the mizuna and a few pickled radishes, onions, and mushrooms. Drizzle with vinaigrette and sprinkle with fleur de sel and *piment d'Espelette*.

PIGEON ROSSINI

Serves 10

Active time
1½ hours

Cooking time
5 hours

Chilling time
Overnight

Storage
3 days

Equipment
6-in. (16-cm) square baking frame, 1½ in. (4 cm) deep

Mandolin

Butcher's twine

Fine-mesh sieve

Ingredients

Vegetable and quince terrine
1 butternut squash
4 quinces
1 celery root (celeriac)
1¾ sticks (7 oz./200 g) butter
Leaves of ¼ bunch thyme
2 tsp (10 g) salt

Pigeon
5 pigeons
9 oz. (250 g) foie gras
3½ oz. (100 g) caul fat
3 cloves garlic, divided
1 cup (250 ml) olive oil, divided
4 sprigs thyme, divided
5 tbsp (2½ oz./75 g) butter
Salt

Pigeon jus with hibiscus
7 oz. (200 g) white onions
½ head garlic
5 pigeon carcasses (about 2¼ lb./1 kg, see above)
Scant ½ cup (100 ml) olive oil
¼ bunch thyme
1¾ sticks (7 oz./200 g) butter
8 cups (2 liters) vegetable stock, divided
1¾ oz. (50 g) dried hibiscus flowers

To serve
Hibiscus powder
10 roasted unpeeled garlic cloves
10 purple shamrock leaves

PREPARING THE VEGETABLE AND QUINCE TERRINE (1 DAY AHEAD)

Preheat the oven to 325°F (160°C/Gas Mark 3). Place the baking frame on a baking sheet lined with parchment paper. Peel the butternut squash, quinces, and celery root, and cut them into 1⁄16-in. (1-mm) slices using the mandolin. Melt the butter in a saucepan and stir in the thyme leaves. Arrange quince slices in a single layer in the base of the baking frame, overlapping them slightly. Brush generously with the melted thyme butter, then add a layer of butternut squash, brush with melted butter, and add a layer of celery root. Repeat these layers, brushing with butter each time, until the frame is full. Place a piece of parchment paper and a weight on top. Bake for 1½ hours. Carefully remove the weight and let the terrine cool to room temperature in the frame. Replace the weight and reserve in the refrigerator overnight.

PREPARING THE PIGEON

Preheat the oven to 130°F (55°C/Gas on lowest setting). Prepare the pigeons (see technique p. 125, steps 1–15), reserving the carcasses for the jus. Bone the breasts and remove the skin. Cut the foie gras into 5 pieces weighing 1¾ oz. (50 g) each and place each piece between two pigeon breasts. Season with salt, wrap in caul fat, and tie into small roasts using twine (see technique p. 42). Roughly crush the unpeeled garlic cloves. Heat half the olive oil in an oven-safe skillet with 1 clove of garlic, half the thyme, and the butter, then sear the roasts, basting them with the oil and butter until browned. Transfer to the oven and roast for 1 hour. Meanwhile, heat the remaining olive oil with the thyme and 2 cloves of garlic in a large skillet and cook the pigeon legs for 1 hour over low heat, until deeply golden.

PREPARING THE PIGEON JUS WITH HIBISCUS

Peel the onions and cut each one into 8 wedges. Roughly crush the unpeeled garlic cloves. Cut the pigeon carcasses into 1½-in. (4-cm) pieces. Heat the olive oil in a large saucepan and fry the carcasses until pale golden brown. Add the onions, garlic, thyme, and butter, and continue to cook until the carcasses are deeply browned, basting with the olive oil and butter. Pour off the excess fat and deglaze with 2 cups (500 ml) of the vegetable stock to release the browned bits stuck to the bottom of the pan. Add the remaining stock and simmer, uncovered, for 1½ hours. Strain through the fine-mesh sieve into a clean saucepan and reduce until the jus coats the back of a spoon. Add the dried hibiscus flowers and let infuse.

TO SERVE

Remove the frame from the terrine and cut into ½-in. (1.5-cm) slices. Brown the slices on one side in an ungreased skillet over low heat, then cut them in half at an angle to obtain 2 × 2½-in. (6-cm) pieces. Dust hibiscus powder and drizzle a little pigeon jus on each serving plate. Add a pigeon leg and a slice of roasted pigeon breast and foie gras, along with 2 slices of terrine. Garnish with a roasted garlic clove and a few purple shamrock leaves.

GAME

MARINATED HARE STEW

Civet de lièvre

Serves 8–10

Active time
1½ hours

Cooking time
4 hours

Marinating time
Overnight

Storage
3 days

Equipment
Fine-mesh sieve
Immersion blender

Ingredients

1 hare, skinned and gutted, with 1¼ cups (300 ml) blood reserved for the sauce

Marinade

3½ oz. (100 g) white onions

3½ oz. (100 g) carrots

3½ oz. (100 g) celery

Generous ¾ cup (200 ml) cognac

Hare stew

Marinated hare (see above)

Scant ½ cup (100 ml) olive oil

5¼ oz. (150 g) farmhouse slab bacon (*lard fermier*) trimmings

3 cups (750 ml) red wine

6 cups (1.5 liters) brown veal stock (*fond brun de veau*, see recipe p. 16)

1 bouquet garni (thyme, bay leaf, and rosemary)

1¼ cups (300 ml) hare's blood

2 tsp (10 ml) crème fraîche

Olive oil

To garnish

10½ oz. (300 g) baby potatoes

10½ oz. (300 g) carrots

1¾ sticks (7 oz./200 g) butter

1 bunch scallions

1 small celery root (celeriac)

Generous ¾ cup (200 ml) heavy cream, min. 35% fat

5¼ oz. (150 g) farmhouse slab bacon (*lard fermier*)

2 tsp (10 g) salt

To serve

Celery leaves

PREPARING AND MARINATING THE HARE (1 DAY AHEAD)

Cut the hare into pieces (see technique p. 137). Peel and finely chop the onions, carrots, and celery, and place in a bowl with the cognac. Add the hare loins, forelegs, and hind legs, and let marinate in the refrigerator overnight.

PREPARING THE HARE STEW

The following day, preheat the oven to 325°F (160°C/Gas Mark 3). Drain the marinated hare and vegetables, reserving and straining the cognac. Reserve the loins in the refrigerator and pat the forelegs and hind legs dry. Heat the olive oil in a Dutch oven and melt the bacon trimmings, then add the legs and cook until browned. Remove the meat, add the vegetables, and sweat over low heat for 10 minutes. Deglaze with the reserved cognac, then flambé. Add the wine and reduce by three-quarters. Add the stock, bring to a boil, and add the forelegs, hind legs, and bouquet garni. Cover and cook in the oven for 3 hours. Drain the meat and set it aside. Strain the cooking liquid through the fine-mesh sieve, return it to the pan, and reduce until it coats the back of a spoon.

PREPARING THE GARNISHES

While the hare is stewing, prepare the garnishes. Wash the potatoes and peel the carrots. Cut both diagonally into 2-in. (5-cm) slices. Heat the butter in a skillet until melted and cook the potatoes and carrots until tender and lightly browned. Trim the tops of the scallions 2½ in. (6 cm) from their ends and quarter them lengthwise. Place in a saucepan of cold, salted water, bring to a boil and cook for 5 minutes. Peel the celery root, cut it into ¾-in. (2-cm) dice, and cook in a saucepan of boiling, salted water for 25 minutes. Drain and return to the pan, then add the cream, and process to a smooth purée using the immersion blender. Cut the bacon into ¾-in. (2-cm) dice, place in a saucepan of cold, salted water, and bring to a boil. Drain and repeat twice more. Drain the bacon on paper towels, then brown it all over in a skillet.

TO FINISH AND SERVE

Whisk the hare's blood and crème fraîche gradually into the sauce in the Dutch oven; keep it warm but do not let the sauce boil, as it will curdle once the blood has been added. Heat a little olive oil in a large skillet and brown the hare loins for 5 minutes on each side. Transfer the loins to the sauce in the Dutch oven so they are coated. Serve the meat immediately, arranging it attractively on serving plates with a generous amount of sauce and the garnishes alongside, topped with a few celery leaves.

HARE ROYALE

Lièvre à la royale

Serves 10–12

Active time
1½ hours

Cooking time
18½ hours

Storage
2 days

Equipment
Meat grinder + medium grinding plate
Disposable pastry bag
Trussing needle
Butcher's twine
Fine-mesh sieve
Rondeau pan large enough to hold the stuffed hare + lid
Spaetzle maker (or colander with ⅛-in./3–4-mm holes + bowl scraper)

Ingredients

Hare
7¾–9-lb. (3.5–4-kg) hare, skinned
Salt and freshly ground pepper

Farce
3½ oz. (100 g) lean slab bacon (*lard maigre*)
9 oz. (250 g) fresh pork belly (*poitrine de porc fraîche*)
About 7 oz. (205 g) hare leg meat (see above)
5¼-oz. (150-g) lobe foie gras
1¾ oz. (50 g) black truffles (optional)
Heart, liver, and lungs of hare (see above)
1½ tsp (7.5 g) salt
¾ tsp (2 g) freshly ground pepper
1 tbsp finely chopped parsley
½ tbsp finely chopped sage

¾ tbsp finely chopped rosemary
½ tbsp juniper berries
2¾ oz. (75 g) confit shallots
2 cloves confit garlic
2 tbsp (1 oz./30 g) butter
2 tsp (10 ml) Armagnac
1 × 14-oz. (400-g) lobe foie gras
7 oz. (200 g) caul fat

Hare broth
2 onions
2 carrots
3 shallots
Cloves of 1 head garlic
1 stalk celery
3 tbsp (1¾ oz./50 g) butter
Hare bones (see left)
Hare forelegs (meat and bones, see left)
3 qt. (3 liters) full-bodied red wine
3 qt. (3 liters) brown stock, veal (see recipe p. 16) or game

Sauce
2 cups (500 ml) tawny port
2 tbsp (1 oz./30 g) butter, at room temperature
3½ oz. (100 g) foie gras
Scant ½ cup (100 ml) hare's blood (see left)
Salt and freshly ground pepper

Spaetzle
9 oz. (250 g) fromage blanc
1¾ cups (8 oz./225 g) all-purpose flour
3 eggs
1¼ tsp (6 g) salt
¼ bunch parsley, finely chopped
1 scant tbsp (10 g) poppy seeds

PREPARING THE HARE (1 DAY AHEAD)

Cut open the hare through the belly to remove the giblets. Reserve the heart, liver, and lungs for the stuffing and the blood for the sauce. Carefully bone the entire hare, making sure you keep the body intact, so that it can be formed into a ballotine shape. To do this, place the hare on its back and remove the bones from the saddle one by one, being careful not to pierce any holes through the back. Season inside with salt and pepper. Cut off and bone the forelegs and hind legs (see technique p. 137), reserving the hind leg meat for the stuffing and the foreleg meat for the stock. Reserve all the bones for the stock.

PREPARING THE FARCE AND STUFFING THE HARE (1 DAY AHEAD)

Cut the bacon, pork belly, and hare meat into pieces and grind them together through the meat grinder fitted with the medium grinding plate. Cut the 5¼ oz. (150 g) foie gras, truffles (if using), and the hare's heart, liver, and lungs into ½-in. (1-cm) pieces and stir into the ground meat mixture. Stir in the salt, pepper, parsley, sage, rosemary, and juniper berries. Peel and finely chop the confit shallots and garlic. Melt the butter in a saucepan and sauté the shallots and garlic briefly. Add to the farce. Pour in the Armagnac and stir to incorporate, then transfer the farce to the pastry bag. Lay the hare flat on its back, snip off the tip of the pastry bag, and pipe farce over the whole of the inside of the hare. Cut the foie gras lobe in half lengthwise and remove all the veins. Cut it into small pieces and scatter evenly over the farce. Roll up the hare into a ballotine (log) shape and stitch it closed using the trussing needle and butcher's twine. Wrap the caul fat around the ballotine and tie it like a roast, ensuring an equal width from end to end (see technique p. 68).

PREPARING THE HARE BROTH AND COOKING THE HARE (1 DAY AHEAD)

Peel and finely chop the onions, carrots, shallots, garlic, and celery. Heat the butter in a Dutch oven and brown the hare bones and forelegs. Add the chopped vegetables and continue to cook for an additional 10 minutes. Add the red wine and flambé, then reduce by two-thirds over medium heat. Add the broth and let simmer for 3 hours. Preheat the oven to 200°F (100°C/Gas Mark ¼). Strain the hare broth through the fine-mesh sieve into the rondeau pan, without pressing down. Submerge the stuffed hare in the broth, cover the pan, and place in the oven. Let cook for 15 hours.

PREPARING THE SAUCE

After the stuffed hare has cooked for 15 hours, remove it from the pan and let it cool. Reduce the hare broth until thick. In a small saucepan, reduce the port until it is syrupy and about 4 tbsp (60 ml) remain, then add it to the reduced hare broth. Stir the butter and foie gras together and add them to the pan. Stir until mixed in, then stir in the hare's blood. Do not let the sauce boil once the blood has been added, as it will curdle. Season with salt and pepper, then strain through the fine-mesh sieve into a clean large saucepan. Cut the stuffed hare into ¾-in. (2-cm) slices and place in the sauce to glaze them.

PREPARING THE SPAETZLE

Place the fromage blanc, flour, eggs, and salt in a large bowl. Beat for 3 minutes to strengthen the mixture and ensure it holds together when cooked. Bring a large pan of salted water to a boil and fill a large bowl with ice water on the countertop alongside. Place the spaetzle maker over the pan of boiling water and push the dough through it into the water (alternatively, use a colander and a bowl scraper). When the spaetzle rise to the surface of the water, scoop them out with a slotted spoon and transfer them to the bowl of ice water to cool them quickly and prevent further cooking. Drain the spaetzle and spread them over a clean dish towel to dry.

TO SERVE

Just before serving, sauté the spaetzle in a little butter, then sprinkle with the parsley and poppy seeds. Serve the hare royale slices in the sauce, with the spaetzle on the side.

CHEFS' NOTES

You can add a couple of dark chocolate *pistoles* or drops (⅕–¼ oz./4–8 g) to the sauce at the last minute for a richer color and flavor.

RABBIT WITH FAVA BEAN RIGATONI

Lapin de garenne et rigatonis aux fèves

Serves 4

Active time
2½ hours

Cooking time
1 hour 20 minutes

Storage
3 days

Equipment
Fine-mesh sieve
Food processor
Disposable pastry bag
Immersion blender

Ingredients

Rabbit

3¾-lb. (1.7-kg) rabbit, preferably Garenne or Rex du Poitou, skinned and gutted

1 onion

5 tbsp (2½ oz./70 g) butter

Generous ¾ cup (200 ml) Sauvignon-type white wine

8 cups (2 liters) white poultry stock (*fond blanc de volaille*, see recipe p. 19)

3½ oz. (100 g) shiitake mushrooms

Fava bean rigatoni

32 pieces dried rigatoni

9 oz. (250 g) shelled fava beans, fresh or frozen

15 mint leaves

Generous ⅓ cup (3¼ oz./90 g) ricotta

2 tbsp (1 oz./30 g) lightly beaten egg (about ⅔ egg)

⅔ cup (2½ oz./70 g) dried breadcrumbs

Generous ¾ cup (2¾ oz./80 g) grated Parmesan

Ramson garlic coulis

3½ oz. (100 g) ramson garlic leaves (or basil)

Strained rabbit cooking juices (see left)

⅔ cup (150 ml) heavy cream, min. 35% fat

3 tbsp (1¾ oz./50 g) butter, cut into small pieces

Salt and freshly ground pepper

To serve

Generous ½ cup (2 oz./60 g) grated Parmesan

3½ oz. (100 g) cooked fresh fava beans, outer skins removed

Ramson garlic leaves

Parsley-infused oil

PREPARING THE RABBIT

Cut up the rabbit (see technique p. 137). Peel and finely chop the onion. Warm the butter in a sauté pan over medium heat until melted and foaming, then add the rabbit pieces and sear them without browning. Add the onion, lower the heat, and sweat until softened but not browned. Deglaze with the white wine and reduce by two-thirds, then pour in the stock and add the shiitake mushrooms. Cover and let simmer for 15 minutes, then remove the saddle meat to prevent it from drying out. Cover the pan again and continue to cook for 45 minutes, until the rest of the meat is tender. Strain the cooking juices through the fine-mesh sieve into a bowl for making the coulis. Cover the rabbit meat and set aside. Reserve the shiitake mushrooms for serving.

PREPARING THE FAVA BEAN RIGATONI

Cook the rigatoni in boiling salted water following the instructions on the package, then drain. Bring a large saucepan of water to a boil, add the fava beans, and cook until just tender. Drain, cool by running cold water over them, then remove the outer skins. Purée the fava beans with the mint leaves, ricotta, egg, breadcrumbs, and Parmesan in the food processor. Transfer to the pastry bag, snip off the tip, and pipe into the rigatoni until filled.

PREPARING THE RAMSON GARLIC COULIS

Using the immersion blender, purée the ramson garlic leaves with the cooking juices. Strain through the fine-mesh sieve into a large saucepan and reduce until thick. Add the cream and bring to a boil. Let boil for a few minutes, then gradually whisk in the butter until smooth. Adjust the seasonings if necessary. Place the rabbit pieces in the coulis and bring to a simmer over low heat.

TO SERVE

Preheat the oven to 300°F (150°C/Gas Mark 2). Place the stuffed rigatoni in a baking dish in a single layer, sprinkle with the Parmesan, and heat in the oven for 10 minutes. Ladle the coulis into shallow bowls for serving. Arrange the rabbit pieces, stuffed rigatoni, and shiitake mushrooms over the coulis and scatter over a few fava beans. Top with a ramson garlic leaf and finish with several drops of parsley-infused oil.

GAME AND FOIE GRAS PIES

Tourte de gibiers et foie gras

Makes 6

Active time

1½ hours

Cooking time

1 hour

Resting time

20 minutes

Storage

2 days

Equipment

6-in. (15-cm) pastry
cutter

Ingredients

Filling

3 shallots, unpeeled

5¼ oz. (150 g) button
mushrooms

3½ tbsp (50 ml) duck fat
(or peanut oil)

2½ oz. (70 g) horn-of-
plenty mushrooms

2 tbsp finely chopped
parsley

10½ oz. (300 g) pork
neck

9 oz. (250 g) boneless
duck leg meat

7 oz. (200 g) raw foie
gras, deveined

5¼ oz. (150 g) mallard
duck breast (or duck
magret)

1¾ oz. (50 g) pork loin
(*filet de porc*)

2½ tsp (12 g) salt

1½ tsp (4 g) ground
black pepper

Scant ⅓ cup (70 ml)
cognac

Puff pastry

1½ lb. (700 g) puff
pastry (store-bought
or homemade)

Egg wash

1 egg yolk

1 egg

1 pinch salt

To serve

Generous ¾ cup
(200 ml) poultry jus,
warmed

A few frisée leaves

4 red endive leaves

Vinaigrette of your
choice

PREPARING THE FILLING

Preheat the oven to 325°F (160°C/Gas Mark 3). Place the shallots on a baking sheet lined with parchment paper and roast them for 40 minutes, or until completely tender. Meanwhile, cut the button mushrooms into ¼-in. (5-mm) dice. Heat the duck fat (or peanut oil) in a skillet and sauté the button mushrooms until softened and browned. Stir in the horn-of-plenty mushrooms and parsley, then remove from the heat and let cool. Finely chop the pork neck and duck leg meat. Cut the foie gras, duck breast, and pork loin into ¾-in. (2-cm) dice. Place all the meat in a large bowl and stir in the salt, pepper, and cognac. Peel and chop the roasted shallots and add to the bowl, then add the mushroom mixture. Gently stir to combine.

ASSEMBLING AND BAKING THE PIES

Roll the puff pastry to a thickness of ¹⁄₁₆ in. (2 mm). Using the pastry cutter, cut out 12 × 6-in. (15-cm) disks. Place 6 of the disks on a baking sheet lined with parchment paper and divide the filling between them, placing it in the center of each one. Brush the pastry edges with a little water and top with the remaining disks. Press the pastry edges down gently around the filling to remove any air, then cut a hole in the center of each pastry top to allow steam to escape while baking. Score the edges together using the back of a paring knife to seal. To prepare the egg wash, whisk together the egg yolk, egg, and salt. Brush over the pies and let rest for 20 minutes. Meanwhile, preheat the oven to 430°F (220°C/Gas Mark 7). Brush the pies a second time with egg wash. Using the tip of a paring knife, lightly score decorative lines in the pastry tops, starting in the center and working toward the outer edge. Bake for 20 minutes, until golden brown. Transfer to a rack.

TO SERVE

Cut the pies in half and serve with the jus and a frisée and endive salad dressed with the vinaigrette of your choice.

SHREDDED BOAR TACOS

Effiloché de sanglier en tacos

Serves 4

Active time

2 hours

Cooking time

2 hours

Chilling time

30 minutes

Storage

3 days

Equipment

Fine-mesh sieve

Stand mixer + paddle beater

Griddle (optional)

Immersion blender

Sauce dispenser bottle

Ingredients

Shredded wild boar

1½ lb. (700 g) wild boar shoulder

1 onion

Scant ½ cup (100 ml) olive oil

Juice of 1 lime

2 tbsp (15 g) smoked chili powder

2 tbsp (15 g) ground cumin

2 tbsp (11 g) dried oregano

4 cups (1 liter) white poultry stock (*fond blanc de volaille*, see recipe p. 19)

Salt and freshly ground pepper

Wheat tortillas

2 cups (9 oz./250 g) all-purpose flour

½ cup (120 ml) water

½ tsp (2 g) baking powder

4 tsp (20 ml) olive oil

Scant ½ tsp (2 g) salt

Chipotle sauce

1 dried chipotle pepper, soaked overnight in warm water

2 cloves garlic, peeled

1 tbsp (15 g) sweet mustard (preferably Savora)

1 egg white

1 cup (250 ml) grape-seed oil

Finely grated zest and juice of 1 lime

Salt

To garnish

1 red onion

½ bunch cilantro

1 fresh red chili pepper

2 scallions

1 lime

To serve (optional)

Tajín seasoning

PREPARING THE SHREDDED WILD BOAR

Preheat the oven to 340°F (170°C/Gas Mark 3). Cut the boar shoulder into large pieces weighing about 2¾ oz. (80 g) each. Peel and finely chop the onion. Heat the olive oil in a Dutch oven and brown the boar pieces all over. Add the chopped onion and cook for an additional 5 minutes. Add the lime juice, chili powder, cumin, oregano, and stock, and bring to a boil. Cover and cook in the oven for 2 hours, or until the meat is completely tender. Remove the boar pieces from the pan. Strain the cooking liquid through the fine-mesh sieve into a clean saucepan and reduce until syrupy. Shred the meat into a large stainless-steel bowl and stir in the reduced cooking liquid. Adjust the seasonings if necessary. Set the bowl over a pan of barely simmering water to keep the meat warm.

PREPARING THE WHEAT TORTILLAS

Place all the tortilla ingredients in the stand mixer bowl and beat until the dough comes together into a ball. Divide the dough into pieces weighing about 1 oz. (25 g) each—it should make around 30—and shape into balls. Cover and let rest for 30 minutes in the refrigerator. Roll each ball of dough into a 4-in. (10-cm) tortilla, about ⅛ in. (3 mm) thick, and layer between sheets of parchment paper to prevent them from drying out. Cook the tortillas on a griddle or ungreased skillet over medium-high heat for 1 minute on each side, until cooked and browned in places.

PREPARING THE CHIPOTLE SAUCE

Drain the soaked chipotle pepper, cut it in half lengthwise, and remove the stalks and seeds. Place in a bowl with the garlic, mustard, and egg white, and blend until smooth using the immersion blender. Gradually incorporate the oil, blending continuously. Stir in the lime zest and juice, season with salt, and transfer the sauce to the dispenser bottle.

PREPARING THE GARNISHES

Peel and thinly slice the red onion. Wash and stem the cilantro. Wash and thinly slice the chili pepper and scallions. Quarter the lime.

TO SERVE

Reheat the tortillas in the microwave for a few seconds. For each taco, place shredded meat in the center of a tortilla and fold it around the meat. Drizzle sauce over the meat, add the toppings of your choice, and sprinkle with Tajín seasoning, if desired.

LOIN OF VENISON WITH GRAND VENEUR SAUCE

Filet de chevreuil, sauce grand veneur

Serves 6

Active time

2 hours

Cooking time

20 minutes

Resting time

10 minutes

Storage

3 days

Equipment

Fine-mesh sieve

Food processor

Ingredients

Venison

1 venison loin (backstrap)

3½ tbsp (50 ml) sunflower oil

3 tbsp (1¾ oz./50 g) butter

1 clove garlic, peeled

1 sprig thyme

Salt and freshly ground pepper

Grand veneur pepper sauce

3½ oz. (100 g) shallots, finely chopped

1 tsp cracked black pepper (*mignonette*)

Generous ¾ cup (200 ml) cognac

1¼ cups (300 ml) port wine

1⅔ cups (400 ml) game stock (*fond de gibier*)

3½ oz. (100 g) red currant jelly

Parsnip purée

14 oz. (400 g) parsnips

5 tbsp (2½ oz./70 g) butter

3½ tbsp (50 ml) peanut oil

Salt and freshly ground pepper

Honey-roasted parsnips

2 parsnips

3 tbsp (1¾ oz./50 g) butter, melted

2 tbsp (1½ oz./40 g) honey

1 tsp sesame seeds

King trumpet mushrooms

2 king trumpet (king oyster) mushrooms

4 tbsp (2 oz./60 g) clarified butter

Bok choy

2 bok choy

To serve

4 thin slices *lardo di Colonnata* (Italian cured pork fat)

1 tsp cocoa nibs

4 nasturtium leaves

Salt and freshly ground pepper

PREPARING THE VENISON

Preheat the oven to 340°F (170°C/Gas Mark 3). Cut the loin into 4 equal pieces and season with salt and pepper. Heat the oil, butter, garlic, and thyme in an oven-safe sauté pan and brown the loin pieces all over. Finish cooking in the oven for about 8 minutes, basting the meat with the pan juices to keep it moist. It should remain pink in the center. Transfer the meat to a rack and let it rest for about 10 minutes. Leave the juices in the pan for the grand veneur sauce.

PREPARING THE GRAND VENEUR SAUCE

Add the shallots and cracked pepper to the pan used to cook the venison and sweat over low heat for a few minutes. Pour in the cognac and flambé it, then add the port wine and reduce by half over low heat. Add the game stock and reduce by half again over low heat. Stir in the red currant jelly. Reduce the sauce until it coats the back of a spoon. Adjust the seasonings if necessary. Strain through the fine-mesh sieve into a clean saucepan and keep warm.

PREPARING THE PARSNIP PURÉE

Peel the parsnips and remove the fibrous cores (particularly for larger parsnips). Boil in a pan of salted water until completely tender. Drain and place in a food processor with the butter and oil, and reduce to a smooth, velvety purée. Adjust the seasonings if necessary.

PREPARING THE HONEY-ROASTED PARSNIPS

Preheat the oven to 350°F (180°C/Gas Mark 4). Peel and rinse the parsnips and cut into halves or quarters lengthwise, depending on size. Toss with the butter and honey in a baking dish and roast for about 10 minutes, or until tender. Remove and sprinkle with sesame seeds.

PREPARING THE KING TRUMPET MUSHROOMS

Quarter the mushrooms lengthwise and score them with a crosshatch pattern. In a skillet over low heat, cook them for 2 minutes on each side in the clarified butter.

PREPARING THE BOK CHOY

Remove the leaves from the bok choy. Cook them in a large pan of boiling salted water for 3 minutes, then drain.

TO SERVE

Season the venison with salt and a few grinds of pepper. Cover each piece with lardo di Colonnata and sprinkle with cocoa nibs. Spoon a little grand veneur sauce onto each serving plate and arrange the parsnip purée, honey-roasted parsnips, and bok choy leaves over it. Add the venison and mushrooms. Garnish with the nasturtium leaves.

PARTRIDGE SALMI

Salmis de perdreaux

Serves 4

Active time
1½ hours

Cooking time
About 2½ hours

Resting time
10 minutes

Standing time
20 minutes

Storage
24 hours

Equipment
Poultry shears

Fine-mesh sieve

Immersion blender

Teardrop-shaped cookie cutter, 1½ in. (4 cm) long

Instant-read thermometer

Ingredients

Partridge salmi

2 partridges

2 shallots

2 cloves garlic

2 tbsp (30 ml) grape-seed oil

3 tbsp (1½ oz./40 g) butter, at room temperature, divided

1¼ cups (300 ml) cognac

1⅔ cups (400 ml) Syrah red wine

2 cups (500 ml) brown poultry stock (*fond brun de volaille*, see recipe and Chefs' Notes p. 19)

1 bouquet garni (thyme, bay leaf, and rosemary)

4 juniper berries

4 black peppercorns

2¼ oz. (65 g) *mi-cuit* (partially-cooked) foie gras

1 tbsp (15 ml) red wine vinegar

Salt and freshly ground pepper

Bourguignon-style garnishes

3½ oz. (100 g) button mushrooms

3½ oz. (100 g) pearl onions

3½ oz. (100 g) smoked bacon

3 tbsp (2½ oz./45 g) butter, divided

Salt

Foie gras toasts

2¾ oz. (75 g) *mi-cuit* (partially-cooked) foie gras

2 slices sandwich bread

4 tsp (20 ml) olive oil

Salt and freshly ground pepper

PREPARING THE PARTRIDGE SALMI

Preheat the oven to 350°F (180°C/Gas Mark 4). Dress and truss the partridges (see techniques pp. 97 and 134). Peel and finely chop the shallots. Peel the garlic and crush it using the flat of a chef's knife blade. Place the partridges in a Dutch oven and roast them in the oven for 12 minutes, until extra rare (blue) or rare to medium-rare. Let rest for 10 minutes, then remove the birds from the pan. Set the pan with the juices aside for making the sauce. Cut the breasts and legs off the partridges, then French trim the legs to expose the tips of the bones. Place the breasts and legs on a rack set over a baking sheet to catch the drippings. Cut the partridge carcasses, wings, and remaining bones into 1¼-in. (3-cm) pieces using the poultry shears. Warm the oil and 1 tbsp (20 g) butter in a sauté pan, add the cut-up pieces of carcasses, wings, and bones, and cook for 10 minutes, until deeply browned. Add the shallots and garlic, and continue to cook for an additional 10 minutes. Pour off the excess fat, add the cognac, and flambé. Reduce completely over medium heat. Pour in the wine and reduce by one-quarter. Add the stock and bring to a boil, skimming any foam from the surface. Add the bouquet garni, juniper berries, and peppercorns, and let simmer, uncovered, for 1 hour. Strain through the fine-mesh sieve into a clean saucepan and reduce until there is a generous ¾ cup (200 ml) of sauce. While the sauce is still hot, gradually add the *mi-cuit* foie gras and remaining butter, blending with the immersion blender until smooth. Strain through the fine-mesh sieve once more, then stir in the vinegar. Taste and add more salt and pepper as needed.

PREPARING THE BOURGUIGNON-STYLE GARNISHES

Wash the mushrooms and peel the onions. Cut the bacon into ¾-in. (2-cm) lardons, place in a saucepan of cold water, and bring to a boil to blanch them. Drain on paper towels. Warm 1 tbsp (15 g) of the butter in a small skillet over high heat until foaming, then add the lardons and cook until deeply browned. Transfer to a small baking dish. Place the onions in a small (5½ in./14-cm) saucepan and add enough water to just cover. Add 1 tbsp (15 g) butter and a pinch of salt. Cut a piece of parchment paper to fit snugly inside the saucepan and place it over the onions. Cook over medium heat until all the water has evaporated, then remove the parchment paper and continue to cook, stirring continuously, until the onions are evenly golden. Transfer to the baking dish with the lardons. Warm the remaining butter in a small skillet, add the mushrooms, and cook until lightly browned. Transfer to the baking dish with the lardons and onions.

PREPARING THE FOIE GRAS TOASTS

Remove the foie gras from the refrigerator and let it sit at room temperature for 20 minutes. Preheat the oven to 325°F (160°C/Gas Mark 3). Using the cookie cutter, cut out 4 teardrop-shaped pieces from the sandwich bread. Place them on a baking sheet lined with parchment paper, brush with the olive oil, and season with salt and pepper. Toast in the oven for 10 minutes. Press the foie gras through the fine-mesh sieve into a bowl, then whisk it until creamy.

TO SERVE

Preheat the oven to 200°F (100°C/Gas Mark ¼) and reheat the Bourguignon-style garnishes. Heat the sauce to 176°F (80°C), add the partridge legs and breasts, and finish cooking them for 5 minutes. Top the toasts with the foie gras. Arrange the partridge in shallow bowls with the sauce, Bourguignon garnishes, and toasts. Serve immediately.

APPENDIXES

INDEX

Acknowledgments

We would like to thank **Marine Mora** and the **Matfer Bourgeat Group** as well as the **Mora** store for the utensils and equipment.

www.matferbourgeat.com
www.mora.fr

Rina Nurra wishes to thank the following people:
Flammarion and Clélia, her editor, for her trust and kindness;
Audrey, for her invaluable assistance and her impeccable organization;
Chefs Stéphane, Bastien, and Alexander, for their enthusiasm, their good humor, and their recipes, which are always so inspiring and delicious;
The brand Le Creuset, for their superb Dutch ovens and pans, which we will never grow tired of using;
Hélène Kalmes, without whom this collaboration would not have been possible;
Marie Nurra, for her ceramics, which tell a story by themselves.